EVICTING DEMONIC SQUATTERS & BREAKING BONDAGES

Noel and Phyl. Gibson

PUBLISHED BY —
Freedom in Christ Ministries Trust
P.O. Box 436,
Drummoyne, N.S.W., 2047
Australia.

ACKNOWLEDGMENTS

Unless otherwise stated, all Scripture quotations in this publication are from the Holy Bible, New International Version. Copyright @ 1973, 1978, 1984, International Bible Society.

Special thanks are extended to Marj. Tharratt for her sacrificial efforts in time and energy as she deciphered handwriting, and typed the manuscript.

To our good friend Graham Chaseling who designed the cover as a love gift to his Lord, we also say a sincere thankyou.

And to a special friend, who, as mentor has been extraordinarily patient, albeit ruthless in evaluation and advice, our grateful thanks.

Noel and Phyl. Gibson

FIRST PRINTING	1987
FIFTH PRINTING	1990
SIXTH PRINTING (Revised)	1991

PREVIOUS PUBLICATIONS BY NOEL C. GIBSON

'The Fisherman's Basket'.
A 281 page text-book of evangelism both in the open air, and by other methods. Published by Freedom in Christ Ministries Trust

'Konfused'. A teenage tract published by the American Tract Society.

'The Answer in 20 Minutes'. A Gospel tract published by Moody Press in the 'Acorn' series.

'From henceforth thou shalt catch men'. Lectures on soulwinning.

'He shall glorify Me'. Studies on the filling and control of the Holy Spirit.

'He that winneth souls is wise'. A practical 5'S' plan of salvation for soul-winners.

'Open Air Evangelism'. A booklet prepared for elective seminars for the Lausanne Congress on World Evangelisation (1974).

A variety of childrens' tracts.

ISBN 0 7316 0179 3

F.R.P. PRINTING
5 College Street, Wendouree, 3355
Phone (053) 393737

FOREWORD

In the summer of 1980 I had the great pleasure of meeting Noel and Phyl Gibson at the Youth With A Mission discipleship training school in Kona, Hawaii. As Rev. Gibson was expounding the Word of God and sharing experiences of ministry in God's service, I saw the Spirit of the Lord come upon him and release him into a new ministry. In front of my eyes, I saw God move in Rev. Gibson's life so that he had profound words of knowledge. The power of God was manifest in signs and wonders for healing, resulting in dramatic moves of His Spirit. God reminded me of two scriptures; Psalm 103:5 "who satisfies your years with good things, so that your youth is renewed like the eagle", and also Haggai 2:9 "the glory of this present house will be greater than the glory of the former house". (NIV) Since that time, I have followed Noel and Phyl Gibson's ministry in God, and have just been amazed at how God has blessed his loyal servants with profound insight into people's lives.

At first as one considers this book one may be offended and think "Oh, no, this is just another demon chaser", but I would encourage the reader to consider the principles that are contained in it. Such insight and wisdom come only after years of diligently seeking God to see the Spirit moving in people's lives. I would encourage the reader not to be critical, but to study these principles in the light of God's Word. I have no doubt that they will be fruitful, and that the resulting freedom will be confirmed by God. It is to this end that I commit the 103rd Psalm, verses one through five, to the reader:

> "Praise the Lord, O my soul;
> all my inmost being, praise his holy name.
> Praise the Lord, O my soul,
> and forget not all his benefits.
>
> He forgives all my sins
> and heals all my diseases;
> He redeems my life from the pit
> and crowns me with love and compassion.
> He satisfies my desires with good things,
> so that my youth is renewed like the eagle's."

I can only relate that this association with Noel and Phyl Gibson has opened my eyes to the understanding of what God is saying in His Word about freeing His Church and equipping His saints to claim their birthright in the Lord Jesus Christ.

Donald R. Tredway M.D., Ph.D.
Professor and Chairman
Department of Obstetrics and Gynaecology
Oral Roberts University Research Centre.
Medical Director,
Hillcrest Fertility Centre,
Tulsa, Oklahoma, U.S.A.

CONTENTS

PART ONE

Satanic and demonic activities examined

Theme - Satanic and demonic activities examined.

"Give us help against the adversary, for vain is the help of man. Through and with our God we shall do valiantly, for he it is who shall tread down our adversaries." (Psalm 108:5, 6)

CHAPTER 1.

Getting acquainted

Hi there! Thank you for picking up this book. Let me introduce ourselves. I'm Noel, and Phyl has been my five star partner for the past forty two years. We have served God together in evangelism, Bible teaching and counselling for the major portion of our married life. You may have noticed from the back cover that we have reached that stage of life when the promise to 'still bear fruit, and remain fresh and green' is very meaningful (Psalm 93:14). When we retired in 1982, the Lord just 're-tyred' and re-programmed us. We believe the best is yet ahead (Psalm 92:12-15).

Just in case you are wondering what ever would have caused us to become involved in a deliverance ministry, let me assure you we did not choose it; we were pushed into it! But before we tell you how that happened, there are three reasons for wanting to share with you what God has been teaching us.

Firstly, blessings are only frozen assets until they are shared with others. The Lord Jesus shared his blessings with the apostles, and they in turn passed them on to us. We just want to confirm the twentieth century reality of the authority and power Jesus passed down to us.

Secondly, we firmly believe that spiritual ministry to members of the Body of Christ should ideally be channelled through those whom God has appointed as shepherds over each church, or group of believers. When the needy have to go elsewhere for deliverance they often feel a sense of disloyalty to their own church, and their pastors in turn feel threatened when God uses 'outsiders' for this purpose. The contents of this book are therefore dedicated to every pastor, minister, counsellor, and spiritual leader who is willing to examine the Biblical and practical evidences to be outlined with an open mind and a willing heart ready to obey what the Spirit of God may reveal.

Thirdly, if the volume of the writers' ministry is any indication, there is a tremendous need for deliverance to be ministered to God's people everywhere. At present the burden is carried by so few.

But, praise God, there are encouraging signs throughout the Body of Christ. For years now, Phyl and I have been teaching these principles and ministering freedom in Christ Jesus both in Australia and a number of overseas countries. We have been encouraged to find a growing interest amongst pastors and counsellors particularly of 'main-stream' churches, often as a result of seeing people dramatically change through deliverance. In view of this, there has been an increased willingness to re-examine traditional beliefs and personal prejudices, and reach out for viable answers to vexing problems.

The materials have been arranged in sections to suit the appetites of all readers. Neither of us claim to have all the answers. We do have unanswered questions, and we have made mistakes as we have learned. But with the Psalmist's 'praise of God in our mouths, and a double-edged sword in our hands' (Psalm 149:6) we constantly praise God for his discernment, power, and authority (Luke 17:10, 1 Corinthians 1:31).

You will note that the term 'freedom in Christ' is often used in place of the word 'deliverance', which has gathered some unfortunate connotations over the years. One cannot help but wonder if the Lord himself may not have been embarrassed at times over some methods used, and noisy deliverance sessions. Despite that, people have been released, and God must be glorified by the freedom gained. Wrestling with demonic powers will always be spiritual warfare, and fear of confrontation has allowed Satan to maintain his oppression, by default, for far too long.

The word 'deliverance' was certainly very meaningful in New Testament days when people were not only freed from demonic powers, but healed and made whole personalities. This is not nearly so evident today. By replacing 'deliverance' with 'freedom in Christ', the writers aim to introduce not only the concept of total release from all forms of demonic activity, but also the positive concepts of wholeness and progressive discipleship.

When God does the pushing, it is perilous to resist.

It happened like this. Around twenty eight years ago, while in the Chief Post Office in Wellington, New Zealand, I happened to meet a big man whom I had led to Christ some time before during regular prison visitation. I soon learned he was in all sorts of problems because of his sexual lust. Before coming to Christ he had spent much time and money in red light districts, and he found it very difficult to control his fleshly desires. I realised that words of advice would be about as effective as trying to stop a charging bull with a lassoo of knitting wool. The only thing I could think of was to suggest we have some special prayer together, so I invited him home. Phyl and I prayed for S. . . . . . in our bedroom away from the children. Prayer began quietly as the big man knelt at an ottoman, but once we hit the problem of lust, tranquility slipped out. S. wrestled so violently with that piece of furniture that we were sure it would disintegrate. But suddenly he dropped full-length on the floor and began to snake his way over the carpet. We had no answers, so prayed all the harder for spiritual understanding. So we began to learn just how much power was in the name of Jesus in such circumstances (Mark 16:17).

I later asked a doctor friend of mine for his advice. He didn't have answers, but he certainly gave much encouragement to continue seeking them from God. He told me that on occasions a patient would seem to bring an evil atmosphere into his surgery, and that even after the patient had seen a psychiatrist the evil sense remained. He reasoned that if medical science couldn't resolve the problem, then God alone must have the answers. From that time onwards the Lord brought to our home a trickle of people who needed some form of spiritual release. With little understanding but a lot of faith, we saw person after person released from a variety of demonic problems. God was gracious to us in those learning days. He kept away the people with real complications!

At that time I was heavily involved in open air evangelism. On most Sunday afternoons the voluntary workers who assisted in the outreach returned home for a buffet meal before returning for the evening programme in the centre of Wellington city. One evening, one of the afternoon contacts joined us for the meal. He appeared to be very friendly, and went out of his way to express his appreciation for the hospitality. He listened attentively during devotions, and sat quietly through the prayer session which followed during which I silently bound the spirit of lust Phyl discerned in him as he entered our home. When the last amen had been said, the young man jumped to his feet, spun around, and with contracted pupils menaced me. He shouted something about being able to see through me and knowing the person I really was, before rushing out of the house and up to street level. Shortly afterwards as we were leaving for the city I met him walking slowly back down the path. I told him that I knew his reactions had come from the spiritual forces inside him, and asked whether he wished to be set free. He just glared, and shouted "NO; let US alone", then turned and ran off. He was taken back to the city, and disappeared into the night.

It seemed at the time that God was pushing us into the deep end, but in retrospect, He was directing our footsteps into the pathway of His choice. He has certainly walked with us every inch of that way, gently teaching, guiding, encouraging, preserving, and empowering.

A greatly respected brother who spends a lot of time in deliverance once said to me; "Never be known just for a deliverance ministry". I am sure it was mature advice as setting people free is only one aspect of the liberating power of the Gospel. However, because of the increasing numbers of people who realise their need for freedom, it sometimes becomes impossible to avoid a major time allocation. Because Phyl and I were under this pressure we set three days apart to seek God's will for us, individually. We both felt we needed a word from the Lord before planning our future. At mid-day on the first day we shared our guidance. We had each received such overwhelmingly clear direction to continue the ministry that we hardly needed to continue, but we did so. The balance of the time only served to confirm our conviction that there was to be no turning back, no matter how much time we spent in asking the Lord to set his people free.

Like Israel of old, the visible Church has never been free from Satanic and demonic opposition. Surrounded by apathy or hostility, infiltrated with divisions, relativism, legalism, intellectualism, rationalism, idolatry and sinful practices, the work of the evil one's practices abound. If, as some believe, the Loadicean experience is a picture of the end-time church, there can be no doubt as to who is behind the wretchedness, poverty, blindness, and nakedness Jesus Christ foretold (Revelation 3:17).

After God had driven the Hebrews into captivity because of their idolatry and other detestable practices, he commissioned Ezra and Nehemiah to rebuild the walls of Jerusalem, and re-sanctify its temple. Their work was constantly opposed by an evil trio (Nehemiah 2:19). Two of them, Sanballat and Tobiah were descendants of Lot through his incestuous relationship with one of his daughters while under the influence of alcohol. The third opponent was Gershom, an Arab descendant of Abraham through Hagar the Egyptian. Together, they discredited the work of God, verbally opposed the re-building, and constantly delayed re-construction using every tactic they could think of. Even when the work was completed, Tobiah sneakily waited until Nehemiah was visiting Babylon, then manipulated a relative to give him board and lodgings in one of the rooms of the temple itself. Nehemiah learned of this on his return, and was furious. He ordered all Tobiah's belongings to be unceremoniously dumped in the street, then had the defiled space cleansed and refilled with offerings, incense, and temple furniture (Nehemiah 13:7-8).

The re-building of the walls of God's possession, and the re-cleansing of his Church today are similarly being opposed by a trinity of spiritual evil.

These unseen spiritual beings need to be thrown out of God's house, so that it can be cleansed in preparation for the return of its King-High Priest. The sword and the trowel are still indispensable to builders in the twentieth century.

Many books have been written about how to deal with Satan and his demons, and one more is not likely to be greeted with much enthusiasm if the evil trio get their way. And Christian leaders are usually fairly selective in their purchases when there is a variety from which to choose. The teachings of this book present what will probably be a totally new perspective in dealing with demon oppression in the whole personality in one extended period of counselling, rather than the piecemeal fashion of most deliverance sessions. The fact that it deals with demonisation amongst believers adds to its claim for special attention by shepherds and leaders of the flock of God.

The contents of this book belong to the whole Body of Christ, and the response of pastors of main stream denominations in Australia to these teachings has been a considerable encouragement and confirmation of their Biblical basis and practical value. In the letters to the seven churches in Asia Minor, there is a statement which Jesus Christ repeated to John seven times. It is still significant: "He who has an ear, let him hear what the Spirit says to the churches".

In all the writings of David the Psalmist, no passage sums up the subject matter of the following pages better than Psalm forty, verses one to three:-

"I waited patiently and expectantly for the Lord, and He inclined to me and heard my cry. He drew me up out of an horrible pit - a pit of tumult and of destruction - out of the miry clay (froth and slime) and set my feet upon a rock, steadying my steps and establishing my goings. And He has put a new song in my mouth, a song of praise to our God. Many shall see and fear - revere, and worship - and put their trust and confident reliance in the Lord." (Amplified Bible)

"For by him all things were created: things in heaven and on earth, visible and invisible, whether thrones or powers or rulers or authorities; all things were created by him and for him" (Colossians 1:16).

CHAPTER 2.

Fitting the demonic jigsaw together

There was an era in pre-time eternity when Satan and demons were non-existent. Perfection was absolute.

1. THE ORIGIN OF SATAN AND EVIL SPIRITS.

The Scriptures do not specifically state just how some of God's created intelligences became evil powers, but there are references which give some understanding.

(1) The writings of the prophet Ezekiel (chapter 28).

The chapter is devoted to a prophecy against the king of Tyre. When Nebuchadnezzar fulfilled the prophecy and destroyed the city, Ethbaal (also known as Ithabolus) was king. He was a flamboyant character, trimming his clothes and lining the walls of his palace rooms with flashy jewels. So he literally "walked in the midst of stones of fire" (v. 13, 14). And although very great and famous, evil was the cause of his downfall (v. 15, 16).

But no mere human could have completely fulfilled this prophecy for the following reasons:-

(a) The city of Tyre on the Mediterranean coast could never fit Ezekiel's description of 'Eden the garden of God' (v. 13).

(b) The king of Tyre was born of a woman, not created like the personality about whom the prophecy had its major fulfilment. The word 'create' (Hebrew 'bara') is only used to describe the sovereign acts of God, and does not refer to human birth.

(c) As a baby, Ethbaal may have been called a 'little cherub' by his mother, but the comparison would have ended there. A cherub is a winged angelic being, a symbol of the awesome holiness and justice of God (Exodus 25:19-22). Ezekiel's cherub had a divine anointing to fulfil that position (v. 14).

(d) Ezekiel said that the guardian cherub was expelled 'from the mount of fire' (v. 16). Only one of greater power and authority could have done that. God alone could have said: "So I threw you to the earth" (v. 17). Again, whatever Nebuchadnezzar did to Ethbaal could never have fulfilled that aspect of the prophecy.

(2) Ezekiel's harmony with Isaiah's earlier prophecy (chapter 14).

The identity of Ezekiel's 'anointed cherub' comes more clearly into focus when compared with Isaiah's prophecy directed against the king of Babylon.

"How have you fallen from heaven, O morning star, son of the dawn! (KJV - 'Lucifer', Young - 'shining one'). You have been cast down to the earth, you who once laid low the nations" (v. 12).

Isaiah identifies the cause of **Lucifer's judgment** as pride, self idolatry, independence, covetousness, and rebellion (v. 13, 14). As the specific name of Lucifer does not appear in the Scriptures again, but there are many references to a being of the same standing known as Satan or the devil, there are strong grounds for the belief that Satan is the anointed cherub who was rejected for his rebellion against God. Some modern theologians dispute this comparison, but those who belong to the modern church of Satan do not. The devil is worshipped in the names he claims are his own - 'Lucifer' and 'Set'.

(3) The confirmation of Jesus Christ.
(a) "I saw Satan fall like lightning from heaven" (Luke 10:18).
(b) "Depart from me, you who are cursed, into the eternal fire prepared for the devil and his angels" (Matthew 25:41).

(4) The visions of the Apostle John.
(a) "Then another sign appeared in heaven: an enormous red dragon with seven heads and ten horns and seven crowns on his heads. His tail swept a third of the stars out of the sky and flung them to the earth" (Revelation 12:4)
(b) "He seized the dragon, that ancient serpent who is the devil, or Satan and bound him for a thousand years" (Revelation 20:2).
In these two verses, two symbols are used - a dragon for Satan, and stars for angels. Jesus told John that the seven stars in his right hand were the angels of the seven churches (Revelation 1:16, 20). Linking these two symbols suggests that Satan's rebellion was the direct cause of one third of the angels being cast out of heaven.

(5) Other Biblical descriptions.
The other names by which Satan is known indicate the extent of his influence over the earth.
(a) The controller of the systems of this world (1 John 5:19).
(b) The prince of this world (John 16:11).
(c) The god of this age (2 Corinthians 4:4).
(d) The ruler of the kingdom of the air, and the spirit of disobedience in the world (Ephesians 2:2).
(e) The devil who leads the whole world astray (Revelation 12:9).
The angelic beings who joined Satan's rebellion are also called:
(a) the sons of God (Job 2:1).
(b) angels who abandoned their place of habitation (commonly called fallen angels, Jude 6).
(c) demons (KJV - 'devils') (Mark 1:34 etc.).
(d) evil, or unclean spirits (Mark 3:11).
Although the New Testament is silent on the origin of demonic powers, the incredible variety, numbers and evil influence of these spirits are evident from the Living Bible paraphrase of Ephesians 6:12: ". . the evil rulers of the unseen world . . mighty satanic beings . . great evil princes of darkness who rule this world . . huge numbers of evil spirits in the spirit world".
Further information on the nature and activities of Satan and his demonic powers may be found in Appendices A and B in the resources section at the end of this book.

2. GOD SOVEREIGNLY CONTROLS SATAN AND ALL DEMON POWERS.

Angelic beings of every order have been given prescribed authority to fulfil their divine purposes. From the Biblical record it is obvious that angelic messengers always kept within the limits of their authorisation when speaking to those to whom they were sent. There appeared to be no conversational 'chit-chat' (Daniel 10:11-21; Matthew 1:20, 21; Luke 1:11-20; 1:26-38; Acts 12:7-10).

The angels who rebelled with Lucifer remain under God's sovereign control despite having been deprived of their original status. Their hierarchical standing and responsibility to authority also appears to have been maintained under Satan's control (Ephesians 6:12 compared with Colossians 1:16).

(1) Satanic submission to God's sovereignty.

While Lucifer's transposition to Satan is clothed with symbolism, Satan's submission to God's authority is explicit.

(a) The judgments of the Garden of Eden (Genesis 3:14, 15).

After the Satanically engineered fall of Adam and Eve, God delivered a three-fold judgment. Firstly, he cursed the serpent Satan had used to disguise his identity, so that its species had to crawl on the belly from that time onwards (Isaiah 65:25).

Secondly, God established hostility between the woman and her children, and Satan represented by the serpent and his seed (verse 15). This is nowhere more clearly illustrated than when Jesus said to the Jews:

"If God were your Father, you would love me, for I came from God and now am here . . You belong to your father, the devil, and you want to carry out your father's desire. He was a murderer from the beginning, not holding to the truth, for there is not truth in him. When he lies, he speaks his native language for he is a liar and the father of lies" (John 8:42, 44).

Thirdly, God promised victory to the future seed of the woman Galatians 3:16). This refers to the deadly combat with the serpent which took place at Calvary when Jesus Christ crushed the authority of Satan (Colossians 2:15). He triumphantly dealt with sin and its venom of death in resurrection followed by his ascension to heaven.

(b) King David's numbering of Israel (1 Chronicles 21:1).

Two passages need to be compared to understand the part Satan played in the fulfilment of God's will:

"Again the anger of the LORD burned against Israel, and he incited David against them saying 'Go and count Israel and Judah' " (2 Samuel 24:1).

"Satan rose up against Israel, and incited David to take a census of Israel" (1 Chronicles 21:1).

In both accounts, Joab the army commander in chief tried to dissuade David from his intentions, "The king's word, however, over-ruled Joab" (2 Samuel 24:1; 1 Chronicles 21:4). Satan had obviously prevented David from seeing reason, and as a result, seventy thousand men perished; and part of Jerusalem was destroyed by the angel of the LORD (1 Chronicles 21:14-30).

(c) Satan's affliction of Job.

On two occasions in the book of Job angels came to present themselves to God (Job 1:6; 2:1). Whereas all angelic beings in the pre-sin era were also called 'sons of God' (Job 38:7), after the fall of Lucifer, this term is used only of fallen angels as shown in modern translations, or their footnotes. The term is also used in Genesis 6:2, 4. When these angelic sons of God presented themselves to God, Satan their leader went with them.

During the recorded dialogue between God and Satan on the subject of the integrity of Job, Satan twice asked for specific permission to afflict Job in an attempt to prove his insincerity. On both occasions conditional permission was granted, and Satan made maximum use of his destructive power against Job's sons and daughters, his servants, his possessions, and finally, Job's own body. But he was powerless to kill Job, or to prevent the double blessing God gave Job afterwards (Job 42:12-16).

(d) Satan's inability to accuse Joshua the high priest (Zechariah 3:1-10).

The fourth vision God gave to Zechariah the prophet was that of a court scene in which Satan, as accuser, stood alongside Joshua the high priest who was wearing filthy garments as symbols of the sins of Jerusalem. God, as judge, did not allow Satan to speak, but used his own glorious name to reprove the accuser with his accusations: "The LORD rebuke you Satan! The LORD who has chosen Jerusalem rebuke you Satan! Is not this man a burning stick snatched from the fire?" (verse 2). After that rebuke Satan no longer features in the vision.

(e) The written Word of God exposes Satan's limitation of power (Matthew 4:11).

When Satan tempted the newly anointed Messiah in the Mount of Temptation, he tried all he could to find flaws in his human personality. He tempted his physical appetite; challenged his instinct for self-preservation; and even offered to return his conquest of the kingdoms of the world in return for submission. Jesus Christ rebuffed each temptation by quoting Old Testament scriptures. The final challenge came from Deuteronomy 6:13, and because Satan was not prepared to worship and serve the LORD his God, he left, defeated (v. 11).

(f) Satan had to ask for special authority to sift the disciples, as wheat is sifted (Luke 22:31).

It would appear that Satan did everything within his power to ensure that Jesus Christ had as little support as possible from his disciples when facing his trial and crucifixion. (Some of the results are included in the following chapter). While Jesus gave no extra details of the request, he implied that it had been approved as he spoke to Peter: "Simon, Simon, Satan has asked to sift you (plural) as wheat. But I have prayed for you, Simon, that your faith may not fail. And when you (singular) have turned back, strengthen your brothers" (verse 32).

(g) Satan is given authority to afflict members of the New Testament Church.

The Church exists in a world controlled by Satan and his evil forces are intent on destroying anything which brings glory to God. The specifics of the manner in which these evil beings operate in the Church will be shown in a later chapter.

(2) Demonic submission to God's authority.

(a) God used evil angels to punish people in the Old Testament.

(i) The Egyptians.

Asaph openly claims that God used evil angels to afflict the Egyptians for the failure to release his people: "He unleashed against them his hot anger, his wrath, indignation and hostility - a band of destroying angels" (Psalm 78:49). Alternatives are 'evil angels' (KJV), and 'evil spirits' (Berkeley Version).

(ii) The Hebrews themselves.

The writer suggests that it is not unreasonable to believe that God used those very same evil angels to afflict his own people later in their history to fulfil the curses they pronounced on themselves at Mount Ebal as they entered the land of promise (Deuteronomy 27:13-26; 28:15-68). Of particular significance are verses 58-60:

"If you do not carefully follow all the words of this law, which are written in this book, and do not revere his glorious and awesome name - the LORD your God - the LORD will send fearful plagues on you and your descendants, harsh and prolonged disasters and severe and lingering illnesses. He will bring upon you all the diseases of Egypt that you dreaded, and they will cling to you".

In the twenty-seventh and twenty-eighth verses of that same chapter Moses spelled out some of those diseases and sickness as:

"The LORD will afflict you with the boils of Egypt and with tumours, festering sores, and the itch from which you cannot be cured. The LORD will afflict you with madness, blindness, and confusion of mind".

It is little wonder that Jesus Christ had such an extensive ministry of deliverance and healing which he shared with his disciples, because his people had been oppressed by evil spirits for centuries. "God anointed Jesus of Nazareth with the Holy Spirit and power, and . . he went around healing all who were under the power of the devil, because God was with him" (Acts 10:38).

(b) The remarkable vision of the prophet Micaiah (2 Chronicles 18:16-27).

Jehoshaphat, king of Judah became a relative of the infamous Ahab, king of Israel, through marriage. Years afterwards, he visited Ahab in Samaria, and was both feted and pressured to join Ahab in an attack on Ramoth Gilead. Jehoshaphat asked for counsel from the LORD, so Ahab assembled his prophets, who, because they were on his pay-roll, all approved of the proposal. But Judah's king was a God-fearing man, and insisted on hearing from a true prophet of God. Ahab yielded to pressure, and called for Micaiah whom he intensely disliked because he was fearless in speaking only by divine revelation. At first Micaiah pretended to go along with the majority, but when pressured by Ahab gave a brief prophecy about defeat in battle. Ahab showed his displeasure, so Micaiah then gave him the full revelation he had received from the LORD. It is one of the most enlightening passages in Scripture concerning God's sovereignty over demonic activity.

In the vision, Micaiah saw the angelic hosts of heaven standing before God on his throne, some on his right hand, and some on his left hand. The positioning of these angels is important, and for greater understanding we need to examine a similar scene Jesus spoke about in which people of all nations will stand before the throne of God, having been sorted as a shepherd separates sheep from goats (Matthew 25:31-46). The righteous who are directed to stand on the right side of the throne are welcomed into the eternal inheritance God had prepared for them since the beginning of creation. To those on the left side, Jesus said the King will say: "Depart from me, you who are cursed, into the eternal fire prepared for the devil and his angels" (verse 41).

In view of the fact that the unrighteous are positioned on the left side of the throne of God, and directly associated with Satan and his angels, the writer suggests that it is not unreasonable to believe that the angels in Micaiah's vision were similarly separated, the faithful on the right, the cursed on the left. When God called for a volunteer to lure Ahab into attacking Ramoth Gilead so that he might be killed in battle (v. 19), there were a number of suggestions until "Finally a spirit came forward, stood before the LORD and said 'I will lure him'. 'By what means,' the LORD asked. 'I will go and be a lying spirit in the mouths of all his prophets,' he said. 'You will succeed in luring him,' said the LORD. 'Go and do it' " (verses 20, 21).

No angel reflecting the glory of God would stoop to enticement and deception. The writer believes that the spirit who volunteered for this assignment, and successfully carried it out, could only have been a demon (or evil spirit), from among those who stood on God's left hand. The implication is obvious. God sovereignly controls demonic powers.

Micaiah's final words of prophecy to the two kings confirms it: "So now the LORD has put a lying spirit in the mouths of these prophets of yours. The LORD has decreed disaster for you" (v. 22).

(c) **God fulfilled Jotham's curse on the Shechemites through an evil spirit (Judges 9:23).**

Jotham was the only surviving son of Gideon when Abimelech (his half-brother through a slave-girl). Aided by the treachery of the Shechemites, he butchered his seventy brothers on a rock in the city. When Abimelech was three years into his usurped reign over Israel, God sent an evil spirit to stir up animosity between Abimelech and the people of Shechem to avenge the treachery and the blood of the innocent victims. As a result, the city was destroyed and its people slain. Abimelech requested his armour bearer to kill him, rather than suffer the disgrace of dying from a cracked skull inflicted by a woman. The record concludes: "Thus God repaid the wickedness that Abimelech had done to his father by murdering his seventy brothers. God also made the men of Shechem pay for all their wickedness. The curse of Jotham son of Jerub-baal came on them" (v.v.56, 57).

(d) **When the Holy Spirit left Saul, God sent an evil spirit to torment him (1 Samuel 16:14).**

This evil spirit was also:-
 (i) a forceful, controlling spirit (Ch. 18:10).
 (ii) a murderous spirit (Ch. 18:10; 19:9-11).
 (iii) a relentless spirit (Ch. 19:9).
 (v) a spirit which caused Saul to seek help by witchcraft practices through the witch of Endor (1 Samuel 28:3-25).

The New Testament epistles contain many warnings of demonic activities within the Church of God indicating the extent to which these powers were permitted to operate after their defeat at Calvary. But that is not the subject under consideration here as we are concerned with the extent to which demonic powers are directed by God to fulfil his will.

(e) The demonic nature of Paul's thorn (2 Corinthians 12:7).

"To keep me from becoming conceited because of these surpassingly great revelations, there was given me a thorn in my flesh, a messenger of Satan, to torment me."

The traditional explanation of Paul's thorn is that Paul suffered from some kind of eye disease. This is based largely on two verses in the Galatian epistle. Firstly, " . . I can testify that, if you could have done so, you would have torn out your eyes and given them to me" (Ch. 4:15). This may have been a statement of sincere appreciation for their willingness to sacrifice their own eye-sight for his benefit, had that been possible. Or, it may have been an expression of gratitude for their genuine desire to help, using a figure of speech no more significant than the many we currently use, such as 'I would give my right arm to be able to do this or that'.

Secondly, "See what large letters I use as I write to you with my own hand" (Ch. 6:11). J. B. Phillips adds the following footnote to this verse: "According to centuries-old Eastern usage, this could easily mean, 'Note how heavily I have pressed upon the pen in writing this!' Thus it could be translated, 'Notice how heavily I underline these words to you' (The New Testament in Modern English J. B. Phillips - Bles and Collins).

Certainly no one can say with any certainty whether tradition or the alternatives given are correct, but the character of the thorn weighs heavily against the traditional explanation. Satan is an expert in covering his tracks. He has already successfully covered his true identity with the caricature image of horns, hooves, and a trident. He has also filled the hearts of many of God's people with fear, prejudice, and opposition to a twentieth century ministry of first century Holy Spirit power and authority. And the last thing he wants believers to accept is the level to which he can buffet, bind, and dominate their lives. A review of what God sovereignly directed in Paul's life through this messenger of Satan is therefore important. If God used a demon then, he obviously is able to do so today. If Paul was not exempt from demonic activity, neither are we.

(i) The objective of the thorn was to cause weakness, not a disease.

The Greek 'asthenia' is translated "a want of strength, inability to produce results" by W. E. Vine in his Expository Dictionary of New Testament Words. The thorn was given to prevent Paul from becoming conceited, not as punishment for sin.

(ii) The thorn did not restrict his teaching or writing ministry as would most certainly have been the case had it been some opthalmic disease.

(iii) The effects of the thorn brought Paul an ample supply of God's grace and power to endure the effects it produced. Although Paul pled with God three times for its removal, God refused each request, promising that his grace and strength would be adequate for Paul to handle, whatever situation the demonic messenger caused (v. 9).

(iv) The thorn caused not one weakness, but many.

Paul never spoke of a singular weakness, such as his eyesight, but weaknesses caused by a variety of events. "That is why, for Christ's sake, I delight in weaknesses, in persecutions, in difficulties. For when I am weak, then I am strong" (Ch. 12:10).

(v) The thorn's nature may be identified by three characteristics.

Firstly, it was sharp and gave physical pain. The Greek word for 'thorn' is 'skolops' which means a 'sharp stake'. This is the only time the word appears in the New Testament.

Secondly, the thorn was not a lifeless piece of equipment, it was 'a messenger of Satan' (v. 7), a demonic personality. The Greek 'aggelos' is translated only seven times as 'messenger', the other one hundred and eight times it is translated as 'angel'. The fact that wherever he went Paul ran into opposition and danger indicates the variety of situations the evil spirit used to buffet him. Paul was shipwrecked three times, in constant danger from people and the elements, harrassed to the point of sleeplessness, starved, and deprived of the comforts of life (2 Corinthians 11:26-38).

Thirdly, the aim of the thorn was to cause constant suffering. The words 'to torment me' come from the Greek 'kolaphizo' translated by 'buffet' in the King James Version. The concept is that of a person being struck a number of blows with a clenched fist. Paul experienced the weakness and pain of this thorn constantly, it was not a once-only experience.

God used people as 'thorns' against the Hebrews of old as a means of inflicting punishment on them (Numbers 33:55; Joshua 23:13; Ezekiel 28:24). When Paul's 'thorn' wasn't marshalling the elements and dangerous situations against him he was stirring up the opposition of individuals and groups of people. The circumcision party from Antioch and Iconium followed Paul to Lystra and agitated the locals to stone him (Acts 14:19); also, the owners of the fortune-telling slave-girl at Philippi caused Paul and his companion Silas to be beaten and thrown into prison because Paul had freed the girl from an evil spirit, ending a cosy little financial racket (Acts 16:16-36). Demetrius the Ephesian silversmith successfully organised a city riot against Paul when he opposed a local goddess whose lineage stretched back to Baal in Babylon (Acts 19:23-41). And then there were the lashings Paul speaks of in 2 Corinthians 11:24, 25. Satan's angel obviously went about his duties with real dedication! The apostle's survival can only be described as a miracle of divine grace. Even being chained to Roman guards did not hinder the flow of divine truth and practical teachings in the prison epistles. Nothing the demon was allowed to do prevented Paul from fulfilling the terms of his anointing (2 Timothy 4:7, 8).

God's direction of demonic affliction in the life of the apostle Paul confirms his sovereignty and his sovereign right to use whatever angelic powers he may choose to fulfil his will in believers, or unbelievers.

3. PRESENT DAY USE OF SATAN AND HIS DEMONIC POWERS TO FULFIL THE JUDGMENTS AND PURPOSES OF GOD.

The Scriptures give no indication that God has changed his modus operandi since the ascension of Jesus Christ. In the absence of any clear statement to this effect, and in view of the increasing evidence of demonic activity in the world, and in the Body of Christ, it is not an assumption but a certainty that God continues his sovereign use of all types of angelic beings.

David the Psalmist provides some insight as to God's methods of dealing with rebellious people. In the first five verses of Psalm 109, David complains to God about those who had lied against him and repaid his friendship with hatred and evil. He then adds "Appoint an evil man (alt. the evil one) to oppose him; let an accuser (alt. Satan) stand at his right hand" (v. 6). David obviously had no doubts about God's sovereign use of Satan as a means of punishing the wicked. In fact he was so confident of this that he prayed: "May this be the LORD's payment to my accusers, to those who speak evil of me" (v. 20).

Solomon either learned this piece of wisdom from his father, or received it separately from God, because he wrote: "An evil man is bent only on rebellion; a merciless official will be sent against him" (Proverbs 17:11). Other translation of the words 'merciless official' are:-
1. 'a cruel messenger', (KJV, NASB, RSV).
2. 'a stern and pitiless messenger', (Amplified Bible).
3. 'pitiless angels', (American Standard Bible).

The Hebrew word 'malak' is translated ninety-eight times as 'messenger', and one hundred and six times as 'angel'. King Saul was certainly afflicted by one such 'pitiless angel' termed an 'evil spirit' after God withdrew his Holy Spirit (1 Samuel 18:10).

God's use of evil angels to afflict the Egyptians and later the Hebrews for their gross rebellion against himself has already been referred to. The distinct possibility that God still uses Satan and his evil spirits to afflict saints who are gross sinners today should not be overlooked (1 Corinthians 11:29).

Paul clearly states that believers who take holy communion while living lives which dishonour the body and blood of Jesus Christ, bring a special judgment upon themselves. He lists physical weakness, sickness, and death as the consequences (v. 30-32). The Scriptures have a history of evil spirits being used to bring about these judgments.

Finally, a reminder that Satan and his angels continue to have access to God's presence.

Calvary disarmed Satan and all his demon powers (Colossians 2:15), but armed God's saints to effectively combat them (Ephesians 6:10-18; 2 Corinthians 10:4, 5). Satanic and demonic access to God's presence has already been traced from Job through the visions given to Micaiah (2 Chronicles 18, and Zechariah in the third chapter of his prophecy).

This continues just as clearly in the New Testament. Paul emphasises the effectiveness of the intercessory prayers of Jesus Christ on our behalf when charges are laid against us and we are condemned in the presence of God (Romans 8:31-35). It is certain that none of God's heavenly host would do such a thing, with the blood of Jesus Christ upon the mercy seat of the heavenly ark of the covenant (Hebrews 9:11-14). The forces of evil can only be responsible. No wonder the heavens have yet to be cleansed from the defilement of the accuser and his followers (2 Peter 3:10-13).

The termination of Satan's access to God occurs in Revelation chapter twelve where Satan and his angels are decisively defeated in a battle with Michael and his angels, and all evil forces are hurled out of heaven:
"And there was war in heaven. Michael and his angels fought against the dragon, and the dragon and his angels fought back. But he was not strong enough, and they lost their place in heaven. The great dragon was **hurled down** - that ancient serpent called the devil, or Satan, who leads the whole world astray. He was **hurled to the earth**, and his angels with

him. Then I heard a loud voice in heaven say: 'Now have come the salvation and the power and the kingdom of our God, and the authority of his Christ. **For the accuser of our brothers, who accuses them before our God day and night has been hurled down** ... Therefore rejoice, you heavens and you who dwell in them! But woe to the earth and the sea, because the devil has gone down to you! He is filled with fury, because he knows that his time is short" (v. 7-10, 12 emphasis added).

Both writers and readers live between Calvary and this event. The conclusions and implications are obvious.

CHAPTER SUMMARY.

1. God created all angelic beings perfect, and for his glory. When Lucifer and a number of supporting angels acted in pride, self-exaltation, covetousness, and rebellion, they were cast out of heaven, but remained subject to God's sovereign will and control.

2. Through deception, Satan led our first parents into rebellion and disobedience to God's command, and stole the spiritual power to rule over his creation. And so Satan became the ruler of this world - the spiritual head of all sinners. Through Calvary, Satan and his forces have been disarmed, and believers spiritually armed - given the power and authority to overcome him and his forces of evil.

3. God has used Satan and demonic powers to fulfil his will and his judgments on those who rebel against him amongst the nations and people of the world, including those who belong to him under the first or second covenants. There is no Biblical evidence to show that God has changed his principles of operation.

4. God's use of a demonic messenger against the apostle Paul shows that believers are not exempt from demonic oppression.

5. The Biblical evidence clearly shows that Satan and demonic powers still have access to the presence of God, where they accuse believers, and will continue to do so until the fulfilment of Revelation 12:7-12.

"And I will put enmity between you and the woman, and between your off-spring and hers; he will crush your head, and you will strike his heel."

(Genesis 3:15)

CHAPTER 3.

Satanic and demonic opposition to Jesus Christ and his disciples

When a virgin named Mary gave birth to a son she named Jesus, the angelic message of peace and goodwill on earth brought no joy to the god of this world and his principalities and powers. They had anticipated and dreaded this event ever since God had said that 'a seed of the woman' would crush the head of the serpent. Satan knew that such a miracle child could only be Immanuel himself (Isaiah 7:14). Doubtless the hatred and fury of every rejected angelic being boiled over at the sight of Mary cradling incarnate deity, and vain attempts to do away with Jesus (so heading off the foretold clash) must have commenced immediately.

1. OPPOSITION TO JESUS CHRIST HIMSELF.

Had it been possible to intercept Satan's orders to his demonic powers, I imagine they may have been something like this:-

(1) "Kill Mary's Christ child".

King Herod the Great, a very unkindly soul nicknamed 'the butcher', made the first move. When some Eastern astrologers told him that they were following a moving star to find the birthplace of a baby born king of the Jews, he felt very threatened (Matthew 2:2). He feigned a desire to worship also, but when the Magi gave him the slip (under divine directions), he slaughtered all the baby boys in Bethlehem and surrounding districts under the age of two years to rid himself of a potential rival (Matthew 2:16). What Herod probably didn't realize was that he was being dominated by a murderous spirit acting under highest orders from the kingdom of darkness (John 8:44). Satan was even more threatened by Jesus than Herod was.

Many years later, during the public ministry of Jesus Christ, the Pharisees warned him that another Herod (Antipas) wanted to kill him. Murder was obviously a hereditary method of disposing of opposition in that family! Jesus knew that Antipas was also working under higher orders, and showed his fearlessness of demonic threats by asserting his power over them! "Go tell that fox, I will drive out demons and heal people today and tomorrow, and on the third day I will reach my goal" (Luke 13:32).

(2) "Stir up the religious Jews and make them want to kill him".

After Jesus had returned home to Galilee, he went into his home town synagogue at Nazareth, with Satan hot on his heels. When Jesus had read from Isaiah's prophecy, and claimed to fulfil what was written, the spirits of envy, jealousy, resentment, and murder filled the hearts of his listeners. They drove Jesus out of the town towards a cliff top where they had every intention of hurling the supposed imposter to his death. But Jesus simply walked through the frenzied crowd and went on his way (Luke 4:29, 30).

(3) "Make a scene in the synagogue, and challenge his authority".

After Nazareth, Jesus went to Capernaum on the Sabbath, and was mocked and challenged by a demon-possessed man in the synagogue. "Ha!" he shouted, "What do you want with us, Jesus of Nazareth? Have you come to destroy us? I know who you are - the holy one of God." Jesus ordered the demon (not the man) to be quiet, and to come out (Luke 4:34). Jesus never permitted demons to testify to his deity because they had rejected his sovereignty in pre-time eternity (Luke 4:41; 8:28).

(4) "Drown him".

The next demonic attack took place one evening on the sea of Galilee (Mark 4:35-41). A squall threatened to swamp the disciples' boat while Jesus slept peacefully in the heaving stern. The fearful disciples woke their master and accused him of not caring that they might drown. Recognizing the demonic nature of the storm, Jesus immediately rebuked the powers causing the high wind and waves, using the Greek word 'epitimao', meaning 'be muzzled or gagged'. This word was used against demons on other occasions, such as when the demon-possessed worshipper was released and healed in Capernaum (Mark 1:25). Again, when Jesus rebuked Peter's mother-in-law's fever and she immediately got up, fit and well (Luke 4:39). Also when a deaf and dumb spirit was cast out of a boy (Luke 9:42).

The disciples marvelled at the sudden calm, but obviously did not understand that there had been a spiritual victory in which demons had been exposed and defeated. "They were terrified and asked each other, "Who is this? Even the wind and waves obey him" (Gr. "harken submissively" v. 41).

(5) "Defy or distract Jesus whenever possible".

Dr. Luke writes some excellent case notes in explaining the greatest recorded case of deliverance Jesus accomplished in his ministry (Luke 8:26-29). Because the controlling demon gave his name as Legion, and a Roman legion contained between three and six thousand men, it is reasonable to believe that there were that many demons in the man. The maniac's uncontrollable behaviour and the later destruction of two thousand demon-possessed pigs support this. This spirit Legion actually audaciously interrupted Jesus when he was ordered to leave. He both challenged the authority of Jesus Christ, and tried to win concessions by asking for leave to enter the pigs rather than the abyss.

Demons haven't changed. Some years ago the writers were praying over a heavily demonised friend when a demon used the man's voice to ask permission to enter a dog which had just commenced a dismal howl. Permission was twice refused, and finally the demon told not to ask again. The dog stopped howling, and the prayer time continued. The dog in question lived on the opposite side of the street at a house with a high front gate. Several days later someone failed to latch the gate correctly and the dog escaped. It immediately ran across the road and savagely mauled a child playing on a lawn. The child required a considerable number of stitches to the head. The police destroyed the dog, and the writer felt confirmed in his decision not to permit demons to enter a predatory animal. A medical missionary from the Solomon

Islands once shared that he had released demons from an islander into the sea, and had seen an area of water suddenly churned up by fish leaping and thrashing about.

(6) "Stop the encounter God has arranged - at all costs!"

The agony and victory of Calvary began amongst the olive trees of a garden. Each Gospel supplies important details of the composite scene:-

(a) Matthew emphasizes the triple request Jesus made to his Father to remove the cup he was facing, providing it was the Father's will (Matthew 26:36-45).

(b) Mark tells us that Jesus was deeply distressed and overwhelmed with sorrow, to the point of death (Mark 14:32-41).

(c) Luke alone writes that an angel from heaven appeared and strengthened Jesus, and that in his anguish his sweat was like drops of blood falling to the ground (Luke 22:39-46).

(d) John makes it clear that after the events in the garden, and in the presence of the disciples, Judas, and the arresting band of soldiers, Jesus openly stated his intention to drink the cup the Father had given him (John 18:11).

The writer of the Hebrews includes a verse which would appear to complete the Gospel accounts. "During the days of Jesus' life on earth, he offered up prayers and petitions with loud cries and tears to the one who could save him from death, and he was heard because of his reverent submission" (Hebrews 5:7).

The events of the Garden of Gethsemane are certainly holy ground for prayerful consideration. Throughout his life Jesus constantly spoke of his forthcoming death in Jerusalem, but it is clear from what he said that he was going to lay his life down, not have it taken from him (John 10:17, 18). On one occasion he spoke of "the cup I am going to drink" as a figure of speech for the death he was going to suffer (Matthew 20:22).

As we examine the facts of Gethsemane we find a saviour who is anguishing so greatly over a cup he was about to drink that Dr. Luke describes his sweat as like drops of blood falling to the ground. His cry to his Father was "Father if you are willing, take this cup from me, yet not my will, but yours be done" (Luke 22:42). This seems inconsistent with all that Jesus Christ had previously said, unless he indeed faced a substitute cup of premature death which would have prevented him from becoming the Passover Lamb of God. This could only have been cleverly engineered by the one who had most to lose by having his head crushed by the seed of the woman. It is the writer's belief that this was indeed so. Let us look at the facts again:

(i) Jesus committed himself to lay his life down, symbolised by drinking a cup.

(ii) In the Garden Jesus was deeply distressed and troubled, saying, "My soul is overwhelmed with sorrow to the point of death" (Mark 14:33,34). The synoptic writers all agree that Jesus cried to his Father to remove the cup he was faced with drinking, provided it was the Father's will. That cup could well have been death by loss of blood in the Garden, because:

(iii) An angel came and strengthened him (Luke 22:43).

(iv) Almost immediately afterwards Judas and the soldiers arrived. Peter showed his loyalty with his sword, an ear was healed, and Jesus uttered these words - "Shall I not drink the cup the Father has given me?" (John 18:11).

There seems to be little doubt that the first cup was given by the same hand that had vainly tried to kill him on so many previous occasions. He has always been a murderer (John 8:44). Paul warns all believers to beware of substitute cups: "You cannot drink of the cup of the Lord and the cup of demons too" (1 Corinthians 10:21).

2. SATANIC INFLUENCE OVER THE DISCIPLES OF JESUS CHRIST.

(1) Satan put words into Peter's mouth.

Shortly after Peter received divine revelation concerning the deity of Jesus Christ, he treated Jesus as an ordinary human being by taking him aside and rebuking him for talking about his future death and resurrection. He may have been declaring the common Jewish expectation of the Messiah, or assuring Jesus that his disciples would stand by him to prevent his death; but what he said was certainly not divine revelation. Jesus recognized the subtlety of the evil one, and so he addressed him in his reply to Peter - "Out of my sight, Satan! You are a stumbling block to me; you do not have in mind the things of God, but the things of men" (Matthew 16:23).

(2) The Satanic discipleship test.

Close to the end of his ministry Jesus warned Peter that Satan was going to test all the disciples just as a farmer sifts wheat from chaff. As a result of this:-

(a) Judas betrayed his Lord.

"Then Satan entered into Judas, called Iscariot, one of the Twelve. And Judas went to the chief priests and the officers of the temple guard and discussed with them how he might betray Jesus" (Luke 22:3, 4). "As soon as Judas took the bread, Satan entered into him. 'What you are about to do, do quickly,' Jesus told him . . . As soon as Judas had taken the bread, he went out. And it was night" (John 13:27-30).

(b) Peter denied knowing his Lord.

Warming himself with the servants in the High Priest's house, Peter vehemently denied knowing Jesus or being one of his followers, and ". . Just as Peter was speaking, the rooster crowed. The Lord turned and looked straight at Peter. Then Peter remembered the word the Lord had spoken to him: 'Before the rooster crows today, you will disown me three times.' And he went outside and wept bitterly" (Luke 22:60b-62).

(c) Peter, James and John slept, while Jesus agonized.

Matthew tells us that Peter, James and John were taken into the garden by Jesus to be close to him and maintain a prayer vigil. But they fell into a deep sleep (Matthew 26:37, 38). When he found them sleeping, Jesus asked Peter, "Could you men not keep watch with me for one hour? . . . Watch and pray so that you will not fall into temptation. The spirit is willing, but the body is weak" (vv. 40, 41). The warning to engage in spiritual warfare and not submit to the tempter could not have been clearer, but they failed to heed it, and were overcome by a spirit of deep sleep at a time of desperate spiritual need (Isaiah 29:10; Romans 11:8).

(d) All the disciples forsook their Lord.

"Then everyone deserted him and fled" (Mark 14:50). John alone represented the apostles at the crucifixion, and was given the privilege of caring for the mother of Jesus (John 19:26, 27).

The manner in which the evil one dominated some of the apostles in the very presence of Jesus Christ must surely call into question the prevalent teaching that believers are beyond the reach of Satan and his demonic hordes. If the apostles fell victim when Jesus was with them, what has changed to prevent this happening to us in whom Jesus Christ is present in the person of his Holy Spirit?

The writers are constantly finding that when the saints hear teaching on the sources and types of Satanic and demonic oppression in their lives, they can't wait to receive freedom. In one medium-sized church, after a brief period of teaching, some seventy people surged forward at an altar call to claim release.

CHAPTER SUMMARY.

1. Satan and his demons tried to discredit Jesus Christ in his earthly ministry. On more than one occasion they tried to kill him, and so prevent Calvary's fulfillment of God's promise that the seed of the woman would deliver a crushing blow to Satan.

2. Satan successfully manipulated the apostles into attitudes, statements, and actions designed to embarrass and hinder the earthly ministry of Jesus Christ.

3. The warning to present day believers is obvious. Satanic and demonic hatred towards God and every member of his kingdom on earth is unending. As the world moves towards the inevitable conflict between the angelic forces and the powers of darkness, God's people need to claim their freedom, and retain it by all means.

"For God was pleased to have all his fulness dwell in him, and through him to reconcile to himself all things, whether things on earth or things in heaven by making peace through his blood, shed on the cross" (Colossians 1:19–20).

CHAPTER 4.

Why the deliverance ministry was so important to Jesus Christ

The only manifestation of power in the life of Jesus Christ which had no Old Testament counterpart was the ministry of deliverance. Certainly, forms of exorcism were practised by some Jews and other nations, but they were mainly linked with occultism. Without question, the ministry of Jesus Christ was unique. He set people free, healed them, made them socially acceptable, and authorised his disciples to do the same, because the need was so great. The ministry of deliverance was strategic to Jesus Christ because:

1. He alone had the authority and power to end Satan's despotic rule over this world, and set the prisoners free (Romans 11:26).

The events of the Mount of Temptation come between the anointing from above, and the commencement of three and one half years of public ministry in which Jesus constantly confronted Satan and his evil spirits. The victory won in the wilderness was the first of a series of victories Jesus Christ gained over Satan and his powers, climaxing in the triumph of the resurrection and ascension to glory.

To understand the significance of this event, we need to go back to the Amalekite attack on the Hebrews after they had crossed the Red Sea (Exodus 17:8-13). The battle was won only by the intercession of Moses on behalf of Joshua and his forces. Standing with Aaron and Hur on a hilltop overlooking the battle, Moses lifted his hands towards heaven. As long as he held them above his head the Israelites won, but when he tired and lowered his hands, the Amalekites won. When Moses was overcome by exhaustion, he sat on a rock, with the two priests standing on either side of him, each holding a hand high until sunset to ensure victory for Joshua.

As a memorial, Moses erected an altar which he named "The LORD is my Banner", because "hands were lifted up to the throne of the LORD" (v.v. 15:16).

After entering the promised land, Israel again needed a special intercessor to enable them to win a battle previously lost at Ai because of the defilement of sin. Once the offending Aachan and his family and possessions had been destroyed, and the people cleansed, God gave them his battle plans. He also said to Joshua, "Hold out toward Ai the javelin that is in your hand, for into your hand I will deliver the city" (Joshua 8:18). Joshua obeyed to the letter, and did not lower the javelin until all the people of Ai had been destroyed (v. 26).

When Jesus Christ went to the wilderness of temptation, as the newly anointed Messiah, he had a much greater task than either Moses or Joshua. Their intercession brought victories in battle, but were symbolical of a much greater spiritual reality. Without human support, Jesus Christ began to grapple with Satan and the forces of darkness.

To be able to set prisoners free spiritually, Jesus had to win not only that first contest against Satan, his demons, and all evil, but also each succeeding contest and the final decisive battle at Calvary. By overcoming the tempter at a time of the most intense physical weakness - after a forty day fast - Jesus began to crush the head of his opponent (Genesis 3:15). With the final victory of Calvary behind him, Jesus Christ returned in triumph to his Father, having provided a four-fold benediction of victory for his people:

(1) Redemption from sin through his blood.

"But now he has appeared once for all at the end of the ages to do away with sin by the sacrifice of himself" (Hebrews 9:26). "In him we have redemption through his blood, the forgiveness of sins . . " (Ephesians 1:7).

(2) Freedom from the devil's grip and influence.

" . . The reason the Son of God appeared was to destroy (Gr. 'luo' - 'to loose') the devil's work" (1 John 3:8b).

(3) Release from slavery to the fear of death.

"Since the children have flesh and blood, he too shared in their humanity, so that by his death he might destroy him who holds the power of death - that is, the devil - and free those who all their lives were held in slavery by their fear of death" (Hebrews 2:14, 15).

(4) Provision of eternal life, and the promise of protection from marauding attacks of the devil.

"I am the gate; whoever enters through me will be saved. He will come in and go out and find pasture. The thief comes only to steal and kill and destroy. I have come that they may have life, and have it to the full" (John 10:9, 10).

In view of this four-fold provision, some readers might say: "If all that has been provided through Calvary, why are Satan and demons still at loose today?" The major reason is that God permits it to be so. God sovereignly determines all frameworks of time, but we do know that God has already predetermined when their power will be destroyed, and their personalities punished in eternal fire (1 Corinthians 15:24-26; Revelation 20:10; 2 Peter 3:10). Meanwhile the Church in general, and we believers in particular, have been given the power and authority of Jesus Christ firstly, to attack the devil's stronghold (Matthew 16:18), secondly, to cast out demons (Mark 16:17), and thirdly, to defeat the powers of darkness by spiritual warfare (Ephesians 6:10-18). Another reason must also be that Satan and evil spirits remain on the loose today because we believers have failed God in not using the power at our disposal.

A careful examination of Scripture will show how effective the work of Calvary is against all the powers of the evil one:

(a) In spiritual authority over Satan.

Jude tells us that even the archangel Michael would not argue with the devil over the disposal of the body of Moses. He quoted a higher authority - "The Lord rebuke you" (Jude 9). The prophet Zechariah tells us that even God himself used the sacredness of his own name against Satan (Zechariah 3:2). But that was before Calvary. The situation has now changed because reconciliation of all things has been made possible through Calvary (Colossians 1:20). The angels now have a new power.

"And I saw an angel coming down out of heaven, having the key to the Abyss and holding in his hand a great chain. He seized the dragon, that ancient serpent, who is the devil, or Satan, and bound him for a thousand years. He threw him into the Abyss and locked and sealed it over him, to keep him from deceiving the nations any more until the thousand years were ended" (Revelation 20:1-3).

(b) In the believer's victory over Satan and demon powers.

When the devil is resisted, he now has no alternative but to leave in a hurry. "Resist the devil, and HE WILL flee from you" (James 4:7 - emphasis added). "In my name they (who believe) will cast out demons" (Mark 16:17).

When Jesus Christ reconciled all things in heaven and earth to himself through his own blood (Colossians 1:20), Satan was left without defences against the Kingdom of God.

The number of times demons verbally resist the commands to go in the name of Jesus is quite surprising. Quite often the counsellee will say something like this - "No I won't"; "Why should I go"; "I'm stronger than you"; "You haven't the power to get me out, I've been here a long time"; "Leave me alone". Four letter expletives are sometimes colourfully added. In view of the fact that people come to be freed, the voices are obviously from the spirits which have them bound. Demons may delay their departure, but not prevent it.

2. The practical priority of deliverance.

The first recorded **public miracle** Jesus performed was to set a demon-possessed worshipper free at a service in the synagogue at Capernaum (Luke 4:31-36; Mark 1:21-27). In that deliverance, Jesus revealed his power and authority.

Jesus Christ was always willing to release people from the devil's grip. The touching story of the release and healing of the woman who had been crippled by Satan and bent over for eighteen years (Luke 13:10-17), shows how compassionate and thoughtful he was for Satan's victims.

3. Jesus Christ knew that his kingdom on earth could not be established without the power of deliverance.

When Jesus ordained the apostles he did more than hand them a preaching licence for the kingdom of God. He also gave them kingdom power to cast out evil, or unclean spirits, and heal all sicknesses and diseases (Matthew 10:1; Mark 3:15; Luke 9:1).

When the seventy were commissioned to go out and preach, and heal the sick, Jesus said nothing about deliverance (Luke 10:1-11), but God the Father gave them power over evil spirits, and they came back fired up because they found that demons had been subject to them in the name of Jesus. They were then given a warning which is important for all who have a deliverance ministry: " . . do not rejoice that spirits submit to you, but rejoice that your names are written in heaven" (Luke 10:20).

The authority and power Jesus conferred on his disciples came directly from his own delegated authority and anointing as outlined by Isaiah (61:1-3). When Saul was similarly ordained he was given the same detailed authority and power.

(i) **Paul preached the same message of the kingdom of God** (Romans 14:17; 1 Corinthians 6:9; 15:50; Colossians 1:12, 14).

(ii) **Paul included the need for deliverance in his Gospel** (Acts 16:18; 26:18; Colossians 1:13).

(iii) **Paul had the same commission to heal from sicknesses and diseases** (Acts 14:8-10; 19:12).

The Gospel of the kingdom includes not only a message of salvation, but the power to make that message totally effective. Obviously Simon the magician had not been released from the dominant spirits of the occult when he came to Christ (Acts 8:13). Had this been so I believe he would not have come under condemnation for covetousness and bribery (verses 18-22).

The Gospel is the power of God capable of bringing people into the fulness of salvation. God expects those who believe to be totally released from all existing Satanic bondages and dominations at the time of salvation. This is clearly foreshadowed in God's promise to Moses that he would deliver his people from bondage into a place of liberty and supply. " . . I have come down **to rescue (or deliver) them from** the hand of the Egyptians AND **to bring them out of that land into a good and spacious land,** a land flowing with milk and honey . . . " (Exodus 3:8 - emphasis added).

Deliverance is indeed a Kingdom ministry. "For he has rescued (delivered) us from the dominion of darkness and brought us into the kingdom of the Son he loves, in whom we have redemption, the forgiveness of sins" (Colossians 1:13-14).

4. Jesus Christ knew that all believers needed to be set free and kept free of the clutches of the evil one.

There are ten Greek verbs with a variety of basic meanings which can be translated by the word 'deliver'. The statement that 'Jesus Christ knew that all believers needed to be set free from the clutches of the evil one' is an inference from the Greek word 'rhuomai' which W. E. Vine defines as 'to rescue from, to preserve from, and so, to deliver' (Expository Dictionary of New Testament Words' - Oliphants). The Lord Jesus used the word twice. Firstly, in teaching his disciples to pray for themselves. " . . but deliver (rhuomai) us from the evil one" (Matthew 6:13). Secondly, when praying to his Father before his crucifixion in John chapter seventeen. "My prayer is not that you take them out of the world, but that you protect (rhuomai) them from the evil one" (v. 15). His great concern was that believers should be preserved from every attack of the evil one.

The apostle Paul uses the same word three times in one verse, with the same connotation - "He has delivered us from such a deadly peril, and he will deliver us. On him we have set our hope that he will continue to deliver us" (2 Corinthians 1:10). Paul expected the deliverance he had received to be a continuing process of release and protection from all that Satan may try to do.

Theologians consider that 'rhuomai' is very similar in meaning to the word 'sozo' meaning primarily 'to save', but which also includes the concept of 'deliverance' and 'healing'.

5. Jesus Christ intended the deliverance ministry to continue throughout the Church age.

Most of us know that the Great Commission given to the disciples prior to the ascension of Jesus Christ contained instructions on evangelism, baptism, and discipleship (Matthew 28:18-20). Mark added details of the power of this ministry, and the results to be expected (Mark 16:15-19).

The early church therefore knew that it was expected to continue the deliverance ministry which the apostles had practiced from the time of their call. "In my name they will cast out demons" (Mark 16:17). There is no Biblical evidence for a special 'ministry of deliverance' per se. The apostles simply met the needs of the people as they were required, in the power of the Holy Spirit. Admittedly, today some have to give more time to ministering freedom than they may have desired because of the great need and the general lack of pastoral experience in this field. And regrettably one or two have even used deliverance as a means of validating their 'power-gift ministry'. But any mature, sanctified believer who understands the principles of spiritual warfare may follow the example and instructions of Jesus Christ, and minister freedom in the power of the Holy Spirit.

Some people have been prevented from seeing people set free in the name of Jesus because most modern translations read: "The two most reliable early manuscripts do not have Mark 16:9-20." Fortunately the leaders of the early church were simple men of faith who just got on with the job they were told to do. Textual criticism and rationalism were not amongst the problems they faced; their lives were too involved for such distractions.

Even if writer and reader have divergent views on Mark 16, there is in each generation an unavoidable commission which the Holy Spirit has preserved down the centuries. "Peace be with you! As the Father has sent me I am sending you." And with that he breathed on them and said, "Receive the Holy Spirit. If you forgive anyone his sins, they are forgiven; if you do not forgive them, they are not forgiven" John 20:22,23).

That mantle now rests on every anointed leader within the Body of Christ. The anointing carries with it both responsibility and accountability. It also brings a divine promise into focus: "I tell you the truth, anyone who has faith in me will do what I have been doing. He will do even greater things than these because I am going to the Father. You may ask for anything in my name, and I will do it" (John 14:12, 13).

There is no more thrilling personal confirmation of the inspiration of Scripture than to see demonic powers leave the lives of saved and unsaved in the authority and power of the name of Jesus Christ.

On one occasion during a deliverance session in Hawaii, a demon cried out several times: "Don't use that name, don't use that name." The voice died away half way through a word, when commanded to be silent in the name of Jesus Christ. Even if some Christians don't believe Jesus has given us his authority, the demons certainly do.

CHAPTER SUMMARY.

The deliverance ministry was important to Jesus Christ, because:-

1. He alone had the authority and power to deliver his people from Satanic and demonic domination and every form of oppression. God has no alternative.

2. The need was so great amongst the people, that priority was given to deliverance and healing.

3. Deliverance is necessary for the extension of the Kingdom of God.

4. Christians need to be preserved from the evil one so that they can avoid the need for deliverance.

5. Jesus Christ made it clear that deliverance was to be a continuing ministry function of the Church he founded.

"I will confess, praise, and give thanks to you for you have heard and answered me, and have become my salvation and deliverer" (Psalm 118:21 Amplified Bible).

CHAPTER 5.

How could we have been so blind?

A very intelligent and gifted married woman came to see us. She had been visiting a psychiatrist for two years without being able to look him directly in the eyes. She sat with her back to us and talked over her shoulder. Her opening remarks were - "Don't tell me I have demons, or even mention them". So we talked about 'spiritual influences', and 'powers which bound' her, and she was satisfied. The Lord soon set her free, and her psychiatrist discharged her as there was nothing left for him to do. After being freed, she openly talked about what the demons had done to her, without sign of embarrassment.

The sixty four-dollar question which constantly amazes us is - "Why are so many believers blind to the reality of demonic activity amongst Christians?"

We have discovered some answers to this question:

1. Demons cover their existence by deception, so that people concentrate on what they see, or how they feel, and overlook spiritual causes.

The lady just mentioned above is a good example of this. From the Scriptures we see that the crippled woman whom Jesus set free and healed in the synagogue was probably the most surprised of all to hear that it was Satan who had bound her with a spirit of infirmity. All she knew was that she had been unable to straighten up for eighteen years, and that no doctor had been able to help her (Luke 13:11-16). Only yesterday, Phyl and I ministered release to a young woman from a variety of spirits of lust, as well as a spirit of baby bashing and murder. She had been so deeply rejected in utero that her mother had wanted to murder her, and had openly confessed this as she grew up. The woman was intelligent, but had lived with four men for periods of one to several years, and had had sexual relations with another fifteen. She had gone through five abortions by the time she had reached the age of thirty-one years as a form of punishment to men because of her own rejection, and was commencing to beat the child she had decided to give birth to and keep. It was of course, a boy. Her case was complicated by treatment she had received in a mental hospital, and through a sexual involvement with a man deeply into the occult. It was not until she came to Christ that she realised there were demonic causes behind her behavioural problems. Having been born again for less than a year, her faith was uncomplicated by 'demon allergy', a problem common to many Christians.

(1) Fear of demons causes people to deny their existence.

Right from childhood most of us tend to deny what we fear most. In the unexpected tragedies of life, including the diagnosis of cancer, it is normal for the first reaction to be one of denial. "This is not true, it can't be happening to me." Satan and demons are often treated in the same way. The very thought of them may produce fear, and a sense of defilement, so they are rejected.

(2) Spiritual discernment is lacking.

After Ananias and his wife had sold a piece of property, Ananias made a large donation to the Apostles for the common support fund. During the presentation ceremony the Holy Spirit showed Peter that Ananias had not told the truth when he said the gift was the sale price of the land. Satan had filled him with a lying spirit (Acts 5:1-10). Peter's word of knowledge was a manifestation of the same Holy Spirit who indwells every believer today and who is willing to continue manifesting such discernment. The problem is that Satan has cast such a shadow of suspicion over the validity of spiritual gifts today, that he has successfully restricted their use and continued his work under cover, mostly undetected. It is little wonder that the Church has succumbed to humanistic methods of diagnosis and treament of Christians' problems. What is needed is a revival of submission to revelational truth and the exercise of the Spirit's power to set God's people free. This is just what Satan fears most, and actively combats.

(3) Most modern preaching and teaching avoids the subject of demonic activity.

Apart from Pentecostal and 'charismatic' churches, or those dubbed as such by people who oppose their teachings, there is little general understanding on the subject of deliverance except under special licence. Others just avoid the subject, or, like theological ostriches, keep their heads under cover, believing that Satan and his demons really did disappear after the resurrection and ascension of Jesus Christ. Meantime the needy in their congregations are sentenced to spiritual penal servitude, with no provision for parole.

(4) First century faith has largely been replaced by twentieth century rationalism.

When Jesus and his disciples ministered deliverance, shrieks, convulsions, and demonic chatter were frequent manifestations. Today, that is regarded as being in bad taste. We prefer to philosophise, psychologise, rationalise, and use psychiatrists rather than operate by faith based on revelational truth, divine instruction, and example. The Scriptures endorse medical means of healing, but God never intended that medical science should outmode, replace, or downgrade spiritual authority. Actually, they make an ideal partnership when God is given his rightful place as the writers have experienced through working together with the medical profession.

Another faith-diminishing influence is the flood of 'christianised' philosophy and psychology coming from professional humanistic writers whose lives are often filled with atheism, skepticism, and God dishonouring practices.

It would seem that Isaiah's prophecy could well be applied to this generation as well as the one to whom it was written:-

"Go and tell this people; 'Be ever hearing but never understanding; be ever seeing, but never perceiving. Make the heart of this people calloused; make their ears dull and close their eyes. Otherwise they might see with their eyes, hear with their ears, understand with their hearts, and turn and be healed" (Isaiah 6:9, 10).

One major reason for writing this book is to give expression to a heart cry to the Church to re-examine the teachings of Scripture on deliverance. It will have been worth all the time and effort if it helps to bring a revival of obedience to the Biblical instructions to let the oppressed go free. To further this aim, we need to examine what the Word of God says about Satanic and demonic activities amongst God's people.

(a) **In the early church Satan was obviously given power to afflict certain sinning believers, and this power has not been expressly revoked.**

(i) **The Corinthian church sex scandal.**

One of its members had dishonoured his father, by having a sexual relationship with his father's wife. The Old Testament penalty for this was death by stoning (Leviticus 18:6, 8). Paul advised the church leadership to "hand the man over to Satan so that the sinful nature may be destroyed and his spirit saved on the day of the Lord" (1 Corinthians 5:5). The measure may sound extreme, but the brother was later restored to fellowship (2 Corinthians 2:2-11).

The suicidal death of Judas Iscariot shows how merciless Satan may be to those over whom he gains control. "Don't you know that when you offer yourselves to someone to obey him as slaves, you are slaves to the one to whom you obey?" (Romans 6:16).

The Corinthian in question was obviously dominated by an unclean spirit of lust. The Greek 'akathartos' is translated 'unclean' twenty-eight times, and 'foul', twice in the King James Version. In Revelation 17:4, a derivative, 'akathartes', shows the extreme filth of the word. "She had a golden cup in her hand filled with abominable things and the filth of her adulteries".

Because sin comes from Satan, its driving power is obviously demonic. Lustful spirits are among the most common and strongest spirits to oppress and dominate believers. They are stubborn, and often resist the deliverance ministry vigorously. Lust pollutes, brings guilt, erodes spiritual power, and like an avalanche sweeps away will-power and resistance. What pastor has not seen bitter tears, and heard agonised words such as "I didn't want to, but I just couldn't resist it"? Normal counselling methods have about as much power to stop lust as a sandbank to keep out a tidal wave.

Unbridled lust is a disease of epidemic proportions today. Even pastors are having 'affairs' with their parishioners, counsellees, secretaries, and friends. Both Phyl and I have been nauseated at times by the confessions of 'shepherds' of the sheep, or of hurting parishioners who have been sexually defiled by those from whom they sought counsel and spiritual comfort. One such young lady sought help from an ordained minister who was the leader of a Christian community. At the time, his wife was expecting another child, and for three months this wolf in sheep's clothing subjected the young lady to his sexual pleasure while trying weakly to justify his adultery as 'spiritual comfort'.

When lusts of the flesh become energised by demonic power instead of being controlled by the Spirit, some form of moral tragedy is unavoidable.

(ii) **The Ephesian heretics.**

Paul writes that Hymenaus and Alexander had become totally deceived by doctrinal error which had caused them to reject the truth, blaspheme, and make shipwreck of their faith (1 Timothy 1:19, 20). Paul could see that like parts of the body affected by gangrene, these men needed to be cut off from the local church, so that others would not be affected by the spread of their evil doctrine. To do this, he "handed them over to Satan to be taught not to blaspheme".

These men had obviously found the teachings of demons attractive and as a result were taken over by deceiving spirits (1 Timothy 1:19, 20). John the apostle also warns of spirits of 'anti-Christ', and 'falsehood' (1 John 4:1, 6). One cannot but wonder what Paul and John would say if they were to visit the present-day church, and see the profusion of religions, sects, cults, religious ideologies and demonic delusions which press in on the people of God from every side. Every cult is an irrefutable witness to the proliferation of demonic delusion.

We were praying for two born-again sisters whose father had been deeply involved in Christian Science. They were bound by stubborn spirits of scepticism, doubt, and unbelief, which kept them from believing the word of God. Although strong Christians filled with the Holy Spirit, they had to be delivered from hereditary spirits of untruth which strongly resisted faith and revelational truth. We have had the same experience with people whose backgrounds have included strong doctrinal emphases, legalism in Biblical interpretation, Freemasonry, or occultic involvement. Whenever Satan is followed, he will begin to afflict. Unless leaders have the spiritual discernment and authority to release people dominated by deceiving spirits, Satan can draw them away from Christian influence. Anyone who has dealt with cases of doctrinal error will know how difficult it is to break through religious self-confidence which often borders on aggressiveness. Satan keeps them from grasping even the most obvious and simple truths. After an open air Gospel programme, I once spoke with a man who claimed to be one of the seven spirits of God. My amusement turned to disgust, and I bound the spirits of deception in the name of Jesus Christ. The man's mouth flew open and his jaw dropped, but he couldn't say a word. He just shook hands, turned on his heel, and walked away.

2. Satanic and demonic activity was evident in local churches during the first century.

Around 56 A.D., Paul warned the Corinthian believers that false apostles whom he called 'servants of Satan', were masquerading amongst them as servants of righteousness. They were preaching a different Jesus, another Gospel, and representing a different Spirit (2 Corinthians 11:4, 13, 14). Nineteen hundred years later, there is a proliferation of deceptive gospels, messiahs, and "spiritual" experiences. Some demons even boldly claim to be "Jesus".

Actually, by 51 A.D. Paul was teaching that the end-time anti-Christ spirit of lawlessness was already hard at work. He also said there would be a spate of delusive miraculous signs and miracles before the end of the church age (2 Thessalonians 2:7-9). Newspapers, magazines, and television bring such signs into our lounge rooms, but it is so easy to feel secure in our church fellowships, believing we are beyond evil reach. Brethren and sisters, we have been warned!

By the end of the first century, seven local churches in Asia Minor were experiencing some internal or external influence, pressures, or opposition of a Satanic or demonic nature. In Smyrna, Pergamum, Thyatira, and Philadelphia, it was overt (Revelation 2:10; 2:13; 2:20-24; 3:9). In Ephesus, Sardis, and Laodicea, it was covert. While Satan is not named personally, his handiwork is evident (Revelation 2:4; 3:2, 3; 3:5-17).

3. The New Testament constantly warns of the variety of Satanic and demonic strategies we may face.

Satan is the master strategist. Demons just carry out his will. God established an endless state of hostility between Satan, his demons and the seed of the woman in the Garden of Eden (Genesis 3:15). The seed God promised came down through Abraham, Isaac, and Jacob, to Jesus (Galatians 3:16-18).

Because every born-again child of God is also a child of Abraham (Galatians 3:7), we too can expect the same Satanic hatred and opposition. And because of what Jesus Christ did, we can also figuratively crush the head of the serpent by using our delegated authority and power. The Scriptures warn us of some of the well-worn strategems he uses to attack believers:

(a) He tries to bait us through perverting the truth (2 Timothy 2:14-26; 3:8).

(b) The devil attacks Christians who are spiritually indolent and lacking in self-control, as a roaring lion attacks its prey (1 Peter 5:8).

(c) Anger and unforgiveness give him a foothold (Ephesians 4:27).

(d) Believers in the end times are warned of being led astray by demonic doctrines (1 Timothy 4:1; 2 John 7-11).

(e) Idolatry leads to demon worship (1 Corinthains 10:14-22). Demonic idolatry is another feature of the end times. "They did not stop worshipping demons and idols of gold, silver, bronze, stone and wood - idols that cannot see or hear or walk. Nor did they repent of their murders, their magic arts, their sexual immorality, or their thefts" (Revelation 9:20-22). Despite the presence of the Holy Spirit and the visible Church, the world is turning more and more to idolatry and demon worship. Academics often use the halls of learning to spread this anti-God New Age Movement.

(f) Spirits of fear continue to plague Christians just as they did in Paul's day (Romans 8:15; 2 Timothy 1:7).

(g) Paul wrote at length of the believer's warfare against a great variety of spiritual forces exercising power in the heavens and on earth (Ephesians 6:10-18). He speaks of 'the devil's schemes' (verse 11); 'the day of evil' (verse 13); and 'the flaming arrows of the evil one' (verse 16). Surely our own personal experiences with those fiery darts, and the casualties we see around us are warnings that the battle is still raging.

(h) Paul expressed concern that the tempter had caused some believers to lose their faith (1 Thessalonians 3:5). How much greater is that reality in the days in which we live!

(i) Some young Ephesian widows were warned against following the bad examples of those who were following Satan, and providing the evil one with an opportunity to slander them (1 Timothy 5:14-15).

(j) James warns us that there is a spurious wisdom which comes from the devil. He makes it clear that the only way to tell the difference between demonic and Holy Spirit wisdom is the Christlikeness of the speaker (James 3:15-17).

Illustrations of these demonic activities in believers will be given in later chapters.

4. Believers are promised victory over Satan and every demon power.

God does his part. We need to do ours. Having a Bible in the home, and repeating the Lord's prayer is not exactly what God has in mind.

(1) Believers are taught to engage aggressively in spiritual warfare (Ephesians 6:10-18).

We have been raised with Christ (Ephesians 1:19-21), seated with Christ (Ephesians 2:6), and empowered to reign for Christ on earth (Romans 5:17). The spiritual armour (also known as the armour of light - Romans 13:12), is highly effective against every onslaught of the enemy, and victory is promised (Ephesians 6:13).

(2) **Because of the victory Jesus gained, our victory is also assured.**

The authority Adam and Eve forfeited in Eden, was regained at Calvary when Jesus Christ became our ransom (Ephesians 1:7; 1 Timothy 2:6). Satan has no legal claim over the believer living in discipleship. ".. Resist the devil, and he will flee from you. Come near to God and he will come near to you" (James 4:7). That is God's personal guarantee!

(3) **The Lord himself is our preserver.**

"We know that anyone born of God does not continue to sin; the one who is born of God keeps him safe, and the evil one does not touch him (1 John 5:18). Once again the key to preservation is obedience. Sin is rebellion, and makes a believer vulnerable (Ephesians 4:26, 27). God's guarantees are always subject to our unconditional obedience. "But the Lord is faithful, and he will strengthen and protect you from the evil one" (2 Thessalonians 3:3). "The Lord will rescue me from every evil attack and will bring me safely to his heavenly kingdom" (2 Timothy 4:18).

5. The writings of well-known church leaders.
(1) Dr. John Warwick Montgomery.

In January 1978, the Christian Medical Association of the United States of America held a symposium in the University of Notre Dame, New York, attended by members of the Christian Medical Society. They included anthropologists, historians, theologians, missiologists and pastors, all committed to the historical, Biblical, evangelical faith. Those invited held prominent positions in universities, seminaries and well-known mission societies. Dr. John Warwick Montgomery, holder of earned doctorates from the universities of Chicago and Strasbourg, author of more than thirty books and a founding member of the World Association of Law Professors, edited a book entitled 'Demon Possession' from the papers and responses given.

The following has been selected from Dr. Montgomery's reply to a paper given by Dr. William P. Wilson, a professor of psychiatry entitled "Hysteria and Demons, Depression and Oppression, Good and Evil" (Pages 233, 234).

"It is most refreshing to read a paper on demon possession by a professional psychiatrist who does not regard belief in the existence of personal supernatural evil as a hopeless anachronism . . . First, the essayist makes reference to 'certain spiritual giants' who 'refute the notion that Christians can be demon possessed'. I must respectfully disagree with those giants. To be sure Christian believers cannot be torn from Christ's hands by Satan - their ultimate salvation is absolutely assured when they rely solely upon Christ for it (1 John 4:4; Rom. 8:38-39). Moreover the pattern and direction of their lives is set in Christ, so that nothing occurs which is not for the universal best (Matt. 10:29-32; 1 Cor. 10:13). But apart from these magnificent ultimate assurances, Christians are as subject to the evil consequences of a fallen world as any non-Christian. Their physical lives can be snuffed out in a moment by a satanic automobile accident caused by a drunken driver; they can be born blind as a result of satanic venereal disease in a parent; the demonic wars of history can ruin them as readily as unbelievers. The rain of sin, as well as the rain from the clouds, falls on the just and the unjust. Kurt Koch and others have shown beyond dispute that involvement in occult and demonic practices can produce dire emotional and spiritual effects 'to the third and fourth generation' in the families of those who engage in such practices, and that not infrequently, there is a spill-over effect on the community at large when some members of it are practising black arts. As 'The Exorcist' illustrates, on the basis of classical literature on the subject, Satan can even bring about the physical death of the believer in these ways. Christians are no more exempted from such calamities than they are from infections, epidemics, or from the wider evils that are part and parcel of a sin-sick society.

"Why the hesitancy to affirm this obvious truth - reiterated by orthodox Christian dogmaticians from Patristic times through the Reformation to our own day - that Satan can function as a spirit and regularly tries to ape the Trinitarian work of the living God? Does the hesitancy perhaps tie with evangelical reticence to admit to the demon-possession of Christians - based I suggest on the erroneous notion that a personal commitment to Christ ought to clear the inner life completely of satanic influence and create a fortress area of holiness whose ramparts evil cannot scale? Here we witness the great evangelical dualism in action; Satan is given total control of everything external to the Christian heart (politics, society, entertainment, literature, art, etc.) but he is kept from one inviolate Utopia - the inner life of the believer. Here 'perfect separation from the world' is always available when it is successful in separationist church activity and condemnation of non-Christian cultural life in general.

"But this is nothing less than false doctrine! As the Reformers properly maintained on the basis of clear scriptural teaching: Totus homo est caro (the whole man is flesh) i.e. satanic influence, power, and control, cut down the center of even man's psychic life. There is no inner area of safety; no utopian retreat from sin and Satan; no dualistic division of sinful 'world' from inner holiness. Freedom from Satanic wiles must be sought eschatologically - in the new heaven and new earth - not in our present existence under the cross.

"I suggest that a significant degree of emotional immaturity, distress, and even nervous breakdowns among the evangelicals could be traced to this Utopian error. Convinced that his inner life cannot be Satanically worked upon, that only the Holy Spirit can possibly influence him within, the Evangelical tries to keep up an 'I'm so happy' facade which contradicts his real experience and drives him to hypocrisy at best, psychic collapse at worst. Theologically it deflects him from the one proper recourse: constant return in penitence to the cross of Christ. Perhaps to admit (as Dr. Wilson rightly does) that Satan can control the inner life spiritually would not only be a great gain for studies in demonology, but also the path towards recovery of a realistic Reformation view of sanctification on the part of contemporary evangelicals."
(From DEMON POSSESSION, edited by John Warwick Montgomery, published by Bethany Fellowship Inc., © 1976. Printed by permission of Bethany House Publishers.)

(2) Dr. Merrill F. Unger.

Dr. Unger earned his A.B. and Ph.D. degrees at John Hopkins University, and his Th.M. and Th.D. degrees at Dallas Theological Seminary. He held pastorates in New York, Texas, and Maryland. He taught at Gordon College and Gordon Divinity School, and from 1948 to 1967 he was professor of Old Testament Studies at Dallas Theological Seminary.

Dr. Unger is the author of 'Demons In The World Today', 'What Demons Can Do To The Saints', and 'Biblical Demonology'. The following quotations have been taken from 'Demons In The World Today'.

"Christians can and ought to enjoy complete deliverance from the power of Satan and demons as a result of Christ's perfect work of redemption. But what believers can and ought to enjoy are two different things. When Christians fail to recognise what they have in Christ and refuse to appropriate the resulting privileges, they invite defeat and can be held captive by demonic forces to a pitiable degree" (page 183).

"That many regenerated people need to claim deliverance from evil spirits indwelling them is a fact that we would prefer to think is not true, but which is all too true and must be faced realistically by pastors and counsellors who would lay claim to competence and effectiveness in discharging their high and holy calling" (page 187).

"As a result of forfeiting a clear presentation of Christ's redemptive power, and of not using its God-given power to heal and to deliver from Satanic oppression today, the pastoral ministry becomes no more effective than the secular role of the clinical psychologist, the social worker, or the humanistic philosopher. The tragic result is that people who suffer from spiritual, mental, physical or psychic disorders, which only Christ can really cure, are turned over to other professionals for medical or psychotherapeutic treatment which cannot reach the heart of the matter" (page 190). From DEMONS IN THE WORLD TODAY by Dr. Merrill F. Unger. Published by Tyndale House Publishers, Inc. © 1971. Used by permission.

(3) Dr. Kurt E. Koch Th.D.

Dr. Koch is probably one of the best known authors on Christian counselling in demonic realms. In both 'Between Christ and Satan', and 'Christian Counselling and Occultism', there are prolific examples of Christians under demonic oppression.

(4) Corrie Ten Boom.

This well known saintly woman was not stopped by either Nazi guards or demonic spirits. She moved in the realm of freeing people from demonic clutches with thrilling results. She once cried out to the Lord - "Why must I give this message (on the sin and bondage of fortune-telling) when so many of your servants never mention it?" The Lord confirmed her heart in many ways, particularly with the verse - "Be not afraid, but speak, and hold not thy peace. For I am with thee, and no man shall set on thee to hurt thee" (Acts 18:9, 10). Many years ago she wrote 'Defeated Enemies' (CLC) dealing with victory over demonic powers.

(5) Mrs. Jessie Penn-Lewis.

Her 'War On The Saints', written in collaboration with Evan Roberts of the Welsh revival fame, has been a text-book on understanding demonic problems amongst Christians for over seventy-five years. Ahead of its time, and shunned by many, probably mainly because it was written by a woman, the very name of her book confirms the thesis of the writings that Satan constantly wars against believers. Many pastors and counsellors would be shocked if they were to know the extent of that war amongst the people to whom they minister.

(6) The witness of personal experience.

Christians who have sought and received deliverance from the writers include pastors, missionaries, full-time workers, university professors, academics, intellectuals, doctors, nurses, scientists, lawyers, accountants, social workers, psychologists, a psychiatrist, partners in broken marriages, homosexuals, lesbians, drug users, alcoholics, people bound by lust, bestiality, pornography, incest; people with backgrounds of Freemasonry, the black and martial arts, and all forms of witchcraft and occult. Concerning personal problems such as rejection and low self-image, they are countless. What is also very thrilling is the way the Lord releases children.

Only a spiritual ostrich could ignore such a weight of evidence, and refuse to accept the present authority of the Name of Jesus for today's needs.

CHAPTER SUMMARY.

1. In many congregations of God's people there is little recognition of Satanic and demonic activity amongst Christians. This is due to prejudice, disinterest, lack of spiritual discernment, deception of the evil one, and humanistic rationalism.

2. Satan has been given authority and power to afflict sinning believers.

3. No believer is exempt from the hostility and oppression of Satan and demonic powers, but protection and victory is assured through Jesus Christ.

Well known and respected church leaders warn us of the reality of demonic activity amongst Christians today.

4. The practical need for deliverance in people of all walks of life within the Body of Christ confirms the timeless instructions of Jesus Christ to his disciples of every generation.

"When anyone hears the message about the kingdom and does not understand it, the evil one comes and snatches away what was sown in his heart" (Matthew 13:19).

CHAPTER 6.

What Satan and demons do to deceive people about salvation

The whole world is a prison, and everyone in it a spiritual prisoner from birth. Satan is the head jailor, and demons are his prison guards. They serve their master well, and delight in afflicting those under their charge.

"The whole world is under the control of the evil one" (1 John 5:19).

"As for you, you were dead in your transgressions and sins, in which you used to live when you followed the ways of this world and the ruler of the kingdom of the air, the spirit who is now at work in those who are disobedient. All of us lived among them at one time, gratifying the cravings of our sinful nature (or flesh), and following its desires and thoughts. Like the rest, we were by nature objects of wrath" (Ephesians 2:1-3).

We never need to be taught how to sin; it is as natural as breathing. My mother once delighted in telling me that on day two of my life, I showed my temper in no uncertain manner. Having received all the comforts of life, I was put down to sleep, but apparently strenuously objected to the darkness and silence. When the light was turned on I was alleged to have stopped crying, and when it was switched off, I yelled. I think my mother switched the light on and off several times to gather evidence! I cannot recall anyone whispering advice as to how a baby can get its own way. Somehow, I also instinctively had quite some grasp of the ways to manipulate the opposite sex!

When I was a child, there was never a swear word uttered in my home. But on that same good authority, it appears that well before I went to school, my mother was horrified to hear a stream of rather lurid words coming from my mouth. I believe the offending organ was either scrubbed out with soap and water, or some hot English mustard was spread around. The punishment would certainly have been a deterrent, but it didn't eradicate the cause. It appears I also became quite an expert at looking my mother in the eye and denying the obvious. A 'Mr. Nobody' in our home got blamed a lot for my misdeeds. My parents were truthful; I was an expert liar. Very obviously, I had inherited a sinful nature which embarrassed my parents. They had loved me and given me a first-class example, but the inherited nature just took over so often.

Jesus Christ accurately pinpointed the cause of human sinfulness. "You belong to your father the devil, and you want to carry out your father's desire. He was a murderer from the beginning, not holding the truth, for there is no truth in him. When he lies, he speaks his native language, for he is a liar and the father of lies" (John 8:44). So every beautiful, cuddly baby already carries the deadly sin virus.

Satan knows full well that finally he and his demons will be cast into the lake of fire, designed especially for them (Matthew 25:41). He also knows that the ungodly will be sent there with him (Revelation 21:8). So it is obvious that he aims to do all in his power to cause sin and sickness from the youngest age, and to keep his prisoners from understanding the truth and the liberating power of the Gospel.

"And even if our Gospel is veiled, it is veiled to those who are perishing. The god of this age has blinded the minds of unbelievers, so that they cannot see the light of the gospel of the glory of Christ, who is the image of God" (2 Corinthians 4:3, 4).

Some of the means Satan uses to keep people in his spiritual prison include:

1. Making sin attractive, satisfying, and addictive.

Sin is pleasurable (Hebrews 11:25). Pleasure is an offering made by sin at the shrine of self-idolatry to a god who demands continuous sacrifices. Satan supplies not only the desire but the demons to keep the addict wanting more. He also convinces the sinner that to become a Christian will mean the loss of all pleasures in life, and even worse, the loss of friends and social prestige. That is enough to frighten many people, so they regard the Gospel as a plague to be avoided at all costs. The rich young man who couldn't bear to exchange his financial security for discipleship with Jesus is a first century example (Mark 10:21, 22).

2. Preventing people from being able to understand, or believe the truth.

The Old Testament contains many clear statements about the coming of the Messiah, and Jesus Christ obviously fulfilled them all. If anyone should have understood this, it should have been the High Priest, the scribes, elders, and religious leaders. Not only were they blind to the obvious, but they were filled with jealousy, hatred, malice, and murder. Even the resurrection and ascension of Jesus Christ did nothing to lessen the bitterness and antagonism showed to the apostles and early church (Acts 4:2, 18; 5:17, 18, 40).

The same intransigence is often shown today both amongst people in authority and in those who hear the Gospel. Some years ago when assisting other evangelists with an open air Gospel programme in the hippy area of Toronto, Canada, a particularly belligerent young man opposed us. He walked around restlessly, mocking the Gospel, with loud, offensive, obscene, and blasphemous interruptions. Nothing would deter him, not even binding his controlling demons. He gave every indication that he had been totally taken over by Satan who well knows that blasphemy against the Holy Spirit will never be forgiven (Matthew 12:31).

3. Preventing people from trusting Jesus Christ as Saviour.

The writer once shared the Gospel in a home with a family, and challenged any who were not trusting Christ as Saviour to do so. The father asked to see me privately and told me that he realized that he was not truly born again, but having been a vestryman of the Church of England for twenty-nine years, he really felt satisfied and didn't feel the need to go any further. He agreed to let me pray for him. During the prayer, I bound, broke, and loosed the grip of the spirit of unbelief over him. The effect was electric. He jumped to his feet calling out, "I will believe, I do believe". Then falling on his knees, he prayed a sincere and spontaneous prayer of repentance and faith in Jesus Christ. The family told me afterwards that they had seen a change come over him.

An intelligent young man was so bound by intellectualism and rationalism that he was unable to trust Jesus Christ to save him, although he desperately wanted to do so. After being freed from the spirits which controlled his thinking, he received Christ as his saviour by an act of will without any emotion. Later that week he returned for counselling and prayer, and was further freed from deep rejection and demonic problems coming from other sources. He immediately flourished spiritually, and within twelve months was in full-time Christian service.

A deeply rejected and ill-treated teenager used to run away from home, often having to be traced by the police. In foster homes she had been threatened sexually, and was finally raped. She was rebellious, aggressive, and gripped by anorexia nervosa. The court offered her the choice of being cared for by a Christian mission or becoming a ward of the state. She chose the mission, but determined she would not become a Christian. She did, however, agree to come for prayer. God totally freed her from a dominating spirit of anorexia nervosa and other spirits, and without hesitation she received Jesus Christ to be her personal saviour. She received excellent follow up care and plenty of love, and grew spiritually. Had the demonic powers not been broken she could have become a derelict, or taken her life, but certainly would not have become a Christian.

4. Deluding people into thinking that they are saved without a genuine new birth experience.

The parable of the wise and foolish virgins of Matthew chapter twenty-five is the greatest warning against presuming one has eternal security. The five virgins who had brought reserves of oil in case the bridegroom was delayed were the only ones admitted when the bridegroom arrived well into the night.

The two groups of virgins illustrate two phases of the ministry of the Holy Spirit in salvation. First, he enlightens the understanding about personal sinfulness, and to the provision of forgiveness, cleansing, and salvation through faith in Jesus Christ. But awareness of the need and the knowledge of who is willing to fulfil that need is not salvation. This comes with repentance, faith, and discipleship. Many people will be in hell who received knowledge but took no action. The virgins who went searching for oil were shut out and denied entrance (v. 12).

The five virgins who had sufficient oil symbolise those who, by repentance, faith, and discipleship, have Jesus Christ, the source of divine light, in their lives, and the resources of the Holy Spirit to maintain that light (John 8:12; Ephesians 5:8, 9; 2 Corinthians 4:6; Colossians 1:12; 1 Thessalonians 5:5; 1 Peter 2:9).

The parable focuses on the return of Jesus Christ to receive the Church, his bride. A literal interpretation of the parable would mean that of all who claim to wait for his second coming, only fifty per cent of them will enter in, the rest will be rejected. The truth of this awesome prospect has become increasingly evident by teaching and counselling professing Christians. The following illustrations confirm how easy it is to be deluded:

● A young lady who had been deeply involved in Rudolph Steiner's teachings of anthroposophy was attending a discipleship training school. She believed she was a Christian, and so did her friends. But after speaking with her it became evident that she was not saved, but was deluded by a deceiving spirit of error which was really only the tip of her demonic iceberg. She was bound by rejection, lust, the occult, violence through practising Karate, sexual perversion, and manifested a demonic tongue. After deliverance, she was born again, cleansed, physically healed, and filled with the Holy Spirit.

● A twenty-six year old man claimed he was saved because he believed that Jesus Christ was the son of God. Calvary was meaningless to him, and God was too far away to be real. The writer was invited to share in a counselling session but realized the man needed deliverance first of all. The Lord freed him from spirits of religious legalism, idolatry, death, unbelief, rejection, and fears. He then knew that he was saved, and joyfully trusted Jesus Christ as his saviour. When he returned to his room, he picked up his Bible and wrote on the fly leaf 'Born again', adding the place and date.

● An ordained minister from a major protestant denomination became sexually involved with a number of women from his parish churches. With his marriage broken and ministry ruined, he was trying to rebuild his spiritual life. But it was all a self-centred effort, and God featured little. There was much pride, and little real conviction of sin. Believing the Lord had shown me that the man had never really been born again despite his professing to be an evangelical, I ministered deliverance and sent him away to seek God. Within two days he asked to see me again. His first words were, "I believe I have never really been born again." That confirmed the witness in my spirit. He repented, made genuine confession of his sin and hypocrisy, and placed his trust in Jesus Christ on the basis of his substitution at Calvary. I then asked him, "Who is Jesus Christ to you now?" He replied, "My Lord, my Saviour, and my Justifier, and I have never said that before!" Almost immediately he began to talk about being re-baptised.

● A youth worker was constantly seeking assurance of salvation. He had all but wrecked his marriage by constantly, and without justification, questioning his wife about her moral behaviour with other men. He was also close to a mental breakdown. During counsel he seemed totally confused, and the reason soon surfaced. He had been deeply involved in Theosophy, and during deliverance even had a psychic vision of Jesus Christ with a gold cross in his hand. When the last deceptive spirit had been cast out, the man was convinced he had been deceived by false religious spirits, but never saved. Repentance with many tears followed, then genuine faith in the finished work of Jesus Christ. He apologised to his wife for his suspicions and accusations, received her forgiveness, and was renewed in love and tenderness towards her. His deliverance and rebirth saved both his marriage and his sanity.

● A mature school teacher was quite convinced she was saved until asked to define her personal relationship with Jesus Christ. That caused her to see that she was clutching a religious spider's web of her own making, because she had never repented, and the blood of Jesus Christ was meaningless to her. On her knees and in tears after she had been freed from false religious spirits, she spoke out her pride, reliance upon her own good works, and her criticism of others for self-justification. The Lord saved and released her in joyfulness and praise. She went back to tell her fellow mission workers the good news, literally dancing for joy.

Space alone restricts the recounting of many other case histories which highlight the extent to which spirits of delusion have given false assurance about salvation. This calls for a threefold preventative action in evangelism. Firstly, the Gospel must be preached with greater clarity, and challenges to respond made without ambiguity. Secondly, counsellors must be particularly careful to make sure that counsellees clearly understand what faith in Jesus Christ involves. Thirdly, demonic bondages must be broken and dominating spirits cast out at the time of being born again.

Finally, each one of us is responsible to make sure that Jesus Christ is living in us, reproducing his life through us, and that we have the witness of the Holy Spirit within us that this is so (Romans 8:16). "Examine yourselves, to see whether you are in the faith; test yourselves" (2 Corinthians 13:5).

The first of the two diagrams which follow the chapter summary shows the fruit which naturally grows from the root system of the unregenerate life (Mark 7:21-23). The ones shown have all been found to be manifestations of evil spirits. In each example of those who were deluded about their salvation, traditional counselling had been ineffectual, and deliverance was needed before they were able to have a genuine experience of salvation.

The second diagram illustrates what salvation should mean to the believer.

CHAPTER SUMMARY.

1. Because Satan and demonic powers are invisible, people do not understand the extent of their deceptive influence to prevent the new birth experience.

2. Demons gain entry to a life through deliberate sin, and block responses to Christ. Some of their favourite tactics, are scepticism, doubt, and unbelief.

3. Deceiving spirits may cause people to rely on an intellectual understanding, an emotional experience, a deceptive religious philosophy, or some sacrimental experience as false assurance of salvation.

4. The return of Jesus Christ for his Church will reveal the tragic rejection of those who are unknowingly in delusion.

5. Evangelists, pastors who preach the Gospel, and all counsellors have a responsiblity to make sure that when they lead people to life in Jesus Christ, that they also make sure that they are freed from the power of the evil one.

6. Demonic powers are skilled at covering their activities by convincing people that their works are just 'works of the flesh' and will go away after they are saved. Unless the truth is known, and new believers are freed from their demonic domination, a great number of them will be condemned to a lifetime of 'spiritual servitude' until they meet someone who is able to see them set free. God wants all of his children free.

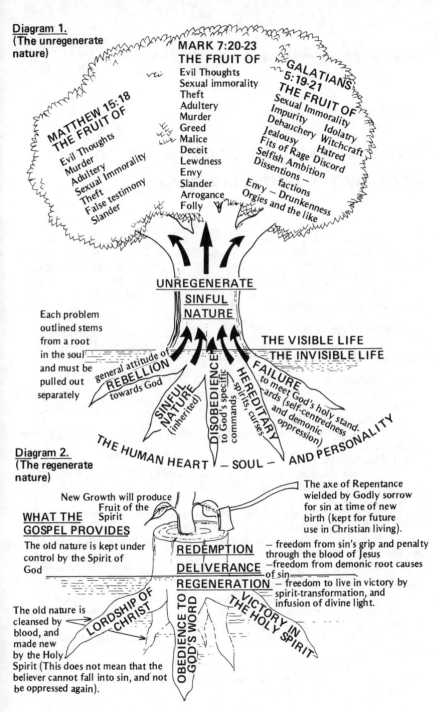

Diagram 1.
(The unregenerate nature)

MARK 7:20-23
THE FRUIT OF
Evil Thoughts
Sexual immorality
Theft
Adultery
Murder
Greed
Malice
Deceit
Lewdness
Envy
Slander
Arrogance
Folly

MATTHEW 15:18
THE FRUIT OF
Evil Thoughts
Murder
Adultery
Sexual Immorality
Theft
False testimony
Slander

GALATIANS 5:19-21
THE FRUIT OF
Sexual Immorality
Impurity
Debauchery Idolatry
Jealousy Witchcraft
Fits of Rage Hatred
Selfish Ambition Discord
Dissentions –
factions
Envy – Drunkenness
Orgies and the like

UNREGENERATE
SINFUL NATURE

Each problem outlined stems from a root in the soul and must be pulled out separately

THE VISIBLE LIFE
THE INVISIBLE LIFE

general attitude of **REBELLION** towards God

SINFUL NATURE (inherited)

DISOBEDIENCE to God's specific commands

HEREDITARY spirits, curses

FAILURE to meet God's holy stand-ards (self-centredness and demonic oppression)

THE HUMAN HEART — SOUL — AND PERSONALITY

Diagram 2.
(The regenerate nature)

New Growth will produce Fruit of the Spirit

WHAT THE GOSPEL PROVIDES

The old nature is kept under control by the Spirit of God

The old nature is cleansed by blood, and made new by the Holy Spirit (This does not mean that the believer cannot fall into sin, and not be oppressed again).

The axe of Repentance wielded by Godly sorrow for sin at time of new birth (kept for future use in Christian living).

REDEMPTION – freedom from sin's grip and penalty through the blood of Jesus

DELIVERANCE –freedom from demonic root causes of sin

REGENERATION – freedom to live in victory by spirit-transformation, and infusion of divine light.

LORDSHIP OF CHRIST

OBEDIENCE TO GOD'S WORD

VICTORY IN THE HOLY SPIRIT

"Rescue me from those who pursue me, for they are too strong for me."

(Psalm 142:6)

CHAPTER 7.

What Satan and demons do to born again believers today

There are few questions which cause more emotive responses than this one:- "Can Christians become demon-possessed?" There are certainly examples of Satan speaking through, or using some of the apostles and early church members to do his will and advance his cause. But apart from Judas Iscariot it is open to question as to whether these individuals were "demon-possessed" in the full sense of the word.

1. Understanding the problem.

In order to reach an understanding we need to look at the basic meanings of the Greek words translated as "demon-possessed".

(1) "daimonizomai", used eleven times.

(Quotations are from the King James Version, with the NIV alternatives in brackets.)

(a) Matthew 4:24

" . . and those which were possessed with devils . . " ("the demon-possessed").

(b) Matthew 15:22

" . . my daughter is grievously vexed with a devil" (" . . My daughter is suffering terribly from demon possession").

(c) John 10:20

"He hath a devil and is mad" ("He is demon-possessed and raving mad").

While early translators chose words which expressed a variety of meanings, modern translators uniformly seem to prefer "demon-possession" to describe all types of demonic conditions.

Well-known Bible authorities have expressed their understanding of the Greek 'daimonizomai' much less rigidly.

(i) Young's Analytical Concordance - "to be demonized, be as a demon."

(ii) Strong's Exhaustive Concordance (1139) - "to be exercised by a demon, have a (be vexed with, be possessed with) devil(s)."

(iii) W. E. Vine's Expository Dictionary of New Testament Words (Oliphants).

- "to be possessed of a demon, to act under the control of a demon. Those who were thus afflicted, expressed the mind and consciousness of the demon or demons indwelling them."

(2) The Greek "echo", used on two occasions.

(a) **Acts 8:7**
"For unclean spirits, crying with a loud voice, came out of many that were possessed with them" ("With shrieks evil spirits came out of many" NIV).

(b) **Acts 16:16**
"A certain damsel possessed with a spirit of divination met us" (KJV). ("We were met by a slave girl who had a spirit by which she predicted the future" NIV).

Although the word "echo" is translated "have" some 607 times in the King James Version, the translators saw fit to use the word "possessed" when linking it with demons. The Revised Version changed the word "possessed" to "had" and "having" respectively. Modern translators have maintained this principle.

(3) The Greek "katadinasteuo" meaning "overpowered".

Acts 10:38
". . who (Jesus Christ) went about doing good, and healing all that were oppressed of the devil; for God was with him" (KJV). ("he went around doing good and healing all who were under the power of the devil, because God was with him" NIV).

The word 'katadinasteuo' comes from root words meaning 'down' and 'under'. James the apostle is the only other writer to use this word, and he does so very effectively. "Is it not the rich who are exploiting you?" (James 2:6).

What conclusions may reasonably be drawn from the basic meanings of these three words used to describe demonic activities with people? The writer suggests:-

Firstly, the word "demon-possessed" has become a classification used to cover every form of demon activity, irrespective of degree. It is rather like the word "prisoner" which applies to all inmates but does not reveal the cause or length of the term being served.

Secondly, the words "possessed" and "possession" in their full sense may well apply to unbelievers who have given themselves over to Satan's control of their lives. He lives in their spirits just as the Holy Spirit lives in and controls believers who make Jesus Lord. The maniac at Gadara (Luke 8:26-39), and the boy whom the disciples were unable to set free (Luke 9:37-43), are certainly examples.

Thirdly, Christians may be harrassed in the extreme (as the Apostle Paul was), or be demonized in a variety of ways, but such activities are more correctly described as "oppression" (KJV) or "under the power of the devil" (NIV).

Regrettably, some sort of defilement has become attached to the term "demon-possessed" and people who have experienced deliverance have either felt, or been made to feel spiritually inferior. The same attitude used to apply to mental patients, until the public became re-educated, and a more appropriate term like "mental health" was coined.

Deliverance releases people from their problem self-image. Dr. Luke makes this abundantly clear in listing some of the people who followed Jesus and ministered to him. "The twelve were with him, also some women who had been cured of evil spirits and diseases: Mary (called Magdalene) from whom seven demons had come out; Joanna the wife of Cuza, the manger of Herod's household; Susanna; and many others. These women were helping to support them out of their own means." (Luke 8:2, 3). Deliverance brings people closer to Jesus Christ than they ever imagined could be possible.

● One twentieth century example of this principle is a young lady whom the Lord drew close to him within seven days of this chapter being written. As a teenager she was drawn into the use of ouija boards, then drugs and the hippy counter-culture. In her travels she went into Eastern religions and Theosophy. Sex became a problem in womanhood, and before she was born again at the age of 34, she had had sexual relationships with hundreds of men, and three abortions. Her rebellion, rejection, and hardness were extreme until the Spirit of God enabled her to repent, with tears. When the Lord freed, cleansed, healed her and gave her self-respect, her joy and gratitude to him knew no bounds.

2. Ways in which Satan and demons oppress Christians.

One of the readings from 'God Calling' by Two Listeners (Publisher, Arthur James), accurately describes his tactics. "The powers of evil watch you as a besieging force would watch a guarded city - the object being always to find some weak spot, attack that, and so gain an entrance. So evil lurks around you watching for some fear. The fear may have been but a small one, but it affords evil a weak spot to attack and enter, and then in come rushing despondency, doubt of Me, and so many other sins."

Paul likens Satan's tactics against Christians to spiritual warfare, in Ephesians chapter six. John Bunyan's classic 'City of Mansoul' took the same theme, and so did Michael Harper in his 'Spiritual Warfare' (Hodder and Stoughton). Based upon the ancient system of warfare, Satan and demonic powers use four main strategies to oppress believers:-

FIRST - The propaganda machine. The key word is INFLUENCES.

By constant subtle propaganda, Satan aims at softening the resistance of the believer's spiritual defence system. He tempts eyes, ears, and other senses to enjoy past, or new sinful desires.

The word 'influences' sums up this type of activity. It comes from a Latin word, 'influens, influentis' meaning 'to flow in'. The Concise Oxford Dictionary even links it with astrology - 'supposed flow from stars - of ethereal fluid affecting character and destiny of man'.

Christians are constantly being tempted by both subtle and brazen attractions to give way to the desires of the old nature. Spiritually weak Christians who take the demonic bait will fall. Believers need to keep themselves spiritually clean, wear the armour of God, and resist all influences.

SECOND - Bold attacks in attempts to breach defences. The key word is AFFLICTIONS.

Christians, (like unbelievers), are subject to a variety of attacks against the soul and body. The enemy is always out to establish a 'power base', and he employs a variety of tactics:

(1) AFFLICTIONS.

The Concise Oxford Dictionary defines this word as 'distress with bodily or mental suffering'. The Greek word 'thlipsis' is translated "pressures, afflictions, anguish, burden, persecution, tribulation, trouble" (Acts 7:10; 2 Corinthians 4:17; 1 Thessalonians 1:6; 3:7). In Hebrews 10:33, the word is translated 'persecution' by The New International Version.

Demonic afflictions may be mental, emotional, physical, or harassing circumstances. They may be a 'one-off' variety, a chain of problems or accidents, or may even climax in disasters of a financial, personal, or family nature. The fiery darts of Ephesians 6:16, are afflictions. If the demonic cause is not recognized and dealt with, Satan will have established his coveted power base and can be expected to press on for greater advantages.

● A missionary nurse assisted a pastor counselling a young lesbian. The pastor was inexperienced in deliverance, and lacked spiritual authority. As a result, the nurse was attacked and overcome by the spirits of lust and lesbianism. She felt constant guilt and temptation as she was working in a girl's school. She heard the writer speak about freedom in Christ at a missionary conference and asked for help. She shared the problem and the Lord released her.

● A 39 year old single man had staying with him two men who had been patients in a psychiatric institution. With a small group of friends, he laid hands on the visitors, and prayed for them. He told the writer, "The top of my head nearly lifted off with incredible power." When the visitors left without showing any improvement, their host felt emotionally heavy, and lost the assurance of his salvation. He tried mind dynamics to obtain relief, and this led him to attend a spiritistic church for a period. When he realized that the church was in deception, he declared his faith in Christ at an evening service, and left. As he walked home in the dark, what looked like golf balls of white light began to rain down out of the night sky on his head. He was so terrified he had to close his eyes and grope along the fence line to avoid seeing them. After he had been released from the afflicting spirits, the assurance of his salvation and his spiritual joy returned.

(2) INFIRMITIES.

"Surely he took up our infirmities" (Isaiah 53:4).

The translators have used a variety of words which illustrate the full meaning of the Greek 'asthenia'.

(a) Sicknesses.

" . . crowds of people came to hear him and to be healed of their sicknesses (Luke 5:15).

(b) Diseases.

" . . and also some women who had been cured of evil spirits and diseases" (Luke 8:2).

(c) Being crippled.

" . . and a woman was there who had been crippled by a spirit for eighteen years" (Luke 13:11). "When Jesus Christ healed her, he said, 'Woman, you are set free from your infirmity.' " (v. 12).

(d) Being an invalid.

"One who was there had been an invalid for thirty-eight years" (John 5:5).

(e) Illnesses.

"Stop drinking only water, and use a little wine because of your stomach and your frequent illnesses" (1 Timothy 5:23).

(f) Buffetings (KJV) torment (NIV).

These were what the demonic messenger was commissioned by God to do to the apostle Paul, and previously likened to the jabbing of a sharp stake (2 Corinthians 12:7).

The devil has certainly taken full advantage of his evil authority over the whole human race by afflicting it with death and all manner of sickness, disease, and afflictions; he well knows the effect these have on the spiritual vitality of Christians. The baffling emergence of new diseases which become resistant to traditional remedies, can quite conceivably be traced to the evil master mind whom Jesus said is a murderer, thief, and destroyer (John 8:44; 10:10).

In addition to God-given natural, medical, and scientific means of healing, the believer has the authority and power of the name of Jesus to bring release from demonic problems.

Two small personal examples illustrate this:-

● Over the years, I have received all types of medical treatment for chronic nasal congestion. The condition became greatly intensified by the unwise over-use of nasal decongestive sprays to the point where I could only sleep upright. A visiting doctor friend saw the problem. He placed his fingers lightly on my forehead and rebuked the spirit of infirmity causing the oedema. The blocked nasal breathing eased very slightly and within a week, the healing was complete. That was five years ago, and I am still rejoicing in a clear nose.

● Some years ago, my wife Phyl suffered from a severe liver condition causing jaundice. Because her gall bladder had been removed many years before, she had difficulty in digesting food, and suffered considerable pain. One night, during a time of family prayer, we were led to take specific authority over the spirit causing her condition. It was bound, broken and released, and she was anointed with oil for healing. After a deep refreshing sleep, she wakened next morning with a deep conviction that her healing had been established. Within a few days, all pain and jaundice had gone, and full digestion returned without any medical aid.

THIRD - The raiding party to immobilize certain essential functions. The key word is **BONDAGES**.

An invading army always aims at crippling vital services to force a country or city to its knees. Telephones, radio and TV stations, food supplies, road, rail, and airport facilities are always prime targets. Satan has the same plan with Christians.

The Christian's vulnerability lies in his thought life, his desires and decision making. Given a chance, Satan will put a bondage on the mind by restricting its ability to think clearly or understand the word of God. He likes to tie up the emotions also, so that a believer will be unable to forgive, or show love which he or she knows ought to be shown. Whenever such a person wants to do right and cannot, there is often a consciousness that 'something' is preventing it. If it were a 'something', then psychology should have all the right answers. But whatever psychology may accomplish by changing attitudes and explaining basic causes, it just does not have the power to release those invading spirit-personalities.

● During prayer, a demon-oppressed Christian had a vision of Jesus Christ coming into his prison cell. He felt Jesus take him by the hand, and lead him outside. He heard the door slam behind them, saw the Lord throw the door keys over his shoulder through the cell grating and heard them drop with a metallic thud on the cell floor. He knew from that moment, he was permanently free.

● A seven year-old boy, being prayed for, had a vision of himself wrapped up in bandages, and unable to walk. He saw the Lord Jesus come to him and cut away the bandages which fell to the ground around his feet. He knew his fears would never again trouble him.

The Biblical word 'bondage' is very meaningful. The Hebrews in Egypt were said to have been "in the house of bondage" (Exodus 13:3; Deuteronomy 5:6; 6:12; 8:14; Joshua 24:7). And Paul used the word 'bondage' (Gr. douleia) to illustrate:-

(a) Jewish slavery to the Law, bound by the spirit of fear (Romans 8:15).

(b) Creation bound by decay, because of sin (Romans 8:21).

(c) The mastery of sin and fleshly lusts which burden the unregenerate (Galatians 5:1).

The writer of Hebrews also uses the word to express the grip that the fear of death had over the people prior to Calvary. By suffering death and breaking Satan's power, Jesus Christ frees people from death and every bondage of fear (Hebrews 2:15). Because of the triumph of the resurrection and ascension, every aspect of demonic oppression in a child of God is an act of trespass.

FOUR - The invasion and capture of a city, and its control by occupational forces. The key word is DOMINIONS (or DOMINATIONS).

The Greek word 'kuriotes' denotes 'lordship' or 'power'. Just as occupational forces impose their directives on the local citizens who are powerless to resist, so do demonic powers literally 'do their thing' in the life of the person they have overpowered. They gratify their own evil natures, such as hatred, anger, violence, fears, lust, addictions, mental problems or a host of other uncontrollable desires or habits. There may be one, two, or even a host of demons of diverse nature dominating an individual at one time. Whatever their names and natures may be, we do know that:

(1) every demonic personality was 'disarmed' (or literally 'unclothed') when Jesus Christ triumphed over them at Calvary (Colossians 2:15). As a result, we now have delegated power over these (John 20:21,22).

(2) every believer now reigns with Christ far above all rule, authority, power, and dominion, to the glory of God the Father (Ephesians 1:21).

When we minister deliverance to believers, demonic powers may verbally refuse to go, or even cause the victim to resist by a show of physical strength. That resistance will cease, and victory will come through standing in the authority of Jesus Christ, and the power of his name.

Believers are expected to walk constantly in the freedom Christ has purchased for them. Satan, that old taskmaster, is always on the lookout to recapture any who may return to enjoy the past lusts of the flesh. He is certainly eager to re-impose old bondages and dominations. The four fleshly danger areas where Satan and his demons have so much success are described in Galatians chapter five:

(a) **Lustful behaviour.**
   "sexual immorality, impurity, debauchery" (v. 19).

(b) **Spiritual unfaithfulness.**
   "Idolatry and witchcraft" (v. 20).

(c) Unrestrained self-expression.
" . . . hatred, discord, jealousy, fits of rage, selfish ambitions, dissensions, factions (the basis of religious sects) (v. 20).

(d) Self-indulgent lifestyles.
" . . . drunkenness, orgies (carousing - Amp.) and the like" (v. 21).

Any consideration of demon oppression in Christians would be incomplete without a brief survey of the human personality and areas of vulnerability.

GOD HAS GIVEN MANKIND A PERSONALITY WHICH REFLECTS HIMSELF.

Firstly, a spirit.
Man's centre of spiritual gravity is his spirit which is immortal (literally deathless), and provides him with a sense of God-consciousness and a faculty of worship. When a person is born again, the Spirit of God brings divine life to the human spirit, and the believer then becomes the temple of God (John 3:6; Romans 8:15; 1 Corinthians 3:16; 16:17; 6:17).

Secondly, a soul.
Man's soul expresses the distinctiveness of his own human personality. It functions closely with the spirit, and after death, spirit and soul appear to be in unity (Luke 16:19-31) The soul appears to have the following inter-related functions:-

(i) **The mind or intellect,** controlling all thought life. It has the capacity to receive wisdom, knowledge, and understanding from the Holy Spirit through the human spirit (1 Corinthians 2:6-16).

(ii) **The heart, or emotional centre** capable of receiving and responding to both divine and human love (Ephesians 3:17; 4:32).

(iii) **The will, or the ability to choose.** Every believer is expected to make the choices which will glorify God's name (Romans 12:1, 2).

(iv) **The conscience, or the inner voice,** which convicts of wrong thoughts and actions and commends those which are right. Believers need to have their consciences programmed with the moral and ethical standards of the Word of God. Consciences may lose their sensitivity, or even be hardened and lose their function (Acts 24:16; John 8:9; 1 Timothy 4:2).

(v) **The senses** of sight, hearing, touch, and smell serve the needs of soul and body. They are also included in what is spoken of as 'the flesh' in the King James Version. "For all that is in the world, the lust of the flesh, and the lust of the eyes, and the pride of life, is not of the Father, but is of the world" (1 John 2:16). The Amplified version puts it this way: "For all that is in the world, the lust of the flesh (craving for sensual gratification) and the lust of the eyes (greedy longings of the mind) and the pride of life (assurance in one's own resources or in the stability of earthly things) - these do not come from the Father but are from the world (itself)".

The body is the physical support system to the spirit and soul. The amount of time, effort, and finance we expend on its desires will be determined by whether we have a life philosophy of 'spirit, soul, and body', or 'body, soul, and spirit'.

The following diagram illustrates the human personality:-

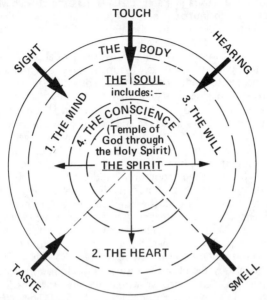

EXPLANATORY NOTES:

* The broken lines indicate the inter-related functions of soul and spirit. All our actions involve the spirit, mind, emotions, will and conscience in varying degrees.

* The Spirit filled and controlled believer will be subject to the direction of the Holy Spirit.

* Satan may bring bondages and dominations to body and soul, but NOT to the spirit, as he could never overcome the Holy Spirit who lives in the believer, particularly the spirit (1 Corinthians 3:16; Romans 8:16).

Before concluding this chapter, one further vital subject needs consideration. Christians are often asked about the place of "the flesh", and "repentance" in the freedom ministry.

The writer understands the following words and terms used in the King James Version as describing the attitudes, actions, and habits of the unregenerate Adamic nature (modern translations in brackets):-

- "the old man" ("old self") Ephesians 4:22.
- "carnal" ("worldly") 1 Corinthians 3:1, 3, 4.
- "the flesh" ("sinful nature") Galatians 5:13, 16.
- "fleshly lusts" ("sinful desires") 1 Peter 2:11.
- "the natural man" ("the man without the Spirit") 1 Corinthians 2:14.

Paul tells us that when a person is born again (or from above), the old nature is crucified with Christ (Romans 6:3). Paul makes it clear that from the moment of new birth we must daily affirm identification with the death, burial, and resurrection of Jesus Christ (Romans 6:11, 12; 1 Corinthians 14:31). The new nature which replaces the "old", "carnal", and "fleshly" nature, will take control provided we allow Jesus to become Lord by his Spirit. In this way the whole personality of the believer is re-programmed by new and righteous attitudes, actions and habits (1 Peter 2:2). Unless the changeover is decisive, and followed by a continuous process of spiritual renewal, the old thought patterns and sensual desires resist the new nature, and may even fight for survival.

A simple illustration may help. Most residential areas have a problem with stray animals, particularly dogs. Normally they are impounded or taken to a society dedicated to animal care. Unless claimed, dogs may be given away, sold, or put down. Imagine that you would like to own a dog. So you go to the pound or R.S.P.C.A., and you find one which suits your purposes well, so you pay the appropriate fees and take the pet of your choice home for some tender loving care. The first night you can't sleep for Tiger's barking. The next morning there are ten newspapers belonging to your neighbours at your front door. When you arrive home that night, a hole has been almost scratched through your highly polished front door, and the front path is covered with your new plants and dirt. You obviously have three choices ahead of you. You can have a breakdown; take the dog back; or break those bad habits by discipline and encouragement, teaching him to obey you. In other words, make the dog understand he has to do your will. As your legal property he no longer has any right to do his own thing. His old nature with its bad habits must be broken and replaced with new responses. So it is with our flesh life. We have been bought by the blood of Jesus, and no longer have personal rights.

From personal experience we would all agree that the lusts and desires of our old nature are even more stubborn than the dog. They NEVER give up. We are all involved in the constant struggle of "the old" versus "the new" as Paul graphically describes in Romans chapter seven. The flesh life neither dies, nor can be cast out through deliverance. Although it certainly can be mastered through Godly living, the flesh is always rebellious. At the slightest encouragement, fleshly or sensuous desires will seek to overthrow the life in Christ. Spiritual awareness and warfare is as needful for spiritual survival as breathing is for living. Paul outlines the blessings of victories by being filled and controlled by the Spirit (Romans 8).

Spiritual victory is not automatic. God has provided each one of us with four clear guidelines, which, if adhered to faithfully, will make us "more than conquerors" as Paul promised (Romans 8:37). They are:

(1) A spiritual understanding of our basic problem.

If any Biblical word has ever been strongly contested, rationalized, and even outlawed, it is the word "sin". But nothing that man can do to convince himself he is not accountable to God can erase guilt which is the spiritual shadow sin casts over the conscience.

Believers live in a sin-cursed world constantly bombarded by temptation. The more they read the Word of God, the more sensitive they become to sin around them and in them. New birth does not return us to pre-fall Eden innocence, but gives us enlightenment, protection, and overcoming victory. Knowing that temptation and lust are a lethal combination, we ought to yield each sin-responsive part of our personality to God so that we can receive his grace to meet each practical need (2 Corinthians 5:17-21). Should we then be confronted by temptation and desire, our first responsibility is to resist the first cause, the devil (James 4:7; 1 Peter 5:9). Our second responsibility is to call upon the Lord for help (1 Corinthians 10:13; Hebrews 2:17, 18). In this way his righteousness is our protection and safeguard.

(2) The death process of repentance.

The foundation of salvation is repentance from past sin, and from the desire to sin (Acts 2:38; Acts 20:21). The foundation of successful living is repenting immediately temptation becomes attractive, and before lust responds and sin is conceived. The Greek 'metanoia' means not only a change of mind and attitude but also implies a change of behaviour as an evidence of the outworking of repentance. John the Baptist expected this (Luke 3:8), and the apostle Paul preached it (Acts 26:20). The daily recognition of the death of our old nature is as essential as being filled and controlled by the Holy Spirit.

(3) A command to obedience.

Obedience is that personal commitment to discipleship which shows our love to Jesus Christ, and glorifies God (John 15:7-14).

In Rotorua, New Zealand, there is a rainbow trout fish hatchery which is a popular tourist attraction. When food is thrown to the fish at feeding time, the water appears to boil with leaping fish. But when the fish are spawning, nothing will stir their appetite. Apart from the occasional flick of a fin, they just seem to be spaced out, suspended in the water.

Believers whose spiritual appetites are fully satisfied in Jesus Christ, are simply unresponsive to the lures of Satan. As darkness cannot displace light, so temptation finds no response in the Spirit filled nature.

(4) The victory of spiritual warfare.

Saul, renamed Paul, was probably more experienced in spiritual warfare than any other apostle. He shared the principles which had ensured his own victory in Ephesians chapter six. By wearing and using items of spiritual armour, believers are promised a threefold victory when the day of temptation to evil comes. Firstly they will be able to stand against Satan (verse 11), then withstand him (verse 13), and finally be still on their feet when the battle is over (verse 13).

The most important aspect of spiritual warfare is that Jesus Christ has ransomed the believer from the curse and penalty of sin (Matthew 20:28; 1 Timothy 2:6). Although the power of sin has been broken, we still need to claim each victory by faith.

In the conquest of Caanan it was God who went before his people and destroyed the nations. All the Israelites did was enter into the victories God had provided (Deuteronomy 31:3-6). Likewise, we members of the Body of Christ have only to believe for, and take by faith the victories Jesus won for us at Calvary (Colossians 2:15). This is how we work out our salvation (alt. deliverance) to fulfil the will of God (Philippians 2:12).

Unless believers actively implement this fourfold plan of activity, they expose themselves to the following activities of the evil one:

(a) Demonic bondages and dominations of the unregenerate life may reappear if freedom was not specifically ministered at the time of new birth (Acts 26:18). These will of course greatly hinder spiritual growth and productivity. Most of the Christian counsellees who request our ministry are in this category.

(b) Christians who flirt with temptation, who claim forgiveness without deep repentance, who obey spiritual principles only when convenient, and who ignore spiritual warfare, are in the gravest danger of becoming oppressed by demonic bondages and dominations.

Despite much present day theological relativism, the Bible defines only two classes of sin - unintentional and intentional. For unintentional sin, atonement was available under God's first covenant of Law (Leviticus 4:3, 13, 22, 27). Under the covenant of grace, forgiveness and cleansing are available to the believer through the blood of Jesus Christ (1 John 1:9).

Under Law, deliberate sin was punished by death (Leviticus 24:18-29). Under grace, deliberate sin carries the sternest warning which should alert each of us to the fact that God regards no sin as trivial (Hebrews 10:26-31).

The writer has personally received tremendous freedom from bondages and hereditary dominations just through the power of the Word of God. The only exemption was the hereditary curse of Freemasonry, which will be explained in a later chapter.

CHAPTER SUMMARY.

1. In describing demonic activities in the lives of believers, the words 'demon-oppression' are far more appropriate than the words 'demon-possession', as evil spirits have no power over a human spirit in which the Holy Spirit lives through the new birth. Demon-possession may indeed be an accurate description for some non believers.

2. Demons may oppress Christians by bombarding them with sensual attractions, a variety of afflictions such as a run of accidents or disasters, sicknesses, infirmities, or allergies, by forcing them to indulge in lustful activities, or frightening them with apparitions, and/or moving things around (poltergeist).

3. Satan may enter and control faculties of the soul, and the body.

4. Jesus Christ has removed from every believer, the rights that Satan and evil spirits had over them because of sin. To maintain the victory which Calvary purchased for them, each believer needs to bring each faculty of the soul, and the body under the constant control of the Holy Spirit. If this is not done, fleshly lust will revive, and the believer can again become subject to demonic bondages and dominations.

"You are my hiding place; you will protect me from trouble and surround me with songs of deliverance" (Psalm 32:7).

CHAPTER 8.

Demon oppression in the local church

How right was the preacher who first said: "There are two sides to the Gospel, the believin' side, and the behavin' side." Ideally, every member of God's kingdom should be an example of his love, peace, and harmony. After all, the Christian life is the original and only valid lifestyle in a demon-afflicted world.

When believers are not released from demonic oppression at the time of new birth, existing demonic problems are simply transferred into the new environment. The use of traditional counselling methods against them is as effective as cutting lawns with a pair of scissors. It's not only tedious but useless. As long as roots remain, growth will continue. **Demons will not go away because they have been renounced. They have to be literally thrown out.**

I am sure that readers who are pastors, counsellors, or spiritual leaders, will have experienced the frustration of exhausting all resources without really helping a needy person. One of three options is usually taken. The first is to refer the counsellee to a Christian psychologist or psychiatrist in the hope that more specialized expertise will solve the problem. Another is to take refuge behind verses of Scripture and shift the blame for absence of freedom to either sin or lack of faith in the counsellee. When there is no improvement, and the counsellee is thrown into unbelief, confusion, and despair, a final desperate third step may be taken. The counsellee is either told that he or she is beyond help, or contact is avoided. Secretaries may even be asked to make excuses in order to prevent further counselling appointments. As a result, Satan gets mileage out of both parties.

Of course there are occasions when a change of circumstances will resolve the difficulty. But when circumstances cannot be changed, and the counsellee has no alternative but to continue facing the basic problem, the matter of the counsellee's reactions to the circumstances have to be resolved. Unless basic intolerances, inadequacies, fears and wrong attitudes are dealt with by removing their root causes, they will readily re-assert themselves, given the right circumstances. The philosophy of the old wartime song says it all: "Pack up your troubles in your old kit bag and smile, smile, smile." Putting on a brave face, and re-locating the kit bag doesn't change its contents one bit. They can always be unpacked in first class condition!

The difference that deliverance makes is that when bondages are broken, and dominant spirits cast out, the Holy Spirit can bring victory through his filling and control. Few Christians who come for prayer have any idea of the extent to which they need freedom. Any other form of counsel will only be of a palliative nature, and will not bring lasting results.

● A married woman who was constantly being rejected found her husband's outbursts of anger and sexual aggressiveness more than she could cope with. Out of desire to honour her marriage vows, she came for counsel. The husband's power to hurt her was broken and she was freed from rejection. After receiving ministry, she found that she was able to control her husband's moods by her spiritual resources, and live with the situation without the previous devastation.

People who spend their lives serving the needs of others sometimes become overwhelmed by the pressures, and feel unable to cope with the constant emotional and physical demands made on them. It has been found that when demonic bondages are broken, they have adequate spiritual resources to meet each challenge.

When a person does not receive release from guilt and shame after there has been genuine repentance and confession, unbelief from a demonic source is usually the cause.

Unless the one forgiven forgives himself or herself, God's cleansing (1 John 1:9) will not be received because of a sense of unworthiness. When the grip of Satan is broken, people who have been deeply involved in the most defiling sins have received totally renewed self-images. The crippling effect of guilt is very real indeed. It is wonderful to watch the Lord spiritually renew those who have been involved in adultery, prostitution, homosexuality, and deviant sexual experiences.

● A married woman regarded herself as a 95% ideal marriage partner, but the 5% failure area became so troublesome to her that she felt it was putting her marriage in jeopardy. It was not a large problem, but she felt constantly beaten by it, despite many tears and much prayer and fasting. When troublesome hereditary spirits were cast out, a sweet change took place in her, bringing her to a new security in which her contribution to the marriage was greatly enhanced.

One of the hindrances to releasing people from demon oppression is that counsellees often have no understanding about the number of problems the evil one is capable of producing in Christians. Few people would seriously dispute Satan's involvement in drugs, prostitution, witchcraft and the like, but by restricting our thinking to what he is known to do in the world, the devil's activities and deception within the church are often overlooked.

Those involved in deliverance are often accused of looking for demons 'behind every leaf, and under every stone'. Substitute the words 'unresolved problem and unconquered habit' for 'leaf and stone' and the truth will be evident. As unpopular as this may be in some circles, there is no shame in upholding the truth.

In his 'Balanced Christianity', Dr. John Stott writes that 'balance' is obtained by standing in an upright position, feet apart, being able to press down with either foot to resist the wind from whichever direction it blows. A precarious balance may also be obtained by placing one foot behind the other, and using the arms as counter-weights. Both methods illustrate how people handle divergent teachings on deliverance. Some try a balancing act between one view or another not delaring an opinion which may offend. That will only lead to a spiritually ineffective no-man's land. On the other hand, by being liberal or conservative, using the particular emphasis the Holy Spirit may dictate in each situation, greater understanding and effectiveness is possible. Godly counselling therefore should not be from one rigid viewpoint, but in sensitivity to the direction of the Spirit of Truth.

To avoid being classified as a 'demon-chaser', it is wise to use as few emotive words as possible. Talking openly about 'demons' and 'deliverance' to a sensitive, fearful or conservative Christian may deflect that person from the only means of full release he or she may ever have.

1. A low key ministry may be effective.

Some demonic influences and bondages may be broken and cleansing ministered without doing what most people associate with deliverance. Intensive prayer does not need to be noisy. A person's hands may be held to avoid any problem that the "laying on of hands" may create. God honours his word and his name, and is not limited to any particular method of release.

● After Phyl's father died, neither Phyl nor I knew how her mother would survive living alone (a choice she had made for herself). She was a fearful person, had never lived alone before, and her house was a little isolated in a small country town. One day while they were sitting opposite one another at the kitchen table, Phyl prayed for her mother. From that moment, every fear disappeared, and until her death some thirteen years later at the age of eighty-four, she lived alone joyously, never showing one sign of nervousness.

● During a children's and adults' mission at a local church, the minister arranged for Phyl and me to have a meal with a lady member of the church. She had a problem which was weighing heavily on her. A neighbour had built a large concrete block wall outside her kitchen window. She had become so paranoid about it that she was pressing her husband to sell the house and move. After the meal while still sitting at the table, we laid the problem before the Lord, and resisted that afflicting spirit of fear. Several weeks later we happened to meet the lady again, and casually asked how she felt about the wall. She gave us a puzzled look, and said, "What wall?"

2. There are ways of speaking of demonic problems which avoid stimulating resistance or giving offence.

● A young man came to talk about his problems. During conversation, it became obvious that there were a number of demonic causes. I was informed that he had already consulted ten pastors or preachers whom he respected. One of them had had experience in deliverance, and had assured him he had no demonic problems. The young man made it very clear that he had lost all confidence in counselling. Without using the word 'demons', the writer spoke of 'spiritual influences' or 'forces' operating within his life, and offered to help if needed. Two weeks later, he phoned. To say he was 'loaded' would be an under-statement. God began a great work in him which took some time. Had a bolder approach been taken, he would not have responded.

3. The problem of the self-diagnosed.

From time to time, anxious people call us, convinced they are 'demon-possessed'. Usually they have read, heard, or felt something which has caused the self-diagnosis. A few key questions will soon show that their fears are groundless. After being reassured, they are relieved and full of gratitude to be given 'a clean bill of health'. Unwise emphasis on demons in preaching, teaching, or counselling sessions may induce fears and false symptoms.

4. The special dangers of those in leadership positions.

The evil one knows that if he can gain an advantage over a shepherd of the flock, he will effectively block his personal ministry, and, even worse, possibly bring dishonour to the name of Jesus Christ, and the testimony of the local church. A missionary and his wife planted churches and pioneered a deliverance ministry in a country where animism and witchcraft still flourished. They were later called to another country where the wife's health deteriorated. Her energy and vitality dropped so alarmingly that her husband felt very discouraged, and was even tempted to give up missionary service. When the demonic bondages and dominions from the first field of service were dealt with, the process of healing and recovery commenced immediately.

One of the most distressing features of a deliverance counselling ministry is to see what devastation Satan is bringing to pastors, spiritual leaders, full-time Christian workers and churches through sexual lust and immoral behaviour. A charismatic song leader used to make excuses for going into the city where he could see blue movies. Pastors have gratified their lustful fantasy in massage parlours. A charismatic leader asked us to minister deliverance to a woman whom he said was enticing him, when in fact it turned out he was subjecting her to his sexual fantasies. A pastor justified having sexual intercourse with a counsellee. A missionary doctor turned a vaginal examination of a fellow missionary into a sexual assault, then pleaded with her not to say anything which would ruin his reputation.

Ministries have been ruined, marriages broken, families scattered, churches divided, and much dishonour brought to the name of the Lord Jesus. Together with the problems of professionalism, pride, and financial greed, there seems to be increasing examples of the type of reprehensible behaviour by self-indulgent shepherds which caused God to give Ezekiel the direst warning (Ezekiel Ch. 34).

Demonic power can only be countered by divine power. The best counselling in the world will no more bring a demon under control than a bucket of water will douse a forest fire. Pride, greed, and lust are just a few of the powerful demonic personalities who buffet the people of God today.

The thrill of the deliverance ministry is not just that people are set free from driving passion which is the nature of demons, but that they are fully cleansed from guilt and the fear of repeating the sinful behaviour. The mercy of God in restoring marriages, families, and ministries after setting the involved parties free, is to his eternal honour and glory. Truly, after freedom comes fulfilment and fruitfulness.

5. The danger of deception.

Another danger for those in spiritual leadership is that undetected psychic spirits may masquerade as gifts of the Spirit. Unless people with hereditary or personal involvement in witchcraft have been released from these spirits, they will not only cause havoc in guidance, but will pass these pseudo-gifts to others through the laying on of hands. Users of such 'gifts' have no consciousness of being deceived. In severe cases, however, they will often have unusual fears, visions, or other problems which are foreign to the Spirit-filled believer. Not only do those who exercise bogus gifts need release, but also those to whom they have ministered, particularly if hands have been laid upon them.

6. To be forewarned is to be forearmed.

A short list of demonic spirits (taken from Appendix C, Chapter 26) should remove any lingering doubts about the demonic nature of some major fleshly problems manifesting themselves within church members or adherents.

(1) **Proud spirits** (Proverbs 16:18). A proud spirit can manifest itself as impatience - self-centredness, rebellion, stubbornness, idolatry (1 Samuel 13:8-13:8-14; 15:14-23). Pride was the primary sin of Lucifer (Ezekiel 28:17).

(2) **Evil spirits** (Luke 7:21; 8:2; Acts 19:12).

(3) **Spirits of divination** (Gr. 'python' Acts 16:16).

(4) **Spirits of error** (1 John 4:6; 1 Timothy 4:1).

(5) **Unclean or impure spirits** (Mark 7:25 etc. Revelation 17:4).

(6) **Familiar spirits** (witchcraft) (1 Samuel 28:3, 8, 9; Deuteronomy 18:11; 2 Kings 23:24; Isaiah 8:19).

(7) **Spirits of heaviness, or despair** (Isaiah 61:3).

(8) **Lying spirits** (1 Kings 22:21-23).

(9) **Perverse (or confusing) spirits** (Isaiah 19:14).

(10) **Spirits of insanity** (Luke 8:26-39).

(11) **Spirits of infirmities, diseases** (Matthew 8:16, 17).

The following examples of demonic activities have been taken from believers' case histories.

(1) Critical and judgmental attitudes which resist all counselling and prayer.

(2) Habits which will not respond to counselling therapy. These include all forms of sexual promiscuity and deviation, frigidity, fantasy-lust and masturbation.

(3) Constant worry, anxiety, and depression.

(4) Fears of all kinds, particularly the stronger ones generally known as phobias. According to surveys, one in every nine persons is troubled with phobias.

(5) Mental problems, schizophrenia, head voices.

(6) Problems arising from hereditary, or personal occultic involvement. These include opposition to spiritual conversation, mockery, having psychic phenomena, terrifying dreams, apparitions.

(7) Addictions to drugs, alcohol, nicotine, gambling, food, excessive physical exercise, and rock music.

(8) Empty religious talk, without deep reality.

(9) Continuous non-pathogenic sicknesses which lack diagnostic confirmation.

(10) A run of accidents, or accident proneness.

(11) Emotional instability with euphoric highs and depressive lows.

(12) An inability to receive God's love, and a continuous low self-image, inferiority and insecurity.

(13) Legalism, harshness, and authoritarian attitudes.

(14) Rebellion, anger, stubbornness, temper and violence.

(15) A relentless unforgiving attitude. Bitterness.

(16) Excessive pride, self-esteem and superiority.

(17) Lack of submission, particularly to authority within the church.

CHAPTER SUMMARY.

1. The deliverance ministry may be misunderstood, misjudged, and misused, but it has been found effective when other methods have failed. The writers have been asked to minister to the most difficult people in some churches as 'test cases' for the effectiveness of the deliverance ministry. God has always honoured the name of Jesus and the principles of his word.

2. Sensitivity to the Holy Spirit's guidance is essential to victory over demonic powers.

3. Spiritual leaders are prime targets for the evil one and his forces.

4. Evidence of demonic activity amongst Christians abounds although it is mostly unrecognized as such.

PART TWO

The sources and effects of Satanic and demonic oppression

Introduction.

INTRODUCTION.

Parts of the following chapters may raise the eyebrows of some conservative Christians, psychologists, psychiatrists, and members of the medical profession. Spiritual explanations for problems generally regarded as having genetic, pathogenic, or psychological causes tend to be rejected, or at least treated with skepticism if they challenge accepted beliefs.

It is with a sense of humility and abounding gratitude to God that the writers share some of what the Holy Spirit has been increasingly teaching us and doing for us in our counselling ministry over many years. Every reader has the right to question the logic and accuracy of Scriptual interpretations but what God has done in the lives of many people is beyond question or doubt.

Rather than presenting a string of case histories in an attempt to support Biblical interpretations, Biblical principles will be laid down, then confirmed by illustrations from counselling experience.

The following chapters will explain some results of Satanic or demonic oppression from conception to old age, as the following diagram shows:-

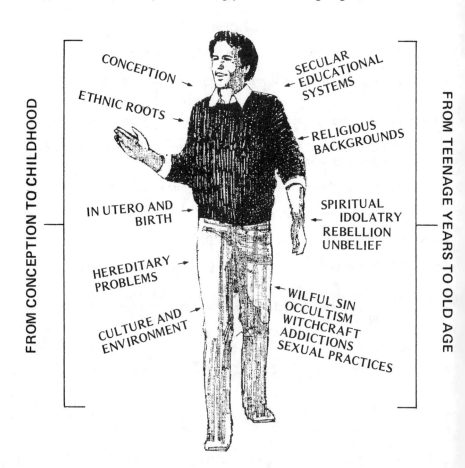

FROM CONCEPTION TO CHILDHOOD

FROM TEENAGE YEARS TO OLD AGE

CONCEPTION →

ETHNIC ROOTS →

← SECULAR EDUCATIONAL SYSTEMS

← RELIGIOUS BACKGROUNDS

IN UTERO AND BIRTH →

← SPIRITUAL IDOLATRY REBELLION UNBELIEF

HEREDITARY PROBLEMS →

CULTURE AND ENVIRONMENT →

← WILFUL SIN OCCULTISM WITCHCRAFT ADDICTIONS SEXUAL PRACTICES

"The fathers have eaten sour grapes, and the children's teeth have been set on edge" (Jeremiah 31:29).

CHAPTER 9.

We are all slaves to hereditary bondages and dominations

Most of us have heard of, and have maybe even cringed from fond parents (or doting grandparents) who insist on eulogizing some characteristics they believe they see in their baby or toddler. The suggestion of hereditary influence is hardly subtle, and congratulations are of course accepted, demurely.

Hereditary problems are usually admitted with both reluctance and self-defence. Using a firm but muted tone out of the side of the mouth, or in a loud whisper behind a hand, you usually hear something like this: "He's got his father's bad temper", or, "He's as stubborn as his old grandfather used to be".

For good or for bad, none of us can avoid showing our family's features and character strengths or weaknesses. The only variable factor is the degree of influence.

So that both writer and reader can have a common understanding of terms which will feature in this and succeeding chapters, the following definitions are quoted from The Concise Oxford Dictionary (Oxford University Press).

Heredity "Tendency of like to beget like; property of organic beings by which offspring have nature and characteristics of parents or ancestors; genetic constitution of an individual."

Hereditary "Descending by inheritance; (of disease, instinct, etc.) transmitted from one generation to another; the same as or like what one's parents had (hereditary greed, hatred)."

Gene "(Biol.) Unit of heredity in chromosome, controlling a particular inherited characteristic of an individual."

Genetic code "System of storage of genetic information in chromosomes."

1. The evidence of hereditary sin passing from Adam to Noah.

The Cain Syndrome (Genesis 4:1-16).

The root of sin was planted deeply in human nature through the events of Genesis chapter three. Eve was deceived by the serpent, while Adam made a conscious choice to disobey the explicit command of his God (1 Timothy 2:14).

The hereditary influence of their sinful nature became tragically obvious to the parents when they lost the first two sons born to them after the close of the Eden era. Both boys had obviously been taught about the ways of God. The younger son Abel chose to live within God's guidelines and offered blood sacrifices to God. Cain the elder, determined that he would not be dominated by good example or advice. Knowing his mother had been deceived into taking forbidden fruit, Cain deliberately chose to give God a fruit offering. When God accepted Abel's offering and rejected Cain's, the eldest son exploded with anger, jealousy, and depression. God tried to reason with him, promising him acceptance if he made the right offering, but warning him that if he failed to conquer the sin that was crouching like an animal to overpower him, it would control him (v. 7). Unfortunately, Cain's judgment was so blurred by his hurt pride, resentment, bitterness, and desire for revenge, that he turned his back on God's grace and planned his brother's murder. Using deception, he lured Abel out of the sight of others and killed him violently (v. 8). When God asked Cain where his brother was, he was brazenly evasive, and finally resorted to a lie. God then cursed Cain for fratricide, and drove him from the ground stained by his righteous brother's blood. Full of self-pity, Cain became a restless wanderer on earth with the mark of the curse upon him (v. 12-15).

Cain is therefore the first Biblical example of parental sin becoming the binding and dominating force in the next generation. Despite the testimony of his righteous brother, and the reasoning of a merciful God, Cain was unable to respond. John said he "belonged to the evil one . . ", and, "his own actions were evil" (1 John 3:12). Within the first two generations we therefore have clear evidence that 'original sin' had become ongoing 'hereditary sin'; and that the power of that sinful nature came from none other than the evil one himself. This is indeed an important truth, and basic to understanding the grip of Satan and sin in human nature. It is no surprise that Jesus later said to the Jews who were the descendants of Abraham, "You belong to your father, the devil, and you want to carry out your father's desire" (John 8:44). The five-fold nature of Satan reproduced in Eve, was now standard human behaviour (pride - self-idolatry - independence - covetousness - rebellion).

Before continuing the hereditary chain of sin, a brief comment on the difference between the attitudes and conduct of Cain and Abel is appropriate. Many Christian and non-Christian families have at least one child who shows the 'black sheep syndrome' - the rejection of righteousness for a path of self-indulgence. In all generations parental suffering for the sins of children is part of the hereditary curse of sin.

Within 1656 years of Adam (calculated by the ages given in Genesis chapter five), the disease of sin had so penetrated the human race by hereditary contamination that:
> "The LORD saw how great man's wickedness had become, and that every inclination of the thoughts of his heart was only evil all the time. The LORD was grieved that he had made man on the earth, and his heart was filled with pain" (Genesis 6:5, 6).
> "Now the earth was corrupt in God's sight and was full of violence. God saw how corrupt the earth had become, for all the people on earth had corrupted their ways" (Genesis 6:11, 12).

God then wiped out mankind and all creation, saving only Noah, seven members of his family and sufficient living creatures to provide sacrifices for sin and yet continue their species.

After the flood, Noah offered animal sacrifices. God responded to his servant in a way which makes it obvious that while the flood dealt judgmentally with sinners, the principle of sin in the human race was as virulent as ever. The LORD smelled the pleasing aroma and said in his heart: "Never again will I curse the ground because of man, **even though every inclination of his heart is evil from childhood.** And never again will I destroy all living creatures as I have done" (Genesis 8:21, emphasis added).

2. Hereditary sin continues from Noah to the Tower of Babel.

After the flood Noah returned to cultivating the land, and in due course, was able to make wine from the grapes of his own vineyard. Wine obviously caused Noah to become indecent, and in one night of over-indulgence, he fell into a drunken sleep completely naked, his genitals exposed. Some time during the night, his son Ham walked in and appeared to gain some sort of sexual satisfaction in seeing his father naked. Instead of showing the respect his father deserved by covering his body and removing his shame, Ham walked outside and told his two brothers about what he had seen. (The dishonour Ham showed to his father was later to become a crime punishable by death when the Law was given to Moses, Deuteronomy 27:16). Shem and Japheth dissociated themselves from Ham, by respectfully covering their father, without looking at his naked body.

When Noah wakened, he was obviously told about what had happened, and took what appeared to be an astonishing attitude. Instead of judging Ham directly, he placed a curse on Canaan who appears to have been the fourth, and youngest, son (Genesis 10:6).

Obviously Noah had either learned from God, or intuitively knew, the principle of children suffering for the sin of a parent, long before God thundered it from Mount Sinai (Exodus 20:4-6).

A quick look at the descendants of the children of Ham (listed in Genesis 10:6) shows that each son showed the effects of Canaan's specific curse.

(1)   **Cush,** the eldest, was the father of Nimrod, (from the Hebrew root 'marad' meaning 'to be stubbornly resistant to authority'). To the Israelites, the name Nimrod suggested he was a rebel against God. Certainly Babylon and Nineveh were centres of idolatry featuring Baal and Ashtoreth, two demonic heathen deities which afterwards defiled God's people. Cush later became identified with Ethiopia.

(2)   **Mizraim,** the second son, is associated with Egypt where his descendants settled. Egypt was deeply involved in magic and witchcraft during the time of Joseph, when the descendants of Ham persecuted the children of Israel through Shem.

Mizraim was also "the father of the Casluhites from whom the Philistines came" (v. 13). This means that Goliath (Young - 'exile or soothsayer'), was a descendant of Ham. He and the Philistines with their heathen demonic gods certainly afflicted God's people.

(3)   **Put (Phut).** Little is known about this man except that his family settled in Libya (Nahum 3:10). Some of them served as mercenaries with the king of Tyre (Ezekiel 27:9, 10). Ezekiel's lament against the king of Tyre is a corollary dealing with the fall of Lucifer (Ezekiel 28:11-19).

(4)   **Canaan,** the fourth son, fathered eleven nations who settled in the land reserved by God for his people (Genesis 10:15; Leviticus 25:23; Deuteronomy 32:8, 9). The Canaanites settled on the Mediterranean sea coast from Sidon in the North to Gaza in the South, then moved inland towards Sodom, Gomorrah, Admah and Zeboiim, even as far as Lasha (v. 15-19). Their immorality and idolatry were to be the greatest trial to the Israelites until they were wiped out, or became slaves to the Semites, the children of Shem, as prophesied by Noah (Genesis 9:25-27).

But it was the degrading homosexuality of the Canaanites on the plain which brought God's fiery judgment upon those sons of Ham (Genesis Ch. 19).

Without question, all the sons of Ham suffered from the family curse, and became involved in demonic idolatry and promiscuity. But it was the descendants of Canaan - upon whom the curse was specifically pronounced - who became the most morally degraded, and suffered the greatest judgement.

According to the genealogy of Genesis chapter eleven, verses ten to thirty-two, some 367 years after the flood, God called Abraham. Some time before this, hereditary pride, self-idolatry, independence, covetousness, and rebellion against God united the people into building a tower, or ziggurat for self-protection. It is believed to have been associated with worship of the starry hosts. The confusion of languages began a global drift, allowing the curse of sin to spread by heredity to all inhabited parts of the world.

3. The principle of hereditary sin operated in the families of the patriarchs.
(1) Abraham and his son Isaac.
When Abram and Sarai and their family left Haran for Canaan, they were half-brother and half-sister, as children of Terah by different wives. They were also husband and wife, which later presented Abram with a very special problem. Because Sarai was very beautiful, he feared that if it were publicly known that they were married people may dispose of him to get Sarai. Thus he planned a little ruse he later explained in these words: "And when God had me wander from my father's household, I said to her (Sarai), 'This is how you can show your love to me: Everywhere we go, say of me, 'He is my brother.' ' " (Genesis 20:13). It was of course, only half the truth, therefore deception, misrepresentation, self-protection, and distrust in God's promise to make him into a great nation (Genesis 12:2). Abram's lie worked in Egypt until God showed him up (Genesis 12:14-20). Unashamedly Abram used the same trick later against Abimelech King of Gerar (Genesis 20:2-13). On both occasions, to Abram's shame, God mercifully preserved the innocent people from committing adultery.

From that time onwards a spirit of deception has featured in Abram's descendants. Some believe this is evident amongst all Arabs who have descended from Abram through Hagar. No-one could deny the evidence in Isaac, the child of promise, who married a very beautiful relative Rebekah. When husband and wife retraced Abraham's steps to Abimelech king of the Philistines, Isaac repeated his father's deception even more brazenly because of the same fear (Genesis 26:7-11).

We may be sure that Abraham and Sarah never did share the details of their family shame with Isaac. The only logical explanation would appear to be that when Isaac was conceived, his father's genes contained a code which programmed fear and deception in later life.

(2) Jacob and his sons.
Isaac and Rebekah were actually cousins, as Rebekah's father was a son of Nahor, Abraham's brother (Genesis 24:24). Rebekah's brother was Laban (Genesis 29:10), for whom Jacob served fourteen years without wages in order to marry his first love, Rachel. On the wedding night, Laban induced Jacob to take leave of his senses (presumably through alcohol) and switched Leah for Rachel.

Like two peas out of one pod, brother Laban and sister Rebekah were both hard-hearted deceivers. Rebekah was also a ruthless manipulator of her favourite son Jacob (supplanter) in planning and executing the heartless deception of her aged and failing husband Isaac, so that Jacob could gain his brother's blessing (Genesis 27:1-29).

Jacob himself maintained the hereditary tradition in order to increase his flock and recoup lost wages by manipulating breeding procedures (Genesis 30:25-43). To round off the deception, wife Rachel helped herself to her father's family idols which were tokens used in inheritance, and shamelessly deceived her father when he followed the fleeing families, demanding the return of household gods (Genesis 31:19, 34, 35).

But the family web of hereditary deceit is not complete until we take into account how Jacob's scheming sons deceived their father over Joseph. Their deceit was not in asking the old gentleman to identify the multi-coloured robe, but in helping him to come to the wrong decision. The comfort his sons and daughters then offered him was totally hypocritical (Genesis 37:27, 32-35).

Although God changed Jacob's hereditary name and nature at Penial (Genesis 32:22-32), it was too late to prevent his children from showing the same characteristics. So we have a vivid example of the hereditary transference of sin. When two brothers produce children whose families exhibit such gross deception as we have considered, it would be most interesting to know a little more of their father Terah.

5. God proclaims his laws of hereditary curses and blessings to his people and confirms them in writing (Exodus 20:4-6).

"You shall not make for yourself any idol in the form of anything in heaven above or on the earth beneath or in the waters below. You shall not bow down to them or worship them, for I, the LORD your God, am a jealous God, punishing the children for the sin of the fathers to the third and fourth generation of those who hate me, but showing love to thousands who love me and keep my commandments."

Please note the following:-

(1) God obviously intended that these and the following commandments were to apply equally to the Hebrews, and to the aliens living among them (Exodus 20:10; 12:48, 49; 22:21; Leviticus 18:26; 19:34). This surely established the authority of God's laws over all mankind.

(2) God clearly states that when anyone or anything is worshipped before him, he regards this as hatred towards himself. Such sin God punishes to the third and fourth generation.

(3) The loyalty and love of parents towards God will bring God's blessings to their children up to one thousand generations (Deuteronomy 7:9).

6. Evidences of the seriousness of a parent's sin bringing about the destruction of a whole family.

(1) The families of Korah, Dathan, and Abiram died because of the sin of the heads of their families (Numbers 16).

These three men were in the forefront of over two hundred and fifty well known community leaders who became insolent towards Moses. They challenged his intentions and leadership after the debacle at Kadesh which was caused by the unbelief of ten spies (Numbers 13:31-33).

Moses summoned the rebels, but they refused to respond. God then instructed Moses to warn the assembly to "Move back from the tents of these wicked men! Do not touch anything belonging to them or you will be swept away because of all their sins. So they moved away from the tents of Korah, Dathan and Abiram. Dathan and Abiram had come out and were standing with their **wives, children, and little ones** at the entrances to their tents" (verses 26, 27). Moses then told the assembly that if these people were to die from natural causes then it would be a sign that God had not sent him, but if the earth were to swallow the rebels 'with everything that belongs to them', then the people would know that they had treated the LORD with contempt (verses 29, 30).

The earth then split apart under the tents of those concerned, and they, their families, and all their possessions disappeared forever. The cries of the perishing could be heard by those who were nearby, and they fled in terror. Fire from God then killed the rebelling community leaders (verses 31-35).

(2) The children of Achan died with their father, because of his sin (Joshua 7:1-26).

During the sacking and burning of Jericho, Achan coveted and took for himself some articles which he knew had been devoted to God. Achan ignored the warning of personal and public disaster, and secreted in the ground beneath his tent, a beautiful Babylonian garment, two hundred shekels of silver, and a wedge of gold.

As a result God turned the assault of Ai into a rout, and told Joshua why he had done so. The guilty man was soon isolated, and judgment carried out as follows:-

"Then Joshua, together with all Israel, took Achan, son of Zerah, the silver, the robe, the gold wedge, **his sons and daughters**, his cattle, donkeys and sheep, his tent and all that he had, to the valley of Achor . . Then all Israel stoned him, and after they had stoned the rest, they burned them . . " (verses 24, 25).

In these two instances, the sins of the parents were so serious in God's eyes, that he caused the descendants to be punished immediately. No hereditary sin was allowed to continue through the family line.

7. Evidences of descendants being cursed because of the sin of the head of the family.

(1) The behaviour of Eli the priest cursed his descendants.

"For I told him I would judge his family forever because of the sin he knew about. The guilt of Eli's house will never be atoned for by sacrifice" (1 Samuel 3:13, 14).

" . . . in your family line there will never be an old man"; "all your descendants will die in the prime of life" (1 Samuel 2:32, 33).

(2) The idolatry of Jereboam son of Nebat cursed both his sons, and his nation.

God instructed Ahijah the prophet to deliver a message of judgement to Jereboam, son of Nebat, through his wife:

"You have done more evil than all who lived before you. You have made for yourself other gods, idols made of metal; you have provoked me to anger and thrust me behind your back. Because of this, I am going to bring disaster on the house of Jereboam. I will cut off from Jereboam every last male in Israel - slave or free. I will burn up the house of

Jereboam as one burns dung until it is all gone. Dogs will eat those belonging to Jereboam who die in the city, and the birds of the air will feed on those who die in the country. The LORD has spoken" (1 Kings 14:9-11). Also:

" . . Jereboam enticed Israel away from following the LORD and caused them to commit a great sin. The Israelites persisted in all the sins of Jereboam and did not turn away from them until the LORD removed them from his presence" (2 Kings 17:21, 22).

Only one of Jereboam's sons was buried in peace (1 Kings 14:17, 18), the rest died violent deaths. His evil example was followed by so many fathers and sons who became kings of Israel that Jereboam's evil continued both by example and heredity until Israel went into captivity.

(3) King David's problem with lust influenced Solomon and Amnon.

Lust and murder were the only two blots on the life of an otherwise exemplary king. David's relationship with Bathsheba commenced on a wrong foundation of lust, adultery, murder, cover up, and the death of the child conceived out of wedlock. The first child of their marriage was Solomon, who, in due course showed the lust of his parents on a grandiose scale. David had eight wives, but Solomon had seven hundred wives and maintained three hundred 'stand-byes'. Together they stole his heart from the LORD his God, and led him into idolatry (1 Kings 11:1-13).

Amnon, David's firstborn son, also had such insatiable lust that he deceived and cruelly raped his sister Tamar heaping insult and disgrace upon her by having her thrown out (2 Samuel 13:1-24).

8. Other scriptures which confirm the hereditary nature and judgment of parental sin.
(1)   Leviticus 26:39
"Those of you who are left will waste away in the lands of their enemies because of their sins; also because of their fathers' sins they will waste away."
(2)   Numbers 14:33
"Your children will be shepherds here for forty years, suffering for your unfaithfulness, until the last of your bodies lies in the desert."
(3)   Job 21:19-21
"(It is said) 'God stores up a man's punishment for his sons.' Let him repay the man himself, so that he will know it! Let his own eyes see his destruction; let him drink of the wrath of the Almighty. For what does he care about the family he leaves behind when his allotted months come to an end?"
(4)   Psalm 51:5
"Surely I have been a sinner since birth, sinful from the time my mother conceived me."
(5)   Psalm 58:3-5
"Even from birth the wicked go astray: from the womb they are wayward and speak lies. Their venom is like the venom of a snake, like that of a cobra that has stopped its ears, that will not heed the tune of the charmer, however skilful the enchanter may be."

(6) Isaiah 14:20b, 21
" ... The offspring of the wicked will never be mentioned again. Prepare a place to slaughter his sons for the sins of their forefathers: they are not to rise to inherit the land and cover the earth with their cities."

(7) Jeremiah 32:18
"You show love to thousands but bring the punishment for the father's sins into the laps of their children after them."

(8) Lamentations 5:7
"Our fathers sinned and are no more, and we bear their punishment."

(9) Ephesians 2:1-3
"As for you, you were dead in your transgressions and sins, in which you used to live when you followed the ways of this world and of the ruler of the kingdom of the air, the spirit who is now at work in those who are disobedient. All of us also lived among them at one time gratifying the cravings of our sinful nature (flesh) and following its desires and thoughts. Like the rest, we were by nature objects of wrath."

(10) Romans 5:12, 13
"Therefore, just as sin entered the world through one man and death through sin, and in this way death came to all men, because all sinned - for before the law was given, sin was in the world."

(11) Matthew 27:25
"All the people answered 'Let his blood be on us and on our children' ".

9. Hereditary blessings also stem from faithful parents who honour God.

(1) Phinehas the priest blessed his descendants by his righteousness.

As Balaam left Balak after God had prevented him from cursing the Israelites he gave him some private advice. He suggested that the Moabitish women should tempt the Israelites with idolatry and promiscuity. (Promiscuity was the hereditary sin of the Moabites who were descendants of Lot through incest with his daughter while drunk (Genesis 19:30-38). Balaam left Balak suitably rewarded for his good advice (Numbers 24:25; Jude 11; Revelation 2:14).

Shortly after this, a prominent Israelite openly took a Moabitish woman into his tent, obviously with lustful intentions, even while the rest of the congregation were weeping and confessing their sins. Phinehas the priest was so incensed, he followed them and speared them both with one spear. The Lord then said to Moses, "Phinehas son of Eleazar, the son of Aaron, the priest, has turned my anger away from the Israelites; for he was as zealous as I am for my honour among them, so that in my zeal I did not put an end to them. Therefore tell him I am making my covenant of peace with him. He and his descendants will have a covenant of a lasting priesthood, because he was zealous for the honour of his God and made atonement for the Israelites" (Numbers 25:10-13).

(2) Jehonadab and his descendants.

Jehonadab was a contemporary of Jehu. Together they were responsible for slaughtering many prophets of Baal (2 Kings 10:18-27). After stamping out all forms of Baal worship Jehu became king, but continued the sinful pattern of Jereboam throughout his twenty-eight year reign (verses 28-32).

Jehonadab on the other hand followed the Lord with all his heart. He commanded his family to refrain from all alcohol and possession of worldly goods. Hundreds of years later God instructed Jeremiah to invite the descendant of 'Jonadab, son of Recab' to a wine party in the temple. They went, but refused to touch a drop of the alcoholic beverage. They gave Jeremiah the following reason for abstaining:-

"We do not drink wine, because our forefather Jonadab son of Recab gave us this command: 'Neither you nor your descendants must ever drink wine. Also you must never build houses, sow seed or plant vineyards; you must never have any of these things, but must always live in tents . . .' We have obeyed everything our forefather Jonadab son of Recab commanded us" (Jeremiah 35:6-8).

God used the two hundred and fifty year faithfulness of this family to accuse Judah of their fickleness concerning himself, then rewarded the Recabites in these words:

"You have obeyed the command of your forefather Jonadab and have followed all his instructions and have done everything he ordered. Therefore, this is what the LORD Almighty, the God of Israel says: 'Jonadab son of Recab will never fail to have a man to serve me' " (Jeremiah 35:18, 19).

10. The supporting evidence of sociological studies.

Around the beginning of the twentieth century, a Mr. E. E. Winship published studies of two well known American families of the nineteenth century. His findings have been featured in many publications since that date and are well worth passing on (source unknown).

"Max Jukes was an atheist who married a godless woman. Some five hundred and sixty descendants were traced. Of these:-

310 died as paupers.

150 became criminals, 7 of them murderers.

100 were known to be drunkards.

More than half the women were prostitutes.

In all, the descendants cost the U.S. government one and a quarter million 19th century dollars.

"Jonathan Edwards was a contemporary of Max Jukes. He was a committed Christian who married a godly young lady. Some 1394 descendants were traced. Of these:-

295 graduated from college, from whom 13 became college presidents, and 65 became professors.

3 were elected as United States senators, 3 as State governors, and others sent as ministers to foreign countries.

30 were judges.

100 were lawyers, one the dean of an outstanding law school.

56 practised as physicians, one was dean of a medical school.

75 became officers in the army and navy.

100 were well known missionaries, preachers, and prominent authors.

Another 80 held some form of public office, of whom 3 were mayors of large cities.

One was the comptroller of the U.S. Treasury, another a vice-president of the United States.

Not one of the descendants of the Edwards family was a liability to the government."

11. PRACTICAL PRESENT-DAY EVIDENCE OF GOD'S PRINCIPLES IN OPERATION.

A personal testimony.

My own experience illustrates the effects of converging hereditary influences and their inner struggles for control of my personality.

My paternal family line comes from Northern Irish stock. All my ancestors appeared to have been fine Christians stretching back to the 1859 Irish revival. Both my grandfather and father were open air preachers. God called and anointed me for the same ministry. But there were inner struggles against my separation to holy living. A few years ago I started looking for answers, and learned that my maternal grandfather, despite marrying a Christian, was a very irreligious man until he was saved late in life. He was also lustful, an owner of racehorses, a gambler, an inveterate smoker, and worst of all, he and a number of my uncles were Freemasons.

My Christian heritage was certainly deep and strong. But so were the struggles (won in the Spirit) against the temptations to give way to lust, gambling, the desire to smoke, and a fascination with occultic matters stemming from Freemasonry. The understanding God gave me led me to believe for, and receive, complete freedom from the spiritual influence of each one of those hereditary curses.

Paul rejoiced that his spiritual apprentice, Timothy, was living in the hereditary blessing and faith example of a grandmother, and mother (2 Timothy 1:5). But because his father was an unbelieving Greek, Paul had young Timothy circumcised, probably in deference to circumcision legalists. Whatever the motivation it was an act of submission to God's holy requirements. Unlike Timothy, both my parents and my paternal ancestors were Christians, but there were still hereditary influences for which I needed spiritual deliverance. This is really not unlike the rite of circumcision which sanctified God's people of old.

From personal and counselling experience, I am convinced that practising Freemasons and hereditary spirits of Freemasonry are one of the major hindrances to life and vitality in the professing church today. In fact, the spiritual influence of this blasphemous, idolatrous, and demonic religious system is so serious to the persons, families and churches of those involved, that the next chapter has been set aside to examine it and the curses emanating from it.

(1) **Some hereditary bondages and dominations cause suffering because parents, grandparents, and ancestors have broken God's laws.**

(a) **Occultism and witchcraft practices.**

Some Christians who seek help have had no personal involvement in, but may experience manifestations of psychic sensitivity, de javu, premonitions, occultic visions, or become embarrassed by being able to read people's minds. Some are troubled with blasphemous or mocking thoughts, or find they have a gripping fear of Satan. Demonic influence over these people may be as strong, or even stronger than if they had personally chosen to be involved. Satan believes he has a right to maintain an hereditary grip on Christians.

Familiar (family) spirits, curses placed on families, ghosts (benign demonic manifestations), and even poltergeist (spirit-caused physical disturbances) may also be experienced by descendants of practitioners of the black arts.

A 22 year-old Samoan Christian was filled with aggressive thoughts of murder towards her parents who had rejected her because she had been cursed by her grandmother, a witch doctor. When she was released from that aggressive familiar spirit, she was filled with forgiveness and love for her parents.

The born-again daughter and grandson of an unconverted woman deeply involved in occultism experienced many problems with spirits of psychic control and psychic sensitivity. The Lord freed them both, but the boy needed ministry from time to time to maintain freedom from the psychic control of the grandmother.

(b) **Addictions of all kinds.**

Hereditary addictions control the total personalities of succeeding generations. There are seven major addicitions:-

(i) **Drugs.** Addicts find it easy to become 'hooked' on prescription drugs, even headache pills and powders.

(ii) **Alcohol.**

(iii) **Nicotine.**

(iv) **Gambling.**

(v) **Food** including the inability to resist sweet things, especially chocolate.

(vi) **Compulsive physical exercise.** This is a driving spirit to exercise even late at night when physically tired. The euphoria produced by the brain's production of endorphine switches off the pain registering mechanism, and often masks the physical damage being caused by over-exercise.

(vii) **A spendthrift spirit** which causes an irresistable urge to spend money. From experience it has been found that the basic hereditary spirit must be dealt with. If not, when one addiction is 'cured' another will take its place. For example an addiction to food will often follow release from alcohol or nicotine.

The people whom the Lord has released are too many to mention, but the following are examples:-

● A young lady who had never smoked, found her mouth filled with the taste of nicotine when being set free from a hereditary spirit of nicotine.

● A married woman whom the Lord freed from six hereditary addictions told us, "I just had to spend money. I felt as if a demon was driving me. Now that I am free I am so looking forward to visiting the shops without having to spend a cent."

● A chain smoking mother died of lung cancer. Her daughter did everything in her power to break the addiction. She tried hypnotism and tablets, and went through the Seventh Day Adventist de-toxification programme three times without success. Finally she was delivered, but became such a compulsive and obsessive eater that she was ashamed. Again the Lord freed her, and she had the discipline of the Spirit to live comfortably, free from all hereditary addiction.

(c) **Anxiety, worry, depression, schizophrenia, suicide, and other mental problems.**

A large percentage of those who seek deliverance suffer from conditions such as these, and very few of them do not speak of relatives of past generations having suffered similarly. Apart from certain medically certified causes, and identifiable stress circumstances, most people suffer the hereditary afflictions imposed by Satan for the sinful activities of preceding family members.

A middle-aged manic-depressive who had received shock therapy on a number of occasions and who had been under psychiatric treatment and medication for more than twenty years asked for spiritual help. The roots of his problems were easily traced to hereditary causes. He showed immediate improvement and his psychiatrist considerably reduced his treatment.

Schizophrenia and suicidal tendancies are frequent problems encountered in a deliverance ministry. In nearly all cases, the conditions may be traced back to hereditary sources. By treating them as dominating spirits which have no right to maintain control over Christians despite having been in the family for several generations, the Lord has given many lasting victories.

A young man told me his Christain life was empty and meaningless. His father had committed suicide eighteen months before he came for counsel, and his sister, a medical doctor, had done the same six months previously. He was depressed, and obviously heading toward the same end. But the Lord had other plans for his life. After deliverance from spirits of rejection and suicide, he began to live the Christian life on a level he had never imagined was possible.

A young married man had great problems with his true identity. He had been put down badly by his father who was schizophrenic. When delivered from the hereditary schizophrenic spirit (and rejection), his business and family life improved considerably. He no longer felt divided.

(d) Hereditary sexual problems.

Lust is an extremely powerful hereditary spirit. Some of the children whom the Lord has freed could only have had such desires and habits through hereditary lust:

(i) Some commenced sexual self-stimulation from the age of two years.

(ii) Others developed obsessive interest in their own sexuality and the opposite sex, well before school age.

(iii) Girls have exposed themselves to boys, and boys have interfered with girls by the beginning of school years.

(iv) Boys have shown an insatiable desire for pornography many years before puberty.

Teenage girls and young ladies who have never yielded to their inner drives have confessed to the most depraved sexual thoughts and desires. Mothers who have had babies before marriage and never told their children have found that their daughters unknowingly followed their example, bringing them much guilt and shame.

Time and time again people have received deliverance from sexual spirits which have been in their families for generations. These include:-

Incest by fathers, brothers, grandparents, and other relatives. They have been personally devastated, and subsequent married relationships have often been ruined. An American social worker, and a Scandinavian doctor have both informed us that eighty per cent of prostitutes in their countries had had incestuous relationships forced on them by a parent.

Homosexual and lesbian lifestyles are sometimes introduced by parents or close relatives. Where this is not so, and the lifestyle commences at an early age, hereditary spirits are normally the cause.

Frigidity. This is very much a family affliction passed down from mothers through their daughters to grandchildren. It not only breaks God's laws for marriage but often becomes a vindictive weapon which sometimes ruins marriage. Experience has shown that deliverance and re-education is most effective.

Promiscuity. Sexual philandering by either sex certainly may provide a pattern by example, but normally it is secretive. When children commence that pattern in their teenage years without encouragement, the driving force has found to be hereditary lust. Quite frequently women counsellees will say: "All of my aunties had a baby before they got married, and all my uncles had 'shotgun' marriages".

One twenty-two year-old woman had been continually subject to forced sex by her father between the ages of six and twelve. Although raped at fifteen years of age, she had never willingly had sex with a man, but she experienced deep rejection, was very angry, and verbally aggressive. The Lord freed her, and gave her self-worth.

(e) False and deceptive religious spirits.

When parents or grandparents have been actively involved in atheism, false cults, eastern religions, doctrinal heresies, or religious bigotry, succeeding generations are normally affected. They may manifest varying degrees of strong unbelief, antagonism, mockery, spiritual confusion, doctrinal argumentativeness, error, or may falsely claim to be born again.

A young lady with a Christian Science family history had to be delivered from spirits of sacrilege, deception, unreality (because of the denial of pain), unbelief, and a bondage on her emotions as her life was ruled by mental choices. Then and only then did her life in Christ become meaningful.

Another young lady whose mother had been a Christadelphian for twenty-five years struggled with rejection (as a female), and spirits of unbelief, guilt, and heaviness until freed in the name of Jesus Christ.

(f) Sicknesses and allergies.

Satan has no pity on those who submit to him. Judas Iscariot served him well, then committed suicide. Children and grandchildren of people involved in occultism, Freemasonry, and flagrant anti-God and anti-social behaviour often show family histories of heart problems, stress-related sicknesses, asthma, and strong allergies. Recurrent and predictable patterns of blindness, death, and brain damage have also been traced to curses placed on the families of some who have come for help.

(g) Other problems from hereditary causes.

(i) Some counsellees have asked for freedom from excessive anger, temper, and violence. In every case, a parent (usually the father) has been found to have had the same problem, and the person seeking help usually the victim. Child-bashing is often hereditary.

(ii) Passive men usually marry dominating women. Their sons are normally passive, and their daughters manipulative. In marriage, the children unconsciously choose partners of similar temperament to their parents and continue the cycle. In Christian marriage this reverse of God's order often causes relationship difficulties. It is the 'Eve syndrome', a clever manipulation of the serpent (Genesis 3:1-6).

(iii) Pride of heritage, intellectual arrogance, haughtiness and class snobbery are all alike detestable to God. They may be learned of course in the family home, but pride is also a hereditary sin. As such it is a curse, and a great hindrance to usefulness with God.

The writers recognize that there will be some psychologists, social workers, medical specialists and theologians who may offer alternative explanations for such experiences. But in fact, the majority of the people who seek assistance from us have already unsuccessfully sought help from many or all of these counsellors and have reached such a point of desperation that they are willing to accept the reality of spiritual forces operating in heredity. Without any form of publicity other than the testimony of those whom the Lord has freed, we find we are unable to keep up with the growing list of people who request a deliverance ministry for themselves, their relatives, or their children.

CHAPTER SUMMARY

1. The fact of hereditary characteristics has been well established by medical and social research.
2. The Bible records and illustrates the principle of the passing down from one generation to another of original and ancestral sin, and its punishment. The Law given to Moses only confirmed what began in the Garden of Eden.
3. Sociological studies confirm the word of God (not that it needs authentification by man).
4. Present day deliverance from evil spirits is simply the continuation of the ministry of Jesus Christ carried out by those who follow him (John 20:21; Mark 16:17). Deliverance frees from hereditary bondages and dominations.

". . They have set up their detestable idols in the house that bears my Name and have defiled it" (Jeremiah 7:30).

CHAPTER 10.

Freemasons curse themselves, their families and the churches

To readers who are practising Freemasons, this chapter heading may be highly offensive. To unsuspecting relatives, and those who may benefit from the social and welfare services of the Masonic Lodge, it may cause shock and alarm.

The stark truth of this statement will unfold as we look at the mass of evidence available from Masonic literature and its spiritual casualties.

Freemasons are members of The Free And Ancient Order of Masons, a continuation of the English stonemasons' guild of the Middle Ages. It is thought that the first lodge was established in Scotland in 1600. The first United Grand Lodge was formed at the Goose and Gridiron Tavern in London, England, in 1717. After becoming firmly established in the United Kingdom, the Lodge spread to each of the colonies established by Great Britain, and the United States of America which is now believed to have three and a half million members, a great many of whom are professing Christians. In fact, most non-communist countries now have temples, orders, hospitals, and social institutions prominently displaying the sign of the square and the compasses.

Although the Masonic Lodge, as it is popularly known, is regarded as a secret society, its beliefs and practices have been well documented by its own members, and well researched by others.

It appears that originally the Lodge was a Christian foundation with old charges permeated by Roman Catholicism, and allusions to Noah's Ark, rather than to Solomon's Temple.

Stephen Knight in his explosive exposé of the secret world of the Freemasons, "The Brotherhood" (Granada), refers to a de-christianisation process accomplished by the Constitutions of Dr. James Anderson sponsored by the 3rd Grand Master, the Rev. Dr. Theophilus Desaguliers in 1723-38. The name of Jesus was then omitted from prayers, and a supposedly long-lost name of God was introduced. Blood-curdling oaths to maintain secrecy became part of degree initiation rites, and over a period of time, the rituals crystalized around Solomon's Temple and the myth of the supposed murder of one Hiram Abiff, the chief architect.

Freemasonry claims to be a religion. Probably the most respected exponent of its principles and practices is Dr. Albert G. Mackay, a former High Priest of the General Grand chapter of the USA. The following quotations are from his "Encyclopedia of Freemasonry".

"Masonry is an eminently religious institution and on this ground should the religious Mason defend it . . . The religion of Freemasonry is not Christianity." (Page 618)

"If Freemasonry were simply a Christian institution, the Jew and Moslem, the Brahman and the Buddhist could not conscientiously partake of its illumination: but its universality is its boast. In its language citizens of every nation may converse; at its altars men of all religions may kneel; to its creed, disciples of every faith may subscribe." (Page 439)

The central religious deity who claims the worship of Jew and Gentile, Hindu, Buddhist and Christian alike, is carefully veiled with ambiguity. Members of all religious persuasions are encouraged to believe that their particular deity is indeed the one known by the initials T.G.A.O.T.U. The members of the first three orders to which the highest percentage of members belongs, 'The Entered Apprentice', 'The Fellow Craft', and 'The Mastor Mason', are told that the letters stand for 'The Grand Architect of the Universe'. It is also known as 'The Grand Geometrician', and 'Universal Ruler'. Christians who believe that this 'deity' is Jesus Christ are being deceived into committing idolatry.

Unless a Master Mason is invited to take higher degrees, and reaches the thirteenth degree of 'The Royal Arch (of Enoch)', he may never learn the real name of the Masonic deity. England is a possible exception to this rule as the special revelation is sometimes made on completing the third degree. In practical terms this means that perhaps two thirds of the membership are deliberately kept from knowing the truth, and compromise themselves as worshippers of T.G.A.O.T.U., a deity neither Jewish, Hindu, Buddhist, nor Christian.

The Encyclopedia Britannica Volume 12, page 99, states that in 1780 Masonic Lodges established relationships with 'The Illuminati'. This organisation was founded by Adam Weishaupt in 1776, after he had visited Egypt and imbibed Egyptian mysticism. The Illuminati's 'all seeing eye of spiritual light', features also in Freemasonry, and at the apex of the pyramid on all one dollar notes in the currency of the United States of America. With that mystic basis, the order also claims to draw 'consecration' from the faith of Abraham, prayers of King David, and the sacrifices of King Solomon. Members are promised after death, acceptance in 'The Grand Lodge in the sky'.

The identity of the Masonic deity.

Phase One.

J. Edward Decker Jnr. in his booklet 'The Question of Freemasonry' quotes from Freemason literature: "Man is a god in the making, and as in the mystic myths of Egypt, on the potter's wheel he is being moulded. When his light shines out to lift and preserve all things, he receives the triple crown of godhead and joins the Master Masons who, in their robes of Blue and Gold, are seeking to dispel the darkness of night with the triple light of the Masonic Lodge".

This so called great knowledge and wisdom comes from understanding the secret name of the Deity of Masonry. This is JAHBULON, also known as JAOBULON. Just as the Hebrews knew the sacred name of Jehovah as JHVH, so the Masons use the letters J.B.O. rather than speak their 'sacred' name.

JAHBULON, is a humanistic syncretism of:-

JAH, a Hebrew and Chaldee shortened name for Jehovah which features in the word 'Hallelujah'. "His name is Jah" (KJV Psalm 68:4).

BUL, a Syriac word meaning 'Lord', or 'powerful'. Commentators agree that this word is an abbreviation of BAAL, just as Jeremiah uses BEL (Jeremiah 50:2). Baal was a Babylonian, Syrian, and Canaanite idol-representation of Satan, and was a curse to the Hebrews in the land of promise.

ON, which is generally taken to be an abbreviation for the ancient Egyptian god, Osiris, god of the underworld.

The composition of the name Jahbulon exposes the blasphemous, idolatrous, and demonic nature of the real deity masquerading behind the deceptively bland titles and descriptions of the Bible's Jehovah. This is not usually learned until advanced degrees are reached. For example, during chapter sessions of the Royal Arch degree (13th), an altar cloth is used on which syllables of the names of Jehovah and the Freemason idolatrous deity are made up from cut out letters. (see illustration). When the chapter closes, the letters are again mixed up.

Word Manipulation

The Grand Masonic Lodge of South Australia has published a leaflet in an attempt to refute anti-Freemasonry statements. Its arguments are far from convincing. For example, most Bibles introduce God and creation in ten unambiguous words: "In the beginning God created the heavens and the earth" (Genesis 1:1). To say the same thing, the Freemasons ramble on with paragraphs of obscurantist wording in order to atract people of all faiths:

● **"The Great Architect of the Universe** - acknowledging that he is the designer and planner of the universe."

● **"The Grand Geometrician of the Universe** - implying that, as the Laws of Geometry govern the erection of buildings, so God's Laws of Nature govern the Universe".

Impressive words, but hardly honouring to the personality and holiness of God who made us in his own likeness. But worse is to come:-

● **"The Great Observer** - stating that His all seeing eye oversees all that happens in His world".

We are invited to believe that it is God's 'all-seeing eye' which watches all financial transactions involving the American dollar bill, peers from certain documents of the Masonic and Oddfellows Lodges, and woodenly stares from carvings on certain antique furniture! A modern song sums it up well - "God is watching . . . from a distance". Then there is this:-

● **"The Most High - affirming that His is above all else"**, and **"The True and Living God Most High"** - declaring that for the Freemason God is not an idol made with human hands but is a living God above all else who has said "Thou shalt have no other gods before Me" ".

Of course idols are not limited to those who are hand-made. Jahbulon (JBO) is a conceptual and syncretistic creation of human minds, and cannot be identified with the Bible Jehovah, as Freemasons do not acknowledge any Holy Spirit or Jesus Christ. In fact, the name of Jesus is despised, and never mentioned by loyal Freemasons. A past member who had renounced his vows and left the lodge asking that his name be struck from the register, came for prayer. He told us that he had frequently heard lodge members say blasphemously, "We don't bother about the boy, we go straight to the Father". Others have said that they have never heard the name of Jesus used in any prayer. As no one can approach God the Father except through Jesus Christ (John 14:6), the only other "father" open to direct approach is of course, the devil (John 8:44). The term "Fatherhood of God" is used in a non-personal generic sense, meaning that all humans are his children. But we believers know that God's family is entered only by being born from above (John 1:12).

The sacred writings of a Freemason's faith

Although the Bible is held to be a 'sacred writing' (even to special editions of Masonic Bibles), only a few carefully selected passages are used which support Masonic mythological beliefs, and do not offend members of non-Christian faiths. Their religiously orientated ceremonies include Bible references (particularly in relation to the building of Solomon's Temple), legend, spiritual mumbo jumbo, and outright occultic practices. The publicity leaflet continues:-

● "The Freemason considers the sacred writings **of his faith** the uneering standards of truth and justice, and regulates his life and actions by **its precepts. Those** sacred writings teach him the important duties he owes to God, to his neighbour and to himself".

This leaves each Freemason open to revere the 'sacred' writings of his own religious persuasion. To the professing 'Christian' this means the Bible. To the orthodox Jew, the Torah and Talmud. To the Hindu, the Bhagavad Gita (part of the Mahabharata). To the Muslim the Koran, and to the Latter Day Saints, the Book of Mormon. Freemasonry offends no one's religious conscience.

Edmond Ronayne, a Past Master of a Chicago Lodge, writes these devastating words in his book, "Master's Carpet":-

"All my experience in and out of Masonic Lodges has gone to establish the fact in my mind that Freemasonry, in all its departments, is the most corrupt and wicked, and contains the greatest amount of falsehood of any other institution on the face of the globe. It is positively and absolutely selfish in every single element of its pagan composition, and can truthfully lay no more claim to charity, benelovence or goodness of any other name or description than could say, the heathen organisations which Christian civilisation has long since banished from the world".

With all this in mind it is easy to agree with the statement of a Freemason Anglican vicar who wrote "Light Invisible, A Freemason's Answer to 'Darkness Visible' " (Britons Publishing Co. 1952), under the pseudonym "Vindex". "I for one can never understand how anyone who takes an exclusive view of Christ as the only complete revelation of God's truth can become a Freemason without suffering from spiritual schizophrenia".

Professing Christians who claim to be loyal Freemasons are in as much danger of God's jugment as Lot who lived in the city of Sodom without taking part in the evil of homosexuality. Sodom, and five other cities, Lot's home, and his wife were all destroyed. Lot and his two daughters were saved only because the angels almost dragged them out of the city to safety (Genesis

19:16). The warnings to those who associate with evil in both Old and New Testaments are obvious and ominous:

1. **Deuteronomy 11:26-28.**
   "See I am setting before you today a blessing and a curse - the blessing if you obey the commands of the LORD your God that I am giving you today; the curse if you disobey the commands of the Lord your God and turn from the way that I command you today by following other gods, which you have not known."

2. **2 Kings 17:15.**
   ". . They followed worthless idols, and themselves became worthless . . "

3. **2 Corinthians 6:14-17.**
   "Do not be yoked together with unbelievers. For what do righteousness and wickedness have in common? Or what fellowship can light have with darkness? What harmony is there between Christ and Belial? What does a believer have in common with an unbeliever? What agreement is there between the temple of God and idols? . . . Therefore come out from them and be separate says the Lord. Touch no unclean thing and I will receive you."

4. **1 John 5:21.**
   "Dear children keep yourselves from idols" ('false gods' Amplified Bible, New English Bible).

Probably because of its alleged Biblical associations, Freemasonry has attracted a considerable following from both clergy and church members. Some evangelical ministers have suffered much discouragement and even opposition from office bearers and members who have been active lodge members. One such minister in Victoria, Australia, preached against the lodge, and promptly lost half the male members of his congregation. He, his family, and church, were then 'sent to Coventry' by the Masonic shopkeepers who were in a majority in the community.

The Masonic net is spread far and wide. There are 'The Shriners', 'The Elks', and 'Demolay' for fathers and sons. For the ladies there is the 'Order of the Easter Star' which has as a badge, the horned star of Satan. For the young ladies there are 'Daughters of Job', and 'Daughters of the Nile'. Even the girls are catered for with 'Rainbow Girls'. Both men and women are able to join 'Amaranth', and 'The White Star'. From contacts with people who have been involved in The Manchester Unity Independent Order of Oddfellows, it has obviously a very strong link with the Masonic Lodge. One lady attending a seminar on deliverance said that as a child she sat on a goat to take vows. The Oddfellows also use the apron and a five pointed star which feature in the Masonic Lodge.

A personal testimony.

In the previous chapter I mentioned tracing my maternal lineage to a Freemason grandparent. Two further experiences convinced me that hereditary dominating spirits of Freemasonry were indeed operating in my life.

Firstly, I noticed that when ministering deliverance to Freemasons, I often felt generally confused in my thinking. Also, my forehead felt as if it were being compressed by steel bands. The feelings wore off, but returned the next time Freemasons or their family members came for deliverance.

The second experience occurred when Phyl and I took our house guest who was an overseas medical specialist to a F.G.B.M.I. dinner in a Sydney suburb. I was asked to give thanks for the meal, did so, and resumed my seat.

As the first course was served, I lost consciousness until the end of the meal. Phyl told me afterwards that I ate normally, but appeared agitated, and constantly asked where we were, and why we were there. When told we had brought the guest speaker, I denied ever having seen him before, and expressed great surprise that he was staying with us. Phyl tells me she went up and spoke to the speaker who returned with her and checked my vital signs for any evidence of the recurrence of heart problems, but found none. At the end of the meal he came and prayed for me. As he did so, my consciousness returned, but my mind felt as if it were locked in a black box about 30 centimetres square. The Lord quickly restored all my mental functions, except the memory of what happened during the meal. The following morning I felt that my mind was not functioning with its normal clarity. It seemed to be wrapped in cotton wool. The Lord revealed to Phyl that she should pray over me for mental shock, and when she prayed I was immediately released from every dominating hereditary spirit of Freemasonry and their influence in my life.

There is an unfortunate postscript to this incident. Several years later Phyl herself experienced confusion and tight bands when speaking to people with hereditary Freemasonry spirits. She sought the Lord for an answer and he showed her that my Freemasonry heritage had also affected her through our marriage partnership. I felt convicted, as I regularly teach this principle to others, but I had failed to ask the Lord to free the one closest to me by marriage and ministry. When I did so, she was freed, and both of us have remained free. Since then we have prayed over our daughters, our sons-in-law, and grandchildren, and released them from the curse which continues to the third and fourth generation (Exodus 20:5).

Other testimonies.

● A young man who claimed he was a Christian became very arrogant during a time of counselling, claiming he had never sinned. His father, paternal grandfather, maternal grandfather and great-grandfather, had all been staunch Freemasons. The Masonic spirits were cast out, and the young man was sent away to seek God about his true spiritual condition. Twelve hours later, he returned, broken and repentant. In a flood of tears he was born again, and showed an immediate change of lifestyle.

● A Freemason, whose family was involved in the commencement of the lodge in England, was in severe financial difficulty without fully realising the extent of it. His consultancy had dropped almost to zero, yet he firmly believed it was flourishing. Some 40 or 50 times in all, he would select a client's file and place it on his desk ready for an interview in the afternoon or the next morning. He would then go out for lunch, or go home for the night. Every time he returned, the file would have disappeared and could not be found. Eventually it would turn up unexpectedly in the filing system totally out of sequence. Extreme lethargy also overcame him. After deliverance, he recalled that two deceased family members in other parts of the world had suffered financial disaster. This man had even used trust funds for personal needs as he was so confident that he was going to win a lottery. The devil actually gave him two sets of numbers each week, and supreme confidence that he would win. He got an occasional minor prize but never won anything of substance. Praise God he was set free, together with his wife and children. It should be noted that wives, de facto wives, and even casual sexual partners of masons become affected by demonic powers through sexual relationships.

● A six week-old baby born with brain damage was found to have a heritage of Freemasonry. She was prayed over as she slept. There was only the slightest movement until spirits of infirmities and sicknesses were bound, broken and released. The baby then opened her eyes and began to thrash around with all her limbs, restlessly moving her head from side to side. Since then, God has been doing a steady work of healing.

● During a deliverance seminar, a participant submitted a question which surely provokes some thought. It was, "Freemasonry - could the following be its effects?"

> "My father was a Freemason - also a Christian. I'm not sure that he's ever renounced it, but don't think he goes to any meetings now.
>
> My brother, a missionary, was martyred in 1962 (aged 26).
>
> My sister died of cancer aged 18 in 1964.
>
> My niece, aged 20 - killed in a motor accident 1980.
>
> My mother had a stroke in 1975.
>
> My brother had a stroke in 1985 (aged 46)."

● At a church camp, five men who had been Freemasons, repented and renounced membership with the lodge. They were released, and God immediately began to bring some beautiful reconciliations between some of them and their teenage children.

From acquaintance with a large number of Christians who have been released from the dominant spirits of Freemasonry over recent years, a clear pattern of demonic activity has emerged. The results have been the same, whether the counsellee has been a lodge member, or is the descendant of a member. The following demonic powers need to be dealt with after personal or family Freemason vows and curses have been specifically renounced (in addition to the general renunciation of all Satan's bondages and dominations):

(a) The spirit of Freemasonry and the curse of the Luciferan doctrine.

(b) A spirit, or spirits of Anti-Christ.

(c) A spirit of idolatry.

(d) Spirits of witchcraft and occultism (In severe cases, a spirit of poltergeist may be troublesome).

(e) Spirits of mockery.

(f) The 'all seeing third eye' in the forehead (an Illuminati symbol) may manifest if there has been heavy family involvement.

(g) A spirit of mental confusion.

(h) A spirit of spiritual apathy.

(i) A spirit of emotional hardness.

(j) Spirits of doubt, skepticism, and unbelief.

(k) Spirits of infirmities, sicknesses, and allergies (a most frequent manifestation). Where family membership has been handed down for a long time, and there has been special dedication to the lodge, spirits may cause special destruction in health or financial matters.

(l) A spirit of false religion.

Believers who have broken with Freemasonry and renounced their vows, should write to the lodge asking that their names be deleted from the membership roll. It is also important that all personal regalia (or those handed down in the family) should be destroyed. Associated clothing should be burnt, and metal objects including swords defaced, or smashed and disposed of. Relatives are sometimes superstitious about disposing of these family relics, but they are cursed, and if retained will bring the judgment of God upon the household (Deuteronomy 7:25, 26).

• A pastor friend had a new convert renounce his lodge vows, and advised him to gather his regalia so that he could smash, or burn the items. But he could not find a hammer or a box of matches anywhere in his home or workshop. As a carpenter he had a plentiful supply of hammers and matches. So he used other destructive means, and just as he finished, the telephone rang. It was an urgent call from the local hospital concerning a blood test for his wife who had a serious blood disorder suspected of being terminal. It appeared that for some inexplicable reason a recent blood sample had been destroyed, and another sample was urgently needed. The man took his wife to the hospital immediately, and her blood was urgently analysed. For the first time in two years, the laboratory report showed that the sample was perfectly normal.

CHAPTER SUMMARY.

1. Freemasonry rightly claims to be a religion. Lodges are regarded as 'holy ground', and are supposed to face due East. Its quest is for knowledge of union with God, its standards of worship and prayers are to a divine person, and its members are prepared for the 'Grand Lodge in the sky'. The largest percentage of its membership have been deceived concerning its central deity which is anti-God, and anti-Christ.

2. The central deity of Freemasonry is an object of Satanic syncretism in which the Jehovah of the Bible is blasphemously linked with mythological demonic deities. Worship is therefore idolatrous, and brings Freemasons directly under the curse of God.

3. Holders of the highest degrees in Freemasonry are committed to the belief that Lucifer alone is God. They exalt the one whom God has thrown out of his presence, and for whom the lake of fire has been prepared as eternal punishment.

4. Freemasons who profess to be Christian cause the curse of God to fall also upon their families and their churches because of their gross and blasphemous idolatry.

5. Demonic bondages and dominations in families of Lodge members emphasises the great need for the visible church to be cleansed from all Freemason associations, and all family members delivered from demonic oppression.

Readers requiring further information on this subject will find the following materials helpful:-

(1) 'The Brotherhood" by Stephen Knight. Mr. Knight is a journalist who describes himself as "a neutral investigator holding no brief for Christianity, and no automatic aversion to devil worship" (page 230). His expose is thorough, and his book deals with his claims of Masonic Lodge influence within the Vatican, Scotland Yard, the British police force, and its connection with the K.G.B. He concludes (page 235) " . . . the assurance given to candidates that the name Great Architect of the Universe can be applied to whatever Supreme Being they choose is worse than misleading: it is a blatant lie . . . It is no overstatement to say that most Freemasons, even those without strong religious convictions, would never have joined the Brotherhood if they had not been victims of this subtle trick".

(2) 'The Christian and Freemasonry' by F. G. Hanson and K. N. Shelley (Jordan Books Ltd., 24 Chick Street, Punchbowl, N.S.W., 2196, Australia, published June, 1965). Mr. Hanson, an ex-Freemason, and Mr. Shelley discuss Masonic experiences and claims in the light of Scriptures.

(3) 'The Question of Freemasonry', a booklet by J. Edward Decker Jnr., Free the Masons Ministry, P.O. Box 1077, Issaquah, WA. 98027, United States of America. Mr. Decker appeals to 'Christian' Freemasons, quoting extensively from their own literature and subjecting it to the searching light of God's Word.

(4) 'Should a Christian be a Mason?' by E. M. Storms, with a foreword by Rev. James D. Shaw, a former thirty-third degree Mason (New Puritan Library). This is an excellent scripture-packed examination and denunciation of the craft.

"Although my father and my mother have forsaken me, yet the Lord will take me up [adopt me as His child] " (Psalm 27:10 The Amplified Bible).

CHAPTER 11.

Rejection, the masterpiece of Satanic oppression

During the past several years in which the Lord has directed Phyl and me to allocate more time to evicting demonic squatters and breaking bondages amongst his people, it is difficult to remember one person who was not suffering from some form of rejection. With the majority, rejection was a major factor. With the rest, at least it was significant.

Rejection has numbers of causes and shows itself in a variety of ways. It may be purposely or unintentionally given, and it may be imagined. When Satan caused Adam and Eve to sin, he wrapped it up in anticipatory pleasures and made no mention of the heartache of rejection which inevitably followed. What he had suffered in heaven he was determined to inflict upon earth.

Having prayed for believers of many nations, I have come to this conclusion:
THE GREATEST UNDIAGNOSED, THEREFORE UNTREATED MALADY WITHIN THE BODY OF CHRIST TODAY, IS REJECTION.

Rejection, whether active or passive, real or imaginary, robs Jesus Christ of his rightful Lordship in the life of his children, and robs them of the vitality and quality of life Jesus Christ intended (John 10:10).

Rejection may commence at any time between conception and death. Like some physical sicknesses, its symptoms may not be apparent. In fact, many people are quite unaware they have been suffering from its effects until freed from them. Some of the root-causes and results will become evident in this chapter. The ministry of release will follow in a later section.

1. Rejection may be received by the manner or timing of conception.

Children conceived out of wedlock, in anger, as a result of rape, incest, adultery, or from a drug-dependent relationship will exhibit signs of rejection from birth onwards. Children born to parents who did not want them, who were a strain on the family budget; the last of a large family, and strangely, the middle child of a family, often struggle with rejection.

A woman receiving ministry in Switzerland said she had given birth to three children in three years. She was furious with her husband on the last occasion, and resented the pregnancy greatly. The new-born baby refused to suckle or drink milk from a bottle while being held in her mother's arms. She would only drink from it if it was propped up on a pillow beside her in a carry cot. Even in adulthood, the rejection which began at conception remained as a wall of hostility between mother and daughter.

2. Rejection may be received in a mother's womb.

The circumstances surrounding a pregnant woman and her attitude to her unborn child influence the child in utero. To a lesser degree, a father's pleasure or displeasure may be impressed upon a foetus particularly if, having expressed strong preference for one sex, the child turns out to be the opposite. The in-utero influences of mothers particularly, are well documented in Dr. Thomas Verny's 'The Secret Life of the Unborn Child' written with John Kelly (Summit Books).

● The father of a young married woman who came to us had rejected his wife in marriage. When the mother conceived against her will she rejected her baby in utero. The child grew into adulthood with deep rejection and a hereditary unwillingness to conceive children. She determined to avoid childbirth and what she termed the 'headaches and heartache'. She also rejected her father-in-law because she felt he was trying to manipulate her husband because of his desire for grandchildren.

She suffered from a split identity, intellectualised everything she could, and was driven relentlessly into excessive busyness to attain her self-defined goals which were actually substitutes for maternal instincts. While driven by desires to please God by performance, she was greatly distressed by an inhibiting back pain.

● Another 31 year-old single woman came for counsel. Her mother told her she had hated her in utero, and had wanted to murder her. The girl grew up loathing herself and had tried to commit suicide. The mother later had a mental breakdown, and was diagnosed as a schizophrenic.

● One counsellee freely confessed to having lived with four different men for periods of up to two years and having had casual sexual relationships with another ten to fifteen other men during that time. She also claimed to have had five abortions which she initiated without the knowledge of the men responsible. She reasoned that by depriving each man of the satisfaction of knowing he had fathered a child, she would have pleasure by punishing the opposite sex. This was her method of taking revenge on her father for the rejection she had received from him through her mother.

When she fell pregnant for the sixth time, she determined to keep the child for security and companionship, and live as a solo parent. When she gave birth to a son, she was overcome with anger, and came for help when the child was six months old. She realized she could no longer contain her anti-male rage, and was beginning to abuse her boy physically. She was intelligent, had spent some time at University, but knew that she was unable to control the evil forces within her which obviously commenced in utero. God answered her need.

3. Rejection may be caused by the manner of birth.

Experience has shown that rejection may commence in a child who:-

(1) Is born very quickly, and spends insufficient time in the birth canal to adjust to life outside the womb. Sudden exposure to noise, bright lights, and being physically handled after the security, warmth and relative quietness of the womb can be traumatic.

(2) Is born with instrumental assistance, causing head distortion, or physical injury.

(3) Is born after long and protracted labour in which the mother and baby have both become exhausted.

(4) Is born by Caesarian section. The lack of birth-canal pressure sometimes causes these children to have difficulty in estimating distances between themselves and objects, resulting in frequent accidents, particularly head injuries.

Symptoms of rejection include a constant desire for physical love and assurance of self-worth. One of our grandsons suffered from these problems. Many mothers have confirmed the existence of such symptoms after hearing our testimony.

4. A baby not bonded to its mother soon after birth may receive a sense of rejection.

For the sake of survival some babies are placed in an incubator (humidi-crib) immediately after birth. It may be days, weeks, or even months before their mothers are able to show them mother-love. Other mothers have insufficient milk, or refuse to breast feed their babies, so that no intimate bond is established between them. Whatever the cause, that lack of tenderness and physical bonding causes feelings of rejection. Babies who are not sick, and are well cared for but who cry continuously, are often expressing rejection.

An unusual example of in utero rejection combined with lack of bonding, was seen in a man who told the writer that his mother did not know she was pregnant while carrying him. It appears that his mother was astonished when, on a regular bathroom visit she suddenly gave birth to a one and a half pound baby boy. She placed him in a shoe box and rushed him to the local hospital where he was placed in an incubator. He remained in it for three months. The boy grew up surrounded by sisters, and felt a lot of female oppression. He was in his twenties when he came for help from strong feelings of rejection. He was without emotion and was a homosexual. Although a Christian, he did everything by will-power, and his Christian life was a drag.

It should be noted that A SENSE OF REJECTION AS A BABY OR CHILD GROWS INTO A DEMONIC ROOT UNLESS COUNTERACTED.

5. An adopted child is always a rejected child.

My wife Phyl will be commenting on this subject in dealing with the problems of children, so I will share only two illustrations of adoptive rejection beyond childhood.

(1) 'T' was adopted at birth, and beaten during childhood for every little misdemeanour. As a teenager he felt deeply rejected, and in despair turned to reading literature on occultism. He then tried astrology, cast spells using voodoo dolls, and became haunted by fears. Before he was twenty years old his adoptive father tried to run him down with his utility van at his farm. The Lord freed him from his rejection, fears, the occult, and witchcraft spirits. For the first time in his life he gained a healthy self-image, and was freely able to give and receive love.

(2) 'S' was adopted as a small child by Christian parents. He always loved and respected them, but could never escape feeling rejected. He tried being funny to attract people to him and gain their acceptance. When in his late teenage years the Lord freed him from his rejection syndrome and a spirit of foolishness, he not only accepted himself but felt fully accepted by others. He no longer needed the gimmick of excessive humour to make himself popular.

6. Rejected parents produce rejected children.

Parents who have suffered from hereditary rejection, or who have been rejected before marriage will be unable to share personal warmth with their children. Without doubt they love their children, but because they have had no family example of love, or feel emotionally bound, they are unable to express love physically. It is not uncommon to hear a parent say, "We are not a demonstrative family", or "We aren't the kissing and hugging types", which probably means "We are embarrassed about any show of affection". So the children grow up rejected, insecure, and lacking in self-worth despite being surrounded by materialistic replacements.

So very often counsellees respond to a question about their early childhood relationship with their parents by saying something like this: "I know my father (or mother) loved me because they bought me things", or "they were kind to me". Many feel that by confessing a feeling of rejection in childhood, they are being disloyal to their parents. And sometimes it is hurtful to be truthful, particularly if parents are deceased. But uncovering the truth of hereditary rejection is the first step towards its eradication. All forms of rejection are roots which need to be pulled out.

7. Common causes of rejection in the family home.

In addition to thirteen causes listed in chapter fifteen, the following activities can cause rejection:

(1)   Being born with the sex opposite to what the parents desired. Sometimes a child will dress and act as if he or she were a member of the opposite sex in an effort to please a disappointed parent. I have seen women wear men's overalls, crop their hair short, and drive trucks for this reason. I have also seen the Lord release them into becoming female in every way when delivered.

(2)   A birth deformity, or a physical disability caused by an accident or disease which limits mobility, or prevents participation in sports activities.

(3)   Constant criticism by parents, siblings, or authority figures such as day-school or Sunday-school teachers.

(4)   Unjust discipline, particularly if another family member appears to be favoured.

(5)   Being called names which emphasize embarrassing personal features, such as 'four eyes', 'bugle-nose', 'cauliflower ears', or 'hoppy' if lame in one leg.

(6)   A sick or incapacitated brother or sister receiving prolonged medical care and attention.

(7)   Fathers showing weakness, apathy, or passivity in their authority and responsibility roles.

(8)   Subjection to sexual molestation, or incest.

(9)   A father becoming sexually aggressive to his wife in the presence of his children. One adult told us that when he was a boy, his father had lined him and his three brothers up in their parents' bedroom in front of their mother. He said, "This is how you rape a woman", then tore the clothes off his wife, threw her onto the bed, and raped her in front of the children. As a result, the boys felt rejected, and immediately rejected their father. From that time onwards they respected their mother and did all in their power to protect her.

(10) A spoilt pampered child will end up feeling rejected.

(11) Children who belong to a racial minority will usually feel rejected by the majority amongst whom they live and play.

(12) Speech difficulties caused by a hare-lip, a cleft palate, stuttering, stammering, lisping or an inability to pronounce certain consonants or words will cause the speaker to feel embarrassed and rejected.

(13) Unhappy parents who argue, fight, won't talk to each other, or only speak through their children; the children feel guilty, and responsible.

(14) Parental cruelty. One woman who had six men in turn as her 'dad' while she was growing up, received constant beatings from her frustrated mother until 18 years of age.

(15) Alcoholism in one or both parents.

(16) Failure to be forgiven or trusted by parents.

(17) Bribes or threats to be academically successful.

(18) Being expelled from school, or rejected by a peer group.

(19) Embarrassment over the parents' religious beliefs.

(20) A father showing more attention to his daughter's girl friends than he does to his own daughter.

(21) The destruction of the family home by fire or some natural disaster.

(22) A family member convicted for a serious crime.

(23) A sudden drop in the family standard of living caused by the unemployment, redundancy, or bankruptcy of the breadwinner.

(24) Parents having ample financial resources showing meanness towards their children, causing them to feel ashamed before their playmates. It is even worse when children have to lie, or are forced to steal, to cover for their parents.

(25) Children being constantly left to their own resources either because of the working hours of their parents or their disinterest in their children's welfare.

(26) Parents showing no active interest in the progress of their children's school work, sports activities, or leisure time pursuits.

8. Problems caused by teachers or schoolmates.

(1) Being called deprecating names based on some physical defect, mannerism, or special feature such as: 'Hoppy', 'Blinkers', or 'Four eyes'.

(2) Injustice, by not being believed when telling the truth.

(3) Humiliation in the eyes of peers by being continually picked on by teachers, and made the object of humour or sarcasm.

(4) Being made to feel inferior, when the scholastic record of an older sibling is used in an attempt to produce greater results.

(5) When friends exclude one of their group, and 'send them to Coventry'.

(6) When hearing or eyesight difficulties are not recognised by the teaching staff, and a child is blamed for not responding as expected.

(7) When a child does not understand what is being taught, and being too fearful to ask for help slips behind other students, and is looked on as being 'dumb'.

9. Rejection caused by one's own attitudes.

(1) A sense of shame, guilt, or inadequacy through being unable to become parents.

(2) Guilt and sorrow over unwanted pregnancies or abortions. If the abortions were forced by the male responsible, bitterness and resentment will add to the rejection.

(3) Feeling uncomfortable or ashamed of one's sex, and taking all possible steps to deny it.

(4) Inability to cope with the pressures of the female menopause.

(5) Inability of males to cope with the pressures of the so-called mid-life crisis.

(6) Personal embarrassment over some physical feature causing considerable

rejection and inferiority. The length of nose, size of ears, facial birth marks and injury scars are frequent examples. Some women reject themselves because they are embarrassed by the size of their breasts. Others feel equally rejected because that portion of their femininity is not as noticeable as desired.
(7)   Womenfolk convincing themselves they are unattractive in appearance, and so rejecting themselves and withdrawing from mixing socially. Nearly every person we have counselled for this problem was in fact quite attractive, and was bound by a spirit of self-delusion.

10.   Other causes of rejection in later life.
(1)   Desertion or divorce. The death or unfaithfulness of a marriage partner.
(2)   Mental or physical cruelty caused by a husband or wife.
(3)   Shame caused by a court conviction for a criminal offence. The serving of a prison term.
(4)   Inability to find any long-term relief for mental, emotional, or physical problems after having exhausted all forms of counselling or professional services.
(5)   Incompatible religious ideologies in marriage, involving one partner being forced to comply with the other's wishes.
(6)   A lowering of standards of lifestyle caused by the drinking habits of a marriage partner.
(7)   Rejection in love, or a broken engagement.
(8)   Becoming bed-ridden, or crippled, as a result of disease or an accident.
(9)   Becoming subject to pressures beyond one's ability to control. These may be unexpected business responsiblities through the death or illness of a partner or associate; an unexpected increase in the home workload with a consequent drain on finances (such as caring for the children of relatives).
(10)   Becoming redundant, being sacked for incompetency, or being unable to find employment over a long period.
(11)   Being 'sent to Coventry' by family members, relatives, friends, or fellow employees.
(12)   Being totally let down by people who had been trusted, and whose advice had been totally relied upon. Examples include: the loss of a husband who died intestate; financial embarrassment caused by the failure of investments taken on the advice of a close friend, or being financially cheated by unscrupulous operators.
(13)   An over-fertile imagination particularly if indulging in self-pity.

Rejection is certainly a complicated subject to deal with. Effects are often confused with causes. Root systems sometimes become entwined so that it becomes difficult to determine what is the primary cause of rejection. Some like to distinguish a sense of rejection as passive, and the outward response towards situations and people as active. But the writer does not intend to introduce readers to some of the succeeding phases of rejection reserved for specialist training seminars.

To this point we have only considered the causes of rejection which give the evil one an opportunity of dominating the lives of children, teenagers, and adults. In turning our attention to the personal behavioural patterns which result from rejection, I believe it will become evident that Satan not only causes it, or uses it, but that he is also the power behind its manifestations.

Probably the best illustration of the rejection 'cause and effect syndrome' can be found in the root-fruit system of a tree. The Bible often uses the illustration of a tree to explain human behaviour:

"They will be called oaks of righeousness, a planting of the Lord for the display of his splendour" (Isaiah 63:1).

"He, (the righteous) is like a tree planted by the streams of water, which yields its fruit in season and whose leaf does not wither. Whatsoever he does prospers" (Psalm 1:3, 4). See also Jeremiah 17:7, 8.

"The axe is already at the root of the trees, and every tree that does not produce good fruit will be cut down and thrown into the fire" (Matthew 3:10).

The roots of rejection produce three different fruit-bearing branches. Firstly, rejected people show a variety of aggressive attitudes. Secondly, they suffer from symptoms of self-rejection which may or may not be seen. Thirdly, motivated by their fear of rejection, they make constant attempts to avoid being rejected again. The following lists clearly show the fruit systems:

11. THE THREE BRANCHES PRODUCED BY THE ROOTS OF REJECTION.

1 AGGRESSIVE REACTIONS	2 SELF-REJECTION SYMPTOMS	3 MEASURES TO COUNTER FEAR OF SELF-REJECTION
Refusing comfort	Low Self Image	Striving, achievement performance, competition
Rejection of others	Inferiorities	Withdrawal, aloneness
Harshness, hardness	Insecurity	
Skepticism, unbelief	Inadequacy	INDEPENDENCE,
Aggressive attitudes	Sadness, grief, sorrow	isolation
Swearing, foul language	Self-accusation	Self-protectiveness,
Argumentativeness	and	Self-centredness, selfishness
	Self-condemnation	Self-justification,
Stubbornness, defiance		Self-righteousness
	Inability to or refusal to communicate	SELF IDOLATRY
REBELLION,		Criticism,
fighting	Fear of failure	Judgemental attitudes
		Envy, Jealousy
		COVETOUSNESS
		Self-Pity
	Fear of others' opinions	PRIDE,
	Other fears:	
	Anxiety, worry	ego, haughtiness
	Depression	arrogance
	Negative attitudes	Manipulation,
	Pessimism	possessiveness
	Hopelessness, despair	
		Emotional immaturity
		Perfectionism

These manifestations are certainly not of the Holy Spirit, but are caused by a spirit which focuses on the self life. This is the original Satanic 'I-disease', now a spiritual virus which affects all mankind, including Christians. Satan is certainly having a hey-day!

Based on the understanding God gave us, some of which is outlined in Part One, we came to regard these behavioural problems as being controlled by Satan and his demonic powers. By ministering deliverance from the demonic causes of rejection, and the fruit manifestations of rejection, self-rejection, fear of rejection, and each known problem, we witnessed God set countless numbers free. Since that beginning, thousands have received freedom from rejection and its associated problems as God continues to confirm its demonic power.

1. The spiritual basis for ministering deliverance to believers suffering from rejection.

(1) God provided a sinless substitue for rejected humanity.

"Such a high priest meets our needs - one who is holy, blameless, pure, set apart from sinners . . " (Hebrews 7:26).

(2) Jesus Christ came to free mankind from all the devil's work.

(a) "But you know that he appeared that he might take away our sins. And in him is no sin . . " (1 John 3:5).

(b) "He who does what is sinful is of the devil, because the devil has been sinning from the beginning. The reason the Son of God appeared was to destroy the devil's work" (1 John 3:8).

(3) Jesus Christ bore our sin to give us his life.

(a) "God made him who had no sin to be sin for us, so that in him we might become the righteousness of God" (2 Corinthians 5:21).

(b) "He was despised and rejected by men, a man of sorrows and familiar with suffering. Like one from whom men hide their faces he was despised, and we esteemed him not" (Isaiah 53:3).

(4) Jesus Christ releases those who trust him, from sin and Satan.

(a) "But now he has appeared once for all at the end of the ages to do away with sin by the sacrifice of himself" (Hebrews 9:26).

(b) "How much more, then, will the blood of Christ, who through the eternal Spirit offered himself unblemished to God, cleanse our consciences from acts that lead to death, so that we may serve the living God!" (Hebrews 9:14).

(c) "It is for freedom that Christ has set us free. Stand firm, then, and do not let yourselves be burdened again by a yoke of slavery" (Galatians 5:1).

2. Jesus Christ has given us his authority, his name, and his blood-bought victory to overcome Satan and his demonic power.

(1) "I tell you the truth, whatsoever you bind on earth will be bound in heaven, and whatever you loose on earth will be loosed in heaven. Again, I tell you that if two of you on earth agree about anything you ask for, it will be done for you by my Father in heaven. For where two or three come together in my name, there am I with them" (Matthew 18:18, 19).

(2) "And these signs will accompany those who believe: In my name they will drive out demons . . " (Mark 16:17).

(3) "They overcame him (that ancient serpent called the devil or Satan who leads the whole world astray - verse 9) by the blood of the Lamb and by the word of their testimony" (Revelation 12:11 The Amplified Bible).

3. The following testimonies are to the glory of God, and confirm the living reality of the truths just quoted.

• One young lady for whom we had the privilege of praying was an anorexic, and compulsively walked for about thirty-one kilometres every day. Her depressions lasted up to eighteen months without relief, and she suffered from a very serious type of asthma.

Her mother was an alcoholic, and beat her constantly until she was eight years of age. If she couldn't tie her shoes she was beaten for up to three hours. For not being able to do up the buttons of her dress (because the button holes were too tight) she would be beaten all morning. The mother was nice to everyone except her daughter and her grown-up son. She once tried to kill him with a knife, but he threw her through a window and left home.

The daughter was confined to a room without any warmth, was given little food, and was forced to wear clothes years old. Finally she was ordered to leave home or be committed to a mental institution. The mother died when the daughter was eleven years of age.

The basis of the anorexia nervosa, obsessive exercise, asthma, depression and countless other problems was this incredible feeling of rejection. She had worked for a group of doctors for years. They found they were unable to give her any lasting help and suggested that she try some Christian counselling.

Because the Lord loves his people more than we can ever imagine, he caused our paths to cross and we ministered deliverance from the basic cause, rejection, its manifestations, and then the other problems. Her beauty in God is evident to all. Her asthma is presently at a level of control which does not hinder her work, and she is trusting God for total healing.

• A married woman was having great problems expressing any emotion whatsoever. She was gentle and caring for her husband and family, but had not cried for over twenty years.

As a child she lived in a European country under German occupation. At the age of four years her father was arrested and imprisoned. He was eventually rescued by a clever ruse engineered by her mother. Fear of discovery then gripped the household, and the daughter was not allowed to cry for fear that it would attract Nazi attention. She buried her emotions so deeply that in later life she was greatly embarrassed by any show of emotion, even on television. She was ruled by a spirit of stoicism. Her childhood fear of the Germans was maintained by a fear of the disciplinarian nature of her husband, whom she respected and loved as much as she was able to express.

The whole rejection syndrome came to the surface when the Lord revealed the bondages and dominating spirits common to her childhood and married life. She wept noisily during prayer. She had been an ardent but discouraged Christian for many years.

In exercising the ministry of deliverance with rejection sufferers, make sure you are A ROOT AND FRUIT DESTROYER, not just one who diagnoses or removes objectionable fruit!

CHAPTER SUMMARY.

1. From years of experience in ministering to Christians spiritually crippled by rejection and its manifestations, we have come to an unavoidable conclusion. **The greatest undiagnosed, therefore untreated malady in the Body of Christ today, is rejection.**

2. Rejection may be experienced from before the cradle, even to the grave.

3. Rejection may not have been intentionally given to have been received. It may have real or imaginary causes. The range and intensity of the effects of rejection are variable.

4. Rejection may be recognized by the attitudes and actions shown. It is a root-system which must be removed.

5. Jesus Christ has provided, and given us authority to minister, release to rejection sufferers.

6. A diagrammatic summary of the root-fruit system is shown on the opposite page.

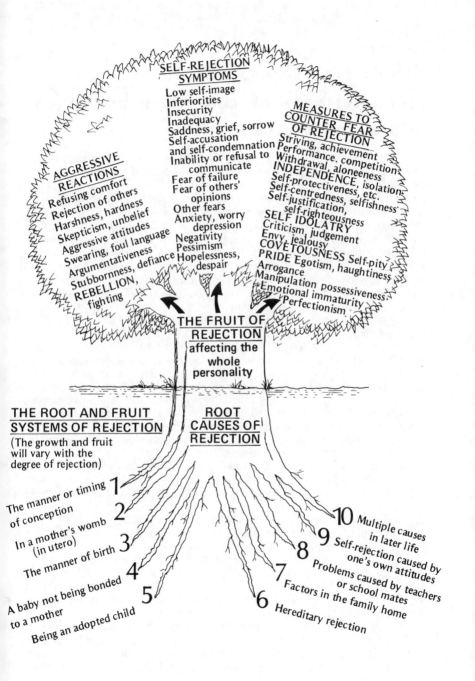

SELF-REJECTION SYMPTOMS
Low self-image
Inferiorities
Insecurity
Inadequacy
Saddness, grief, sorrow
Self-accusation
and self-condemnation
Inability or refusal to
communicate
Fear of failure
Fear of others'
opinions
Other fears
Anxiety, worry
depression
Negativity
Pessimism
Hopelessness,
despair

MEASURES TO COUNTER FEAR OF REJECTION
Striving, achievement
Performance, competition
Withdrawal, aloneeness
INDEPENDENCE, isolation
Self-protectiveness, etc.
Self-centredness, selfishness
Self-justification,
self-righteousness
SELF IDOLATRY
Criticism, judgement
Envy, jealousy
COVETOUSNESS Self-pity
PRIDE Egotism, haughtiness
Arrogance
Manipulation possessiveness
Emotional immaturity
Perfectionism

AGGRESSIVE REACTIONS
Refusing comfort
Rejection of others
Harshness, hardness
Skepticism, unbelief
Aggressive attitudes
Swearing, foul language
Argumentativeness
Stubbornness, defiance
REBELLION,
fighting

THE FRUIT OF REJECTION affecting the whole personality

THE ROOT AND FRUIT SYSTEMS OF REJECTION
(The growth and fruit will vary with the degree of rejection)

ROOT CAUSES OF REJECTION

1 The manner or timing of conception
2 In a mother's womb (in utero)
3 The manner of birth
4 A baby not being bonded to a mother
5 Being an adopted child
6 Hereditary rejection
7 Factors in the family home
8 Problems caused by teachers or school mates
9 Self-rejection caused by one's own attitudes
10 Multiple causes in later life

99

"I will . . make you . . to say to the captives 'Come out' and to those in darkness 'Be free' " (Isaiah 49:9).

CHAPTER 12.

Ethnic traditions, culture, and environment can cause bondages and dominations

Most of us are walking signposts pointing to where we were born or have lived. Some of us may even point in several directions at once! The shape of our face and eyes, colour of skin, texture of hair, style of clothes, eating habits, and speech are often pointers to our ethnic roots and place of birth.

Anthropologists have given us both information and speculation about ethnology (the origins and characteristics of racial and linguistic groups). Unfortunately, many of their propositions have been based upon the unprovable humanistic theory of evolution. The Scriptures on the other hand provide us with divine insight into the beginnings of racial characteristics. This makes it possible to trace certain ethnic groups for thousands of years in Biblical history, and to see clearly how developing nations become influenced by conquered or surrounding cultures and environments.

When God caused language confusion at Babel (Genesis 11:7, 8), he scattered linguistic groups throughout the earth in accordance with his predetermined will. "When the Most High gave the nations their inheritance, when he divided all mankind, he set up boundaries for the peoples according to the number of the sons of Israel" (Deuteronomy 32:8).

Both Jews and Arabs, the two ethnic groups which feature most in the chapters immediately following the dispersion, have Abraham in common as their father. Their respective mothers, Sarah and Hagar, were hostile to each other, and the Arab descendants of Ishmael through Hagar, and the Hebrew children of Isaac through Sarah, have continued that unbroken family tradition right through to the twentieth century.

The angel of the LORD told Hagar four things about the child she was expecting (Genesis 16:11):
(1)   She was carrying a male child, and that his name was to be Ishmael (God hears).
(2)   The boy's nature would be similar to that of a wild donkey.
(3)   He would be against everyone else, and everyone would be against him.
(4)   He would live in hostility towards all his brothers.

The Arab peoples of the world have remained ethnically unchanged since Ishmael had his twelve sons who became tribal leaders. Arab aggressiveness against Israel, the unilateral Arab oil policy shaped by the members of O.P.E.C. who are continually at variance with one another, and the sporadic warfare between Middle East oil nations, are well known.

Sometimes Christians with Arab ethnic roots come for prayer and deliverance. Irrespective of their national identity, all Arabs have certain characteristics which need special attention because of their common ancestry in Ishmael. These include rejection by others and of others; aggressiveness; a fighting spirit; a nomadic spirit; hostility and an argumentative spirit towards others; isolation and withdrawal; pride and arrogance. Because of more recent Islamic influences including polygamy and witchcraft, many other cultural spirits also need exorcising. The characteristics of Ishmael's descendants remain basically as the angel of the Lord told Hagar they would be (Genesis 16:11).

On the other hand, no nation has retained its national language, customs, unit of currency and religious identity more fervently and tenaciously than the Hebrews (sons of Shem) later known as Jews. Their return to the land of promise, their establishment as an independent nation, their subjection to oppression in many countries, and the antagonism and hatred shown towards them by the Arab nations, all prove that the word of God to the patriarchs was inviolable.

Many Causcasians and migrant Asians have ethnic roots in countries other than these in which they were born, or have their residence. The Gospel provides power for the breaking of ethnic bondages and dominant characteristics which would hinder oneness in Jesus Christ, particularly where ethnic backgrounds would make different races natural enemies.

"You are all sons of God through faith in Christ Jesus, for all of you were baptized into Christ and have been clothed with Christ. There is neither Jew nor Greek, slave or free, male or female, for you are all one in Christ Jesus. If you belong to Christ, then you are Abraham's seed, and heirs according to the promise" (Galatians 3:26-29).

1. Ethnic traditions may dominate any one of us.

The world in which The Church exists abounds with prejudices. There are 'white only' policies, and 'black is beautiful' policies. Some countries and ethnic groups actively oppose Christians, or even persecute them in order to preserve their own forms of worship. In multi-cultural countries ethnic groups sometimes cut themselves off from community relationships to preserve their own identity, language, and lifestyle. In some cases this has produced nationalistic reactions which have caused the ethnic groups to feel even more isolated than before. Sometimes even our children at school get caught up in name-calling campaigns directed against the children of immigrants.

Unless this deeply rooted ethnic antipathy is broken by Jesus Christ, local churches can become as deeply divided as the community in which they exist. A Moroccan Arab living in Switzerland came to Jesus Christ through the tender love and care of a Christian couple who took the young man into their home knowing he was an ardent Muslim opposed to Christianity. Since that time he has been constantly subject to rejection as an Arab wherever he has travelled, and sad to say, by some Christians as well. Christian love should be multi-coloured.

2. No one is exempt from cultural bondages and dominations.

Culture may be examined from many points of view, dependant upon the premise of the examiner. The characteristics upon which this chapter focuses mainly concern the moral and spiritual milieu of modern nations or groups. For this purpose culture is defined as "that unique blend of a country's belief systems and lifestyles which identify its citizens wherever they go, and which need to be brought into conformity with Biblical standards when a citizen is born again". Admittedly, this definition may be regarded as simplistic, but it is sufficient to highlight some of the problems which the Gospel uncovers.

The contributory factors which combine to form a cultural identity come from a variety of sources. For example:

(1) The manner in which a national identity commences. As the 'Mayflower' and the Pilgrim Fathers laid strong spiritual foundations in the United States of America, so the 'First Fleet' and its criminal element contributed to the Australian culture, particularly in New South Wales. The continuing effects of these early settlers are discernible in both cultures.

(2) The influences of settlers, land developers, migrants, and traders, produce discernible effects in society structures. China and India are examples.

(3) Primitive religious beliefs, and imported religions with their unique forms of worship all play an important part in cultural development. The Spaniards imposed Catholicism on the peoples they conquered, and British colonizers were usually closely followed by trading merchants and the Church of England.

(4) In reverse, superstition, mythologies, and customs held by conquered or colonised people are sometimes absorbed by the invaders or colonisers. The Romans took pagan deities back to Rome; New Zealand and Hawaii have adopted a religious symbol, the tiki, for national identification.

(5) Countries conquered and occupied in war often exhibit a spirit of heaviness and self-protectiveness. For example, the Koreans, Okinawans, and the Finns still show a reserve to foreigners because of the hurts and memories of the past.

(6) Strong family traditions continue to affect the cultures of countries like China, India, and Japan as they have for centuries.

(7) Struggles for economic survival, a country's financial viability, over-population, poverty, harsh climatic conditions limiting productivity, and reliance upon foreign aid, all affect culture. Some African and Asian countries still show the strong influences of the past.

(8) Class structures, such as the 'haves' and 'have-nots' of society have their effect.

(9) The political scene shapes culture. People under Marxist, democratic, or dictatorial rule reflect these influences in their manner of living.

(10) Immigration broadens the cultural milieu when other ethnic groups introduce new languages, customs, food, religious beliefs and practices. The United States of America, Britain and Australia show this.

(11) Every country is subject to the influences of demonic overlords (Daniel 10:13, 20; Mark 5:10). A missionary in South America saw the proof of this when working in a town where the main street was the border between two countries. People on one side of the street would refuse tracts, while those on the other side would readily accept them. The remarkable fact was that when those who showed aloofness and had refused tracts on one side crossed the border, they readily accepted what was offered.

3. Environmental bondages and dominations.

As ethnic and cultural bondages and dominations come from racial backgrounds and countries of birth and residence, so environmental bondages and dominations come from the more personal circumstances of our daily lives. For example:-

(1) The class of house in which we lived during childhood, the social standing of the neighbourhood, the presence or absence of family status symbols, and

attitudes of peer groups all help shape attitudes and character.

(2) Schools, teachers and educational systems, all affect the personalities of students. Attendance at a private or public school tends to raise or lower the social standing of students in the eyes of some people. Being in a racial or religious minority at school can also have an adverse effect on students. Levels of achievement and the reactions which parents show to them may shape attitudes and habit patterns.

The financial security of the parents will affect the children. Lifelong attitudes and habits may be formed when a family spends lavishly, or has insufficient money to maintain socially acceptable standards of living.

4. Modes of relaxation and entertainment.

(1) **Music,** particularly rock-and-roll and punk rock can pipeline demonic influence to Christians. Backward masking (Satanic subliminal messages record-ed backwards), and the use of witchcraft in marketing practices by recording artists make the medium very dangerous to believers. The demonic power of rock's primitive beat will dominate a Christian as much as an unbeliever, and deliverance from its power is often necessary. Demonic spirits have often vocally and physically resisted us in sessions of deliverance.

(2) **Occultish games** have the power of addiction. One high school student who had been addicted to 'Dungeons and Dragons' for five years asked that the demonic power over him be broken, and he was freed.

(3) **Books and magazines** devoted to space fantasy and supernatural heroism are often the cause of children and teenagers going into fantasy, or developing alter-egos to match their heroes. These have produced both mental and emotional problems which have drastically lowered academic standards in child-ren and produced unreality in adults. Spiritual release from demonic bondage is needed.

(4) **Television programmes and videos** have allowed a tide of filth, violence, occultism, demonism, perversion, and promiscuity to engulf the unwary. Many Christians have been enticed away from their loyalty to Jesus Christ by time unwisely spent with these mind-moulders.

(5) **The printed media** may also be manipulative. When editorial policies, political influences, and personal prejudices influence journalism, truthfulness and objectivity often become sadly distorted.

(6) **Political ideologies** of course affect attitudes, relationships, and living patterns in the family home. As children grow to maturity, they often continue the established family beliefs.

Summary.

The influences of ethnic tradition, culture, and environment have become so identified with our education and personality growth factors that they are an integral part of attitudes, value systems, and lifestyles. Quite often Christians are not aware of this until their attention is drawn to some problem, attitude, mannerism or habit of which they were previously unconscious.

Anger, criticism, self-centredness, and manipulation may be normal cultural attitudes and responses which create no unexpected 'waves' in the worldly community, but when a person is born again into the kingdom of God they are strangely out of place in a community of love. In fact, they are disruptive factors to the unity and harmony God expects of his people. Bondages and dominations of any kind are not the will of God. They belong to the Egypt of the past, not to God's land of promise.

5. God warned the Israelites against assimilating heathen cultural practices.

(1)   "Speak to the Israelites and say to them, 'I am the LORD your God, you must not do as they do in Egypt where you used to live, and you must not do as they do in the land of Canaan where I am taking you. DO NOT FOLLOW THEIR PRACTICES. You must obey my laws, and be careful to follow my decrees. I am the LORD your God" (Leviticus 18:3, 4 - emphasis added).

(2)   "Keep all my decrees and laws and follow them so that the land where I am bringing you to live may not vomit you out. **You must not live according to the customs of the nations I am going to drive out before you. Because they did all these things, I abhorred them**" (Leviticus 20:22, 23 - emphasis added).

In order to protect his people from such influences, God instructed Moses to destroy the people of the land of Canaan, to forbid marriage to any of the local women, and to totally destroy their idols and religious symbols. The people were also clearly warned against being defiled by taking gold and silver from the idols into their home, the penalty being destruction. (Deuteronomy 7:2-5, 25-26).

Because both Israel and Judah disobeyed God and fell into the practices of the nations around them (2 Kings chapters 17 and 21), they were thrown out of their land of promise into captivity. The culturally objectionable practices of the Canaanites had so defiled the city God claimed as his own that he said, "I will wipe out Jerusalem as one wipes a dish, wiping it and turning it upside down" (2 Kings 21:13).

6. New Testament warnings.

(1)   "See to it that no-one takes you captive through hollow and deceptive philosophy, which depends on human tradition and the basic principles of this world rather than on Christ" (Colossians 2:8).

(2)   "Since you died with Christ to the basic principles of this world, why as though you still belonged to it, do you submit to its rules . .?" (Colossians 2:20).
"We were in slavery under the basic principles of the world" (Galatians 4:3).

(3)   "Formerly, when you did not know God, you were slaves to those who by nature are not gods. But now that you know God - or rather are known by God - how is it that you are turning back to those weak and miserable principles? Do you wish to be enslaved by them all over again?" (Galatians 4:9).

(4)   "Therefore come out from them and be separate, says the Lord. Touch no unclean thing, and I will receive you. I will be a Father to you, and you will be my sons and daughters, says the Lord Almighty" (2 Corinthians 6:17, 18).

7. Evangelistic theology agrees that all cultures contain problems.

The Lausanne Covenant, item 10, includes this statement on culture:
"Culture must always be tested and judged by Scripture. Because man is

God's creature, some of his culture is rich in beauty and goodness. Because he is fallen, all of it is tainted with sin, and some of it is demonic. The Gospel does not presuppose the superiority of any culture to another, but evaluates all cultures according to its own criteria of truth and righteousness, and insists on moral absolutes in every culture. Missions have all too frequently exported with the gospel an alien culture, and churches have sometimes been in bondage to culture rather than Scripture."

8. Biblical examples of breaking with cultural conformity.

(1) After Jacob had been reconciled to his brother Esau, God told him to settle in Bethel, and build an altar there. Jacob called his household together, and told them to get rid of everything associated with the culture where they had been living. They washed themselves, changed their clothes, and buried their ear-rings and foreign gods under the oak at Shechem. Once cleansed, the fear of God fell upon the group, and the locals were powerless to follow them or harm them (Genesis 35:1-5).

(2) Ruth, the daughter-in-law of Naomi, the widow of Elimelech the Ephrathite, is a classic example of a person renouncing cultural and religious ties in order to become a Hebrew proselyte: "Where you go, I will go, and where you stay, I will stay. Your people will be my people, and your God, my God" (Ruth 1:16).

Gideon is a sad example of how it is possible to become bound by demonic forces of culture, even after being so diligent in doing God's will. After destroying his father's images of Baal, and killing the two Midianite kings Zeba and Zalmunna who had murdered his brothers, he removed the gold crescent-shaped ornaments from their camels' necks and asked for each of his soldiers to give him a golden ear-ring from their Ishmaelite booty. With the ornaments and ear-rings Gideon made an ephod for worship in Ophrah. As a result, "All Israel prostituted themselves by worshipping it there, and it became a snare for Gideon and his family" (Judges 8:27). The problem was that the defiled gold had been used for idolatrous worship and Gideon's righteousness was insufficient to keep the curse from being effective.

9. Practical examples of breaking cultural bondages over believers.

Some years ago, I was teaching discipleship in Korea. While praying for one of the female students, the Lord clearly said to me, "Break cultural bondages". Without understanding what this meant, but in simple obedience I used the authority of the name of Jesus and broke the young lady's cultural bondages. As soon as I had finished praying, she jumped up and hugged me. At first this seemed to be out of character for anyone with a Chinese ethnic background, but each student with whom I prayed showed the same reaction.

The next country where I obeyed the Lord's instruction was Japan. Here the number involved was greater, and the results even warmer. During this time the Lord began to give understanding about the bondages and dominations caused by Japanese culture, ancestor worship, and religious spirits. From that time onwards I always prayed for Japanese nationals to be released from those spirits before commencing to lead them to Christ. One 71 year old lady, responding to an invitation and kneeling at the front of the church after having been set free, and born again, said, "For 71 years I have been full of darkness, and now I am full of light."

As the Lord confirmed his instruction by freeing more and more people from cultural bondages, so did the realization that all believers in fact need to be set free from the humanistic and possibly demonic contents of their local cultures. This enables them to receive the filling of the Holy Spirit more effectively.

• A Christian university graduate from Mexico asked for her cultural bondages to be broken. She explained later that the experience 'was like being born again'.

• The writer has ministered to nationals of several South Pacific islands where violence and lust are almost second nature. The cultural demonic powers often resist strongly, but the releases gained and changes evident in lifestyles are often quite remarkable.

• In countries where indigenes hold primitive religious rites, or have practising witch doctors, those exposed to their demonic influence, innocently or otherwise, are in real danger of bondage to those spirits. Christians certainly need freedom and cleansing. Many Australians have been freed from dominating Aboriginal spirits. Some were afflicted after attending corroborees, visiting sacred caves, living with Aborigines or in homes built on sacred sites. One or two have become afflicted merely by studying Aboriginal art forms at university.

• New Zealanders similarly have been freed from dominating Maori spirits, and visitors to Hindu and Buddhist temples in Asia have had to be delivered from spirits who gained entry during the visit. Once established, spirits maintain their affliction, even if a person moves from one country to another.

• An indigene from a south Pacific island living with Christians had sexual relations with a local woman when he was studying a foreign language in another country. He had been unable to resist his cultural spirit of lust, and was defiant towards the Christian friends with whom he lived. Finally he asked for deliverance. When freed, he became deeply repentant, and immediately asked his friends' forgiveness for letting them down and resisting their love and counselling.

• Another Pacific islander constantly had strong temptations to use his shovel to kill a fellow Christian working in the garden with him. When he was freed from the driving cultural spirits, he lost all desire to harm anyone.

• Some cultural spirits stimulate the fear of man which restricts Christians from either publicly witnessing for Christ, or from preaching. When the Lord sets them free, they have much joy in personal witnessing and sharing Jesus publicly.

• YWAM Australia holds regular discipleship schools for Asian university students during the university vacation. For several years it has been the writer's privilege to minister to these ethnic Chinese students from various countries. They are nearly always first generation Christians, and their cultural bondages and dominations include spirits of Buddhism, Taoism, Confucianism, and spirits of ancestor worship. The release of emotion and warmth they exhibit after ministry, is quite remarkable. One young lady revisited her parents in Malaysia after deliverance, and testified the following year to the total release she had received from the cultural fear of her parents.

Over the years, the writer has accumulated lists of the most common bondages and dominations in many countries. For certain reasons it is considered inappropriate to include them here. They are released during sessions at specialized training seminars on the deliverance ministry.

Finally, two points need emphasis.

Firstly, to desire freedom from cultural bondages and dominations does not mean that one shows disloyalty to one's country of birth, or citizenship. Deliverance simply releases from background hindrances to a full and free participation in the kingdom of God.

Secondly, freedom enables a change of attitudes and behaviour so that Jesus Christ may be Lord of every aspect of living. To illustrate: suppose you want to have a dog and you haven't much money so you visit an organization which cares for lost and unwanted animals. There you find what you imagine is your ideal dog, and return home with him. Next morning when you go out to collect your morning paper, you find fourteen of your neighbours' papers on your doorstep. On returning home later in the day, to your horror you find there are a number of deep scratch marks on your panelled front door. Do you shoot the dog? Preferably not. You go to work on a programme of discipline to change those bad habits into new and pleasurable ones. In just the same way, Christians must discipline and re-train themselves, so that the habit patterns of the past once released can be replaced by those which glorify Jesus Christ.

Some Christians may have difficulty in deciding whether a particular problem has been caused by cultural factors or is a part of normal daily living. A missionary from Tanzania returned home after twenty years in the field. Every morning he found he had to use spiritual warfare to fight off a spirit of heaviness and depression. He assumed that the experience was normal for every Christian, until a demonic bondage was discerned, and dealt with on a spiritual basis. That was the end of the morning heebie-jeebies!

One of the most successful tactics of the evil one is to drain emotionally and physically afflict, missionaries who serve in fields abounding in various forms of demonic worship. So many of them are invalided home or forced to move elsewhere without realizing that Satan is the primary cause. The writer has seen the Lord set free some of these discouraged servants. Regrettably, he has seen others rationalize the cause and remain bound.

CHAPTER SUMMARY.

1. Ethnic, cultural, and environmental bondages and dominations are very real. Some are humanistic, others are demonic. No country is free of them.

2. Believers need to be released from those things which hold them to the life-moulding processes of the past.

3. Freedom is the key to discipline and re-training.

4. In the Body of Christ, there should be no racial distinctions, colour bars, class systems, inferiority of sexes, power play, or the use of wealth to gain favours. As kings and priests unto God, all believers need to offer him the sacrifices of service with the fragrance of Christlike lives.

"Where is the wise man? Where is the scholar? Where is the philosopher of this age? Has not God made foolish the wisdom of the world?"

(1 Corinthians 1:20).

CHAPTER 13.

Chains of humanism, intellectualism and rationalism

George Bernard Shaw is supposed to have said that his education had been interrupted by his schooling. My father must have appreciated that truth as he often spoke about being educated in 'the university of hard knocks'. Education to most people is a series of stepping stones for reaching acceptable levels of knowledge that lead to financial security, personal fulfilment, and social standing.

Some definitions which contribute towards our systems of education may surprise Christians. For example, the Concise Oxford Dictionary defines the word 'educate' as meaning 'to give intellectual and moral training to', and the word 'education' as meaning 'development of character and mental powers'. So moral standards and character development are important objectives in education. This is precisely where a major problem becomes apparent for Christians. Apart from traditional church schools and the growing number of Christian schools, our educational systems claim to be secular in nature. Again the COD comes to our aid by defining 'secular' as meaning 'concerned with the affairs of this world, worldly, not sacred, not monastic, not ecclesiastical'; also 'skeptical of religious thought, or opposed to religious education'.

Secular education therefore presents the believer with a neatly packaged paradox. How can character be developed with a correct sense of moral values, when the system which claims such responsibility is professedly humanistic, anti-religious and in no way bound to Biblical ethics?

Admittedly, some countries do provide for some part-time religious education in primary schools, or give discretionary powers to teachers to do so. But, generally speaking, the system itself, and the greater percentage of its teaching fraternity, are committed to an academic and scientific approach which is based on natural ethics, rather than one governed by divine absolutes. Philosophy is therefore academic, recognizing the source of wisdom as being from man not God, and choice of lifestyle becomes the responsibility of the student, not of the system or of the faculty.

But this is not the total package of education. Members of the teaching profession are under no code of silence to refrain from voicing their own personal biases, prejudices, philosophies, opinions, and even sexual codes when teaching the system's treasure store of knowledge and scientific data. It is no wonder that humanistic teaching processes are open to become homogenized with atheism, humanism, intellectualism, rationalism, political ideologies, mysticism, holism, occultism, homosexuality, bohemianism, and in general, scorn for Biblical and spiritual values.

These humanistic additives can become a type of intellectual silt which prevents hearers from being able to understand and receive Biblical truth.

Nominal Christians, and those weak in the faith, sometimes stumble, fall, or become confused in such an atmosphere.

Of course this should not be taken as a blanket indictment of all teaching. Some honest teaching and academic staff endeavour to be objective, and there are nominal Christians and born-again believers who uphold the principles of God's word.

From the time that God created man with the capacity to investigate, evaluate, and accumulate knowledge, two major changes have taken place in his mental processes.

Firstly, sin has cut off man's source of true wisdom and knowledge.

When God breathed into the lifeless form of the first man shaped from the dust, his whole being became highly charged with divine life. His mental capacity, for example, was so filled from divine resources that he had no trouble in giving names to all the beasts and birds (Genesis 2:19, 20).

Sin cut off that flow of divine wisdom, knowledge, and understanding. Romans chapter one is a divine commentary on the enormous changes which occurred within man's thought processes and moral conduct as he moved further away from God's intention (vv. 20-32). There are three clear downward steps:

Step ONE. Because mankind deliberately refused to honour God in a manner appropriate to his glory and power, his mind lost its divine input, and became ineffective, godless, speculative, and indulgent in foolish reasonings. God allowed man's thought life to degenerate into the most immoral practices (vv. 21-23).

Step TWO. Mankind rejected revelational truth, and chose to continue believing the plausible lies of Satan, which led him to idolatry and materialism. God then allowed men and women to degrade themselves in homosexual practices (vv. 25, 26, 27).

Step THREE. Finally, man threw off any pretension of dependence upon God and deliberately substituted self-idolatry and self-sufficiency, turning his back on everything that reminded him of accountability to God. Because of this, God allowed him to reap the full measure of evil and wickedness in their many forms. And men and women revelled in it (vv. 28-32).

So man touched spiritual rock bottom, intellectually and morally bankrupt in God's sight. Paul tells us what did happen, while Isaiah the prophet tells us why it happened: "I will destroy the wisdom of the wise; the intelligence of the intelligent I will frustrate" (Isaiah 29:14; 1 Corinthians 1:19).

Secondly, mankind has pursued its own intellectual goals.

Without divine input, man's intellectual function continued prolifically within its own resources in the search for knowledge and wisdom. Some time ago it was claimed that knowledge was doubling every ten years, and judging by the staggering scientific achievements of the last decade, that claim appears reasonable. Man's physical achievements are equally impressive. Feats of endurance and the breaking of sports records once thought impossible, are now a regular occurrence. Yet in conquering his own emotions, passions, and sinful habits, man's mind has produced much advice, but little forward progress. Sin still remains the most effective block to human fulfilment. Being unable to understand God's process of reconciliation through Christ because it doesn't satisfy his non-spiritual, rationalistic understanding, man limps on. His self-confidence is supreme, expecting to solve what only God can do.

Pride is another feature of secular education, as Scripture clearly states: " . . knowledge puffs up, but love builds up" (1 Corinthians 8:1). The arrogance of the Epicurean and Stoic philosophers deriding the Apostle Paul bears this out: "What is this babbler with his scrap-picked learning trying to say?" Acts 17:17, 18 (The Amplified Bible).

It is to the humanistic halls of learning that most of God's people must go in order to qualify professionally. The spiritually sterile nature of what they have to confront is revealed by the Concise Oxford Dictionary:

(1) **Humanism.**

"Devotion to human interests; system concerned with human (not divine or supernatural) matters, or with the human race (not the individual), or with man as a responsive and progressive intellectual being."

(2) **Intellectualism.**

"Doctrine that knowledge is wholly or mainly derived from pure reason; (excessive) exercise of intellect only."

(3) **Rationalism.**

"The practice of explaining the supernatural in religion in a way consonant with reason, or of treating reason as the ultimate authority in religion or elsewhere; theory that reason is the foundation of certainty in knowledge."

(4) **Psychology.**

"The science of the nature, functions, and phenomena of human soul or mind; treatise on, or system of this."

(5) **Philosophy.**

"Seeking after wisdom or knowledge; esp. that which deals with ultimate reality, or with the most general causes and principles of things and ideas, and human perception and knowledge of them."

(6) **Academic.**

"2. abstract, unpractical, theoretical, cold, merely logical."

(7) **Logic.**

"Science of reasoning, proof, thinking or inference."

1. The intrusion and influence of The New Age Movement in educational circles.

Of recent years a great number of occultic philosophies and practices have inexorably been drawn closer together in their efforts to release man into his ultimate objective - deity without God.

It was Marilyn Ferguson who drew the threads together in her "The Aquarian Conspiracy - Personal and Social Transformation in the 1980's" (Paladin). A statement on the dust cover of this book sums up both the contents and the unmistakeable direction taken by the author:

"A great shuddering, irrevocable shift is overtaking us. It is not a new political, religious or economic system. It is a new mind - a turnabout in consciousness in critical numbers of individuals, a network strong enough to bring about radical change in our culture. Marilyn Ferguson describes how this leaderless but powerful underground network challenges the cynicism of our time to create a different class of society based on a vastly enlarged concept of human potential. Its role may well be one of leading us from the present world-wide turmoil to the next step in human evolution."

It is no wonder that academics and intellectuals are being drawn into a circle of support for this de facto relationship between philosophy and experiences of the 'spirit realm'. Outside of Christ, these are of course, demonic. Two of the movement's key words are 'holistic' and 'holism'. In the 1920's the brilliant South African, Jan Christian Smuts, tried to synthesize Darwin's evolutionary theory and Einstein's physics with his own concepts to formulate a theory of evolution of mind as well as matter. He wrote "Holism and Evolution".

Today's 'holistic' medical practitioners deal with aura, biofeedback, hypnotism, meditation, Gestalt therapy and similar practices. Some psychiatrists attend seminars on Eastern mysticism and investigate many occultic teachings and experiences in search of answers to mental illnesses which fail to respond to regular treatment. This descent to 'primitive religion' for 'spirit' answers to modern problems has nothing to do with Christianity but harnesses the power which witchdoctors believe pre-dates the Gospel.

Even the internationally known Dr. Kubler Ross now freely acknowledges her contact with spirit guides and her frequent excursions by astral travel.

The extent of the influence of the New Age Movement's holistic philosphy may be gauged from the following quotation from page 81 of 'Peace, Prosperity, And the Coming Holocaust' by Dave Hunt (Harvest House). The author quotes from a 1979 Education Network news letter of the Association of Humanistic Psychology suggesting that public school teachers incorporate the following activities in their daily routine:-

"The students will: do yoga each morning before class; interpret their astrological charts; send messages via E.S.P.; mind project; astral project; heal their own illnesses; speak with their 'Higher Selves' and receive information necessary for joyful living; lift energies from the power chakra to the heart chakra; practise skills necessary for colour healing; hold an image of themselves as being perfect; receive advice from their personal [spirit] guides; merge minds with others in the class to experience the collective consciousness of the group." ('chakras', are nerve centres).

Believers who pass through educational facilities in which humanistic and demonic influences thrive without gaining spiritual victory against them become bound by them. It is no wonder that humanistic intellectualism, rationalism, skepticism, worldly philosophy and pride, sometimes cause Christians to speak and act independently, resisting the authority of spiritual leadership to whom they are responsible under God.

Both writers are constantly asked to pray for graduates and undergraduates after they realise that a major reason for not being able to receive revelational truth and practical Spirit-given guidance is because faith has an uphill struggle in a mind dominated by intellectualism and rationalism. God never intended his people to become spiritual schizophrenics, struggling to reconcile their secular and spiritual identities.

The principles of the deliverance ministry are certainly more likely to. be challenged by academics and intellectuals than by those who have not had higher education. On almost every occasion when intellectuals have asked for counsel, they have agreed to a time of prayer for deliverance after the spiritual principles have been explained to them. This does not necessarily mean that they have understood or accepted all that has been explained, but they have been prepared to submit to God's Word in faith, and have set aside rationalism so that God's blessing will not be hindered. One of the motives for writing this book has been to expound God's truth to those with the ability to perceive it in the Spirit. We are not concerned about attempting to justify the deliverance ministry by anecdotes and case histories, but praise God for the many victories he has won amongst people who have had the highest academic qualifications and professional expertise. God is never overawed by human ability. Some of the spirits which need to be loosed in this area include:-

(1) heredity spirits of intellectualism, rationalism, humanism, atheism, argumentativeness, and intellectual haughtiness and idolatry.

(2) in some cases bondages to a research mentality, obsessional thinking, obsessive perfectionism, performance orientation, and workaholism.

(3) scepticism, doubt, unbelief, and other anti-Biblical or anti-Christ influences of university life.

If the breaking of cultural bondages does not mean disloyalty to one's country of birth or residence, neither does the breaking of educational bondages mean the downgrading of the knowledge gained by study and research. Only the non-objective humanistic influences, attitudes, and demonic deceptions are involved. Christian intellectuals particularly need the release of the Holy Spirit so that their God-given gifts can be used in humility, and not used in a manner which may threaten their fellow believers.

2. God alone is able to satisfy man's desire for wisdom and knowledge.

Through Calvary, born-again believers may be filled with wisdom, knowledge and understanding through the Holy Spirit. Both Old and New Testament examples show what God is willing to do for those who seek him in sincerity and truth.

(1) **Solomon** asked for and obtained divine wisdom. This made him " . . wiser than any other man" (1 Kings 4:31). He constantly emphasized that the reverential awe (fear) of God is the open door to the treasuries of true wisdom and knowledge (Proverbs 1:7). Throughout the Proverbs, righteous living and faithfulness are shown to be the evidence of such a fear.

(2) **David** acted more wisely and therefore had more success than the officers of King Saul, because the anointing of the Lord was upon him (1 Samuel 18:30).

(3) **Elihu** was a young man with an anointing of wisdom and understanding. He claimed that old age did not automatically mean a person was wise. He openly confessed that the source of his wisdom was the Almighty (Job 32:8, 18).

(4) **Joseph** (Genesis 41:3-40), and **Daniel** (Daniel 5:14), both drew their wisdom from God.

(5) **Paul** prayed that the Ephesian believers would be given the Spirit of wisdom and revelation so as to be able to understand and act upon the fulness of their power and authority (Ephesians 1:17-22; 2:6).

(6) **Stephen** confronted the Synagogue of Freedmen with revelational truth "but they could not stand up against his wisdom or the Spirit by which he spoke" (Acts 6:10).

(7) **James** says that believers may ask for, and receive, divine wisdom by faith, provided they don't doubt (James 1:5). He also says that there are two sources of wisdom. Those who receive what comes from 'below' carry the like-

ness of Satan. Those who receive true wisdom from above show the likeness of Jesus Christ (James 3:15-17).

Vessels whom God has designed to receive his revelational truth and divine wisdom need to be cleansed from all other influences before they can reach their divine potential.

CHAPTER SUMMARY.

1. Secular educational systems are by nature skeptical of religious ideologies and opposed to their teaching.

2. Members of the teaching profession who freely express their antagonism to Biblical teachings and Christian principles may cause attitudes of rationalism and unbelief to develop in believers.

3. Sin has deprived man of his source of true wisdom and knowledge, causing him to seek for humanistic alternatives which may well include demonic influences. The New Age Movement is gaining momentum in academic circles.

4. Christian university graduates may need to be freed from dominating spirits which undermine their faith and cause them to have intellectual and rationalistic attitudes towards God's servants, his word, and their fellow believers.

5. God's wisdom, knowledge, and revelational truth are freely available to those who turn to him instead of seeking spiritual wisdom from humanistic sources.

"Oh, how I love your law! I meditate on it all day long. **Your commands make me wiser than my enemies, for they are ever with me. I have more insight than all my teachers** for I meditate on your statutes. **I have more understanding than the elder** for I obey your precepts" (Psalm 119:97-100 emphasis added).

"Now then, why do you test God by putting on the necks of the disciples a yoke that neither we nor our fathers have been able to bear?" (Acts 15:10).

CHAPTER 14.

Religious spirits of tradition, prejudice and and pride

Surely no one in the New Testament was more of a right wing religious fundamentalist than the young Pharisee named Saul. As a graduate of the Gamaliel School of Judaistic Theology, he said that he had been (Philippians 3:5, 6):
  (i) circumcised on the eighth day, just as the law required.
  (ii) committed to the Pharisaic interpretation of the Torah and Talmud.
  (iii) zealous to a fault, even to the persecution of the Church.
  (iv) blameless in legalistic fulfilment of the law.

A midday encounter with Jesus Christ turned him around completely. His legalism was replaced by love; his persecution of the Church turned into selfless devotion to it; his pride of achievement gave way to humility in all that God had done through him; and his party factionalism was transformed into an intense desire to bring unity amongst the people of God.

If regeneration, and the filling and control of the Holy Spirit had such a profound effect upon Saul, should it not also have a similar effect upon our own lives? If this has not been so, we need to seek out the causes and have them removed.

Some common hindrances to growth and spiritual effectiveness within the Church will be listed in this and the two succeeding chapters.

1. A misunderstanding of the place and function of believers within the Body of Christ.

Prior to the Lausanne Congress on World Evangelization in 1974, the Rev. Howard A. Snyder circulated a paper entitled, 'The Church as God's agent in evangelism'. It included a diagrammatic presentation of The Church and its para-church structures. These included both denominational, inter-denominational and non-denominational structures together with various Church service organisations. Regrettably the spiritual unity and purpose of the Church at worship and service is often overlooked. A type of class system attitude sometimes separates church worship from service.

It is clear from Scripture that The Church (the Body of Christ) comprises only born again believers whether alive, or dead in Christ (Ephesians 2:19-22; 1 Thessalonians 4:16). Any man-made structure beyond that nucleus of believers can only be designated as a para-church grouping. This applies equally to church denominations which attract the loyalty and support of believers to specific patterns of theology, forms of worship and observance; and the societies dedicated to specialist forms of mission, evangelism, or service and support ministries.

To the onlooker, the Church appears to be totally fragmented into many separate and unrelated groups. From God's perspective, the man-made divisions are non-existent. The New Testament reveals there is only one Church founded by Jesus Christ (Matthew 16:18). The growing number of local congregations and missionary outreaches that occurred during the times of the Apostles were never taken to be a fragmentation of the unity of the Body of Christ. Each one was a local expression of the whole. Wherever believers worshipped Jesus as Lord, preached his Gospel, or ministered to people, the Body of Christ was functioning through them.

Unfortunately, the present day non-Biblical lines of distinction drawn between the people who worship and those who serve, almost amount to 'we' and 'they' divisions. It is often most noticeable when people in the practical outreaches of the Body seek personal and financial support from local churches and denominations.

No service for God should be viewed from a 'para-church' point of view. In other words, whatever may have resulted from the labours of any church, mission society, or group of people, should be regarded as a part of the whole, or a manifestation of God's church at work. God may have been pleased to bless and use one or more para-church bodies, but it will be the individual worker and not the human agency which will receive God's reward in eternity. If God is going to remove human divisions in a day to come, we surely need to avoid divisive classifications which ignore the worship and service functions of God's people, here and now.

Before moving to a diagrammatic concept of the Church in operation, it should be noted that all classifications of ministry and spiritual gifts given to the early church were given to the whole Body, not to individual churches or specialist groups. 1 Corinthians 12:4-6 illustrates this principle:

First, **The POSITIONS of authority** (v. 6).
God the Father defines the 'workings' or 'operations' he sovereignly requires for the function of his church (Gr. 'energema').

Second, **The PERSONNEL or appointees to those positions** (v. 5).
Jesus Christ appoints the personnel to carry out the responsibilities of office (Gr. 'diakonia' meaning 'ministries'). Paul states that this was a post-ascension ministry (Ephesians 4:11).

Third, **The POWER for the fulfilment of the office** (v. 4).
The Holy Spirit empowers the incumbents with the power of his grace (Gr. 'charismata').

In practical terms this means that every born again child of God who fulfils his or her divinely appointed position in the Body of Christ, does so as a fellow labourer with God (1 Corinthians 3:9). As such, pride of position, attitudes of superiority, authoritarianism, financial manipulation, lack of co-operation, doctrinal disputations, and personal acrimony ought never to exist between fellow labourers as they sometimes do. Man-made divisions encourage this.

The true function of the Church of God as the writer understands it, is that the essential nucleus of believers (fig. 1), is seen at worship and service through para-church groups (figures 2 and 3).

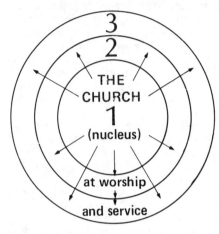

(1)   The Body of Christ, or the Church, comprising every born again child of God.

(2)   Groups of believers gathered together to worship and serve the Lord scattered over the earth. Some are denominationally identified. Some reject any identification other than being believers. Each group is part of the whole.

(3)   All forms of mission outreach or support groups, whether formed by individuals or groups of believers. They include: denominational, interdenominational, and undenominational missions; evangelism; literature; the printed and electronic media; transport; communications; raising of finance; administration; Bible translation and distribution; vehicle maintenance; mission building and vehicle repair; medical work, and hospitals; social work with all age groups; theological and Bible colleges; old age, handicapped, and specialized groups; and doubtless many more as breaking of bondages and dominions of ethnic background, culture, environment and education do not destroy true values as freedom from man-made definitions and their separatist influences will not interfere with God's ministry to others through us. In point of fact, freedom deepens our love, respect, and support for the spiritual work of others. It also gives us greater security in filling our own niche, without being jealous of what the Lord may be doing in the lives of those around us.

God has been sovereignly breaking many of these humanistic barriers ever since the 'charismatic' move commenced in the fifties. Speaking personally, I hardly recognize myself when comparing my spiritual past with the present. I used to be extremely right-wing theologically, prejudiced against spiritual innovation and certainly antagonistic towards all I imagined the fulness (baptism) of the Spirit to mean. I certainly blush when remembering how ignorant and voluble I was. But God in mercy demolished my self-confidence, and gave me an insatiable hunger after himself. He supplied my need through an in-depth experience that freed me from tradition, prejudice and pride and allowed the Spirit of God the control he desired. I certainly gained a new understanding of myself and of others in the Body relationship.

2. The encumbrances of traditions.

Traditions are both inherited and personally cultivated. They are usually held in the highest respect, and the older they are, the more they are established and venerated. A few of course are good. Many are bad. Jesus Christ emphasized the danger of depending on tradition. "You have let go of the commands of God and are holding on to the traditions of men" (Mark 7:8).

From experience, here are some of the more common traditions from which believers need to be set free:-

(1) Defensive denominationalism.

Nobody would want to deny a believer's right to choose a place of worship, but should it become a prison to separate believers from Body life fellowship, it is outside of God's plan. Bondages need to be broken.

(2) Doctrinal obsessions.

Few of us have not been accosted and harrassed by zealots with some doctrinal 'hobbyhorse'. Their chosen topic obviously dominates them, but we find them mostly time-consuming and tedious. Their topics are often irrelevant, or at least unimportant to the real issues of Christian living.

Others are self-appointed watchdogs of the truth and the faith. They berate all whom they feel are speaking contrary to some traditional doctrine, or whose behaviour they judge to be unworthy of the standards cherished by their church or group.

Imbalance is dangerous at any time, but doctrinal imbalance may lead to deception and domination by spirits of demonic doctrines (1 Timothy 4:1). Some danger areas are:

(a) eschatology and interpretations of prophecy.
(b) the place and ministry of women.
(c) the subject of divorce and remarriage.
(d) interpretations of difficult portions of Scripture.
(e) rigidity in matters of the manifestations of the Holy Spirit and healing.

For truth, harmony, and peace, all forms of bondage to excessive or imbalanced viewpoints on non-fundamental truths need to be broken. Deceptive spirits may also need to be released.

(3) Legalism, conservatism, and intolerance.

Prejudice, or fear of vulnerability often cause people to project an attitude of "my mind is made up; please don't confuse me with the facts".

Legalism and point-scoring were at their peak in the first century of Church growth. The Pharisees were experts at dotting i's and crossing t's. Hypocrisy was rampant. They had novel excuses for personal avoidance of rules, and fierce condemnation for others doing the same. Their tradition has survived well, and is active today.

On one occasion we were ministering deliverance to a number of people at one time. An elder of a conservative Christian local church was present. He was openly sceptical of what God was doing in others until religious spirits of legalism and conservatism were bound, broken, and released. The elder immediately began to manifest release, and after a short time the Lord had set him free. He afterwards testified publicly to the release he had received in these terms: "When spirits of legalism and conservatism were named then bound, broken, and ordered to leave, I felt as if there was a rat running around in my stomach. I felt it go up my chest, then on to my shoulder. I was so convinced that a rat was actually on my shoulder that I tore the top button from my shirt in trying to pull it off. I know now that I am free from those spirits. I never believed such a thing was possible." In a few minutes he had changed from being a deliverance skeptic to a believer.

On another occasion a woman who asked for spiritual help revealed that she had been seriously judged and disciplined by church leaders for indulging in sex as a teenager. During prayer, the spirits of legalism and judgment who had entered her years before spoke out strongly, saying, "No, no, we are not going to go!" While the demons were speaking the woman shook her head vigorously from side to side. The Lord soon freed her of these stubborn spirits, and others of hatred, bitterness, fear, accusation of evil, criticism, and opposition to the Holy Spirit which had also dominated her since the time of that judgment.

When the ministry of church leadership becomes a reign of legalism, harshness and judgment, something must be seriously wrong. The Lord freed the woman who had suffered for about twenty years, but one shudders to think of how many others may have suffered similarly.

(4) Reliance on church doctrines which cause false security.

Some of the common excuses used to keep personal workers from pressing the claims of the Gospel come from those who take spiritual refuge behind certain church doctrines. "I have been confirmed", or "I go to mass and receive absolution", or "I am loyal to the church in which I was christened".

Some of these strong doctrinal spirits can cause so much fear in new converts that they withdraw from the follow-up care of personal workers, and return to lifeless churches. Unless those strong spirits are broken, new believers may feel guilty of disloyalty to their previous church teachings.

A Roman Catholic refrigeration engineer who came to Christ through open air evangelism maintained contact with the writer for a brief period, then disappeared. Years afterwards God brought us together quite unexpectedly in another city. He had grown in Christ, married, and become more deeply involved with his church. He freely admitted breaking contact for fear of pressures being placed upon him to leave his family's church.

Another man who was born again through hearing the Gospel out of doors confessed nine months afterwards: "I didn't want to tell you and give a protestant the credit. I wanted it to go to my church".

(5) Bondage to specific forms of worship, and the rejection of others.

The Church of God is full of variety. Believers have: freedom of choice of formal or free worship, baptism by sprinkling or immersion, communion on a daily, weekly, monthly or quarterly basis, liturgical or simple forms of service, the choice of singing traditional hymns or Scriptures in song, silent worship or exuberance with hand clapping, the grandeur of pipe organ, a brass band, orchestra, or percussion and stringed instruments, small or large congregations; one man, pastoral team, or congregation-controlled services, and so on. The Holy Spirit has catered for every spiritual taste. He does not sanction spiritual pride which leads to a spirit of intolerance of others who make choices different from ours. Anything which hinders fellowship, freedom and liberty amongst members of Christ's Body is from the enemy; and many of God's people need release from his works in this area.

(6) Personal prejudices.

(a) Attitudes to Bible translations can become divisive. Some people do not see humour in the old saying which I suspect is because they believe it to be true: 'If the Authorised Version was good enough for the Apostle Paul, it is good enough for me'.

One is for this translation, another for that. Even the number of times the word 'blood' occurs will cause some people to accept or reject a translation.

Prejudice causes division, and division is from the evil one. Recognize and deal with the source, and freedom will result.

An old friend and associate telephoned me interstate recently to apologize for the translation prejudice he had shown in the past, and for any offence which he may have given. God had released him into new freedom in truth and in relationships with fellow believers. I had not allowed our fellowship to be broken on the issue, but I surely appreciated his humility and release.

(b) If there was anything that brought God's judgment upon his people in the Old Testament, it was idolatry. Since then God has not changed, and neither has the extent of idolatry amongst God's people. It has simply changed form. There is idolatry to consecrated buildings and sacred sites; idolatry to images, icons, art forms, music, ceremonies, robes, and regalia; idolatry of the dead, church-created saints, relics, and those in high religious orders. All spirits of idolatry are offensive to God. There must be repentance, confession, and deliverance from each controlling spirit. Jesus Christ alone must be the centre of the believer's worship. A friend used to keep this statement in a prominent place: "Idolatry is trusting people, possessions, or positions to do for me what ONLY GOD CAN DO".

A member of the hippy culture who had freely indulged in marijuana smoking and Eastern mysticism came to know Jesus Christ as his Saviour. Shortly afterwards he found a number of books written by Catholic mystics between the twelfth and seventeenth centuries. Having been raised and educated a Catholic he saturated himself in the old books, and became dominated by the heavy religious philosophies he was reading.

When this man came for prayer it was obvious he was controlled more by these ancient religious mystics than by Jesus Christ. In addition to being bound by spirits of religious idolatry, he had spirits of heaviness and seriousness. He seldom smiled. The Lord freed him, and a new release of amiability and joy immediately became evident.

Jeremiah's word still stands. "This is what the LORD says: 'Cursed is the one who trusts in man, who depends on flesh for his strength and whose heart turns away from the LORD. He will be like bush in the wastelands; he will not see prosperity when it comes. He will dwell in the parched places of the desert, in a salt land where no-one lives' " (Jeremiah 17:5, 6).

3. Some specific sources of deception.

Satan knows Biblical theology very well. He cleverly covers his false doctrines with verses of Scripture so as to deceive the unconverted and non-Spirit-filled believers. It is even worse for people whose parents or grandparents have been involved in false cults, spurious religious sects, or Eastern religions. They will be dominated by those spirits to the third and fourth generation, and will have the greatest difficulty in accepting truth. They will probably show unbelief, confusion, hardness, resistance to truth, and argumentativeness.

In the writers' ministry, believers have been freed from demonic spirits originating from:

(1) **The Watch Tower Bible and Tract Society**, also known as Jehovah's Witnesses, or Russellism.

(2) **Christian Science** and the writings of Mary Baker Eddy. It is not generally known that before Mrs. Eddy founded her false religion she was treated for severe pain by a process of Mesmerism, an early form of hypnotism. After that,

she wrote 'Science And Health', in which error blends with confusion. In her later years, the crippling pain returned, and hypnosis was no longer of any help. She is reported to have died under the influence of morphia. The use of pain-killing drugs effectively cancels everything Mrs. Eddy has said and written about the illusion of pain during her lifetime. The deceptive spirit which she received through Mesmerism continues its work today through her writings.

Believers with a Christian Science background have been released from spirits of unreality, bondage to will-power overriding feelings, unbelief, doubt and scepticism.

(3) The Church of Jesus Christ of the Latter Day Saints (The Mormons).

Joseph Smith introduced the practices of Freemasonry into the church in 1842, 'by divine revelation'. About six weeks previously, he and a thousand or more Mormons had been very unceremoniously expelled from Masonic membership. The reason? Joseph Smith had given himself an unauthorised promotion, moving from the bottom to the top of the Masonic hierarchical ladder overnight. Mormon secret temple ceremonies are loaded with what are clearly Masonic practices. Born again Mormons and their descendants need to be freed from these deceptive spirits. We have certainly seen the Lord victoriously remove them.

(4) Herbert W. Armstrong and his Radio Church of God.

The late Herbert W. Armstrong was dubbed 'Mr. Confusion' on the North American continent. The spirits of confusion, deception, error, false doctrine and unbelief, as well as the controlling spirit of the cult itself need to be ejected from ex-members, adherents and descendants.

(5) The Christadelphians.

Those who have had any involvement with this sect which rejects the Trinity and believes their future paradise is upon this earth, need special release. They have spirits of deception, legalism, hardness and harshness, guilt and unbelief, as well as being unable to express their emotions.

(6) Cults, philosophies and religions with direct links with the occult.

(a) Theosophy.

(b) The Rosicrucian Fellowship (AMORC).

(c) Scientology, whose definition of God is 'knowing that you know that you know'.

(d) Spiritistic churches. Some even claim to be evangelical, and their ministers prophesy over flowers brought by members of the congregation. A woman, involved as a child with her parents was recently freed from a strong psychic spirit which caused her to have fear, to sense presences, hear voices and experience feelings of de javu. She had been a Christian for many years.

(e) The Church of the New Jerusalem (Swedenborgism).

(f) The Family of Love, formerly the Children of God.

(g) Egyptology, and pyramid mysticism.

(7) Eastern religions.

(a) Islam. Some common spirits are anti-Christ, hatred, violence, lying and deceit, fatalism, superstition, pride, inferiority of women, religious legalism, etc.

(b) The Bahai faith.

(c) Hinduism. This demonic form of worship is like an octopus. Its tentacles reach into: the Hari Krishna movement, Ananda Marga, Divine Light Mission (Maharaji Ji) and the profusion of swamis, gurus, and holy men offering peace and 'divine life' to their followers. The recently disbanded Ragneeshis is an example. Bagwan Shri Ragneesh collected followers by the thousands, and dollars by the millions.

(8) Controlling leadership.

Sadly, there are some Christian communities and movements where strong leading personalities dominate the lives of members even to the control of decision making. When those who have been hurt under such pressures summon sufficient courage to leave, they need special ministries of release and healing to be able to fellowship freely with others. We have seen the Lord release some from spirits of domination, rejection, legalism, guilt, self-accusation, condemnation, hurts, and unworthiness. Some have also needed release from unforgiveness, resentment, and bitterness. Sadly, a few have been subjected to a form of sexual slavery, and need deep releases from lust, fornication, adultery, shame, guilt and worthlessness.

Two young ladies come immediately to mind. They had both been crushed through their experiences in separate groups. One had been subjected to sexual relationships against her will, and her sense of defilement made her withdraw from people as much as possible. Both these lovely young ladies longed for release from the dominating influences of their groups, and to have inner cleansing, self-respect, the ability to make right choices, and release in the Holy Spirit. The Lord met their desires in every way.

Spiritual freedom is the blood-bought right of every believer. The responsibility to ensure that believers are set free rests squarely upon the shoulders of every pastor and spiritual leader.

CHAPTER SUMMARY.

1. Religious spirits of tradition, prejudice, and pride may take control because of wrong teaching, doctrinal obsession, strong denominational beliefs, deception, imbalance, prejudice and idolatry.
2. Cults, eastern religions, and mysticism cause people to be bound and dominated by spirits of religious deception.

"The evil deeds of a wicked man ensnare him, the cords of his sin hold him fast. He will die for lack of discipline, led astray by his own great folly" (Proverbs 5:22,23).

CHAPTER 15.

Deliberate sin -
baited with temptation a Satanic trap

To commit sin is to defy God. It is offensive to God's holy nature and to his will for his people. When a Christian yields to temptation, the evil one's trap snaps shut, and he is delighted. Sin hands Satan the right to apply a bondage, to afflict, or control some part of a believers's life.

"Don't you know that when you offer yourselves to someone to obey him as slaves, you are slaves to the one whom you obey, - whether slaves to sin which leads to death, or to obedience which leads to righteousness?" (Romans 6:16).

Through Calvary, Christians have been totally freed from slavery to sin, but that liberty must be maintained by obedience. Wilful sin brings a believer back into slavery again and limits his effectiveness and witness for Jesus Christ. Repentance will bring forgiveness and cleansing, and provide a legal basis for release from Satan's grip. The Scriptures also solemnly warn us that continued rebellion and open rejection of Jesus Christ is a repudiation of salvation and the blood of Calvary. If persisted in, it may lead to the most dire judgment (Hebrews 10:26-29).

There are very many defeated Christians who are slaves to soulish and physical bondages, and to driving forces which have come to them because of wrong choices. The following are some of the open doors through which Satan walks to rob believers of freedom and bring them under his domination. They have all been encountered many times during counselling.

1. **Rebellion, defiance, and disobedience.**

"For rebellion is like the sin of divination, and arrogance like the evil of idolatry" (1Samuel 15:22, 23).

The fall of Lucifer, the fall of our first parents, and the fall of all believers, follow this pattern. Jesus said that obedience to his commandments is a means of expressing our love to him (John 14:23). It also turns out to be our greatest means of protection from the evil one (1 John 5:18). When sinful attitudes and habits cannot be broken by repentance, cleansing, faith and will-power, it is because there is a strong spiritual force blocking freedom. Only deliverance can bring that release.

A Christian young lady who had been deeply rejected in childhood was restored to the Lord after being involved in a number of sinful pleasures. She was set free from dominating spirits through the prayers of a number of Christians over a period of time. She later backslid, and deliberately went back to the sins from which she had been released. In her backslidden state she attended my lectures. She could not look me directly in the eye, and at times left the group to be physically sick. She later said that she had felt totally confused, but was still able to identify seven major areas in which she was under Satanic domination.

She requested a deliverance session which was lengthy; God not only set her free but remade her life. She told us that she knew she had literally fulfilled Matthew 12:43-45. When she had been freed in the first instance, she had not allowed God to replenish her spiritual house and so Satan worked to re-occupy it; the result; seven other spirits entered. Those spirits certainly put up the greatest resistance during our prayer time and caused her a lot of physical pain before the Lord set her free. The spirits she named were:-

(1)   a spirit which drove her to seek pleasure in both sex and gluttony.
(2)   self-idolatry, and hedonistic pleasures.
(3)   divination and mind control.
(4)   unbelief and mockery.
(5)   rejection and rebellion in greater strength than previously.
(6)   anger, rage, and self-hatred.
(7)   temptation to commit suicide. Death always appeared to be attractive to her.

When she was freed, cleansed and her spiritual 'house' refurnished by the Spirit of God, her peace, joy, and love to others was most evident to those who knew her.

Christians who knowingly and wilfully sin expose themselves to dangers.

2. Scepticism, doubt, and unbelief.

Satan is highly successful in using this trio to hinder or cut off the believer's lifeline of faith in Jesus Christ, his Word, and the power of his Spirit. Satan well knows that without living faith, consciousness of the 'new birth' will quickly fade into a mere memory. He aims to choke off Christian fellowship, Bible reading and prayers, and to re-activate logic and rationalism which quickly undermine the authority of God's word, and the power of his Spirit.

Without exception, one hundred per cent of those who come for deliverance suffer from unbelief to some degree. Demons will frequently cause a counsellee to burst out in the middle of prayer, "It's no use, nothing is going to happen", or "I don't feel anything at all". These spirits also cause discouragement and depression. When spirits of scepticism, doubt, and unbelief are evicted, the process of rebuilding faith commences. It often begins with the counsellee's confession, "I choose to believe."

3. The family of spirits hiding behind unforgiveness.

Jesus Christ insisted that forgiveness is not a once for all experience, but a never-ending process (Matthew 18:22).

The spirit of unforgiveness is quick to take advantage of a grudge. It usually opens the door to the rest of its evil family. The number of spirits which enter and dominate the person who stubbornly refuses to forgive will depend on the circumstances which caused it. But they include resentment, bitterness, hatred, anger, revenge, violence, and murder. Some people who have sought ministry have had every one of these spirits.

The subtlety of unforgiveness is that when it grows to the point of bitterness, the person gripped by it just cannot forgive, even if they desperately want to. That demonic power often vents itself angrily as it is cast out, but out it must go. There is a clear warning of the dangers of this problem:

"See to it that no-one misses the grace of God and that no bitter root grows up to cause trouble and defile many" (Hebrews 12:15).

The 'Sydney Morning Herald' of the 16th May, 1986, carried a story about a twenty-seven year old man who stabbed his uncle to death. He claimed his uncle had ruined his life by raping him at the age of seven years, and that when his uncle made a homosexual proposition to him he 'just went berserk after years of breakdowns and traumatic experiences which followed the rape experience'. Most churches have hurt members who harbour unforgiveness, resentment, and bitterness. They often resist normal counselling methods. Some of the worst results are physical problems, particularly arthritis, ulcers, sleeplessness, and phobias. Deliverance needs to be received before hurt people can be expected to forgive.

4. Playing with fire. Self-indulgences which become addictions.

When choice is replaced with compulsion, a person is an addict. Addicts are normally the last to realize and admit they have a problem. Believers are not exempt from the hold that seven major addictive spirits may exert over them. Addiction sometimes commences through an intense desire to escape from an impossible situation, or through loneliness, disappointment, grief, or anger. It can even come from a desire to punish one's self or a loved one for a real or imaginary wrong. Some are just weak-willed in handling temptation and find themselves trapped with no way of escape. Once trapped, some try will-power, or ask for help from every available source. Sadly, those who don't find it often lapse into the hopelessness and despair of defeatism.

Habits may be broken in various ways but addictions have demonic power. The seven major additions are:

(1) Alcohol.

Social drinking may meet personal and social needs of unbelievers, but it is not God's way. Paul's advice is "Do not get drunk on wine which leads to debauchery. Instead be filled with the Spirit" (Ephesians 5:18).

The first drink may be the first step on a downward path strewn with defeat, lies, cover-up, and financial ruin leading to addiction. Addicts need deliverance from dominating spirits and the drink habit pattern needs to be broken.

(2) Drugs.

It is quite possible for a person to become addicted to prescription drugs without the prescribing doctor or themselves being aware of the process. Christians are therefore not exempt from becoming unintentionally drug dependent.

A Bible College student confessed to me that his relatives once laced his drink with L.S.D. as a joke because he was a Christian. He said that from that time onwards he had suffered from periods of mental disorientation.

No believer should deliberately dabble in any form of drug experimentation. The abundant life Jesus gives has the power to resolve the problems which drive people to drugs. Of all known methods of release or control, deliverance from the dominating spirits is surely the quickest, and most permanent.

(3) Nicotine.

In some countries smoking is an acceptable practice for Christians. However I have never heard of anyone smoking in God's house as an act of worship!

The habit is expensive, harmful to health, and the cause of lung cancer, mostly addictive, offensive to non-smokers, and frequently an introduction to drinking and other problems. Deliverance is effective and permanent, providing the addict genuinely repents of self-indulgence and is willing to glorify Jesus Christ in all desires and habits.

(4)   Gluttony.

This self-centred habit may commence through boredom, disappointment, rejection, or hurts real or imaginary. The habit of over-eating is most difficult to break despite a profusion of diet plans, health foods, and exercise programmes. Many people have lost weight through deliverance from dominating spirits. Some have maintained their weight loss, while others have gradually gained weight again when self-pity undermines their self-discipline.

The writers have found one or two cases of demonic gluttony affecting thin people. The sufferers eat abnormally at meal times and between meals without showing any increase in weight. They give off an unusual body odour which clings to their clothes.

It has also been found that anorexia nervosa and bulimia are both demonic afflictions. Numbers of women suffering from these problems have been released by Jesus Christ, and returned to normal eating habits and healthy living.

(5)   Gambling.

While this is normally a hereditary driving force, the problem may be triggered by a desperate financial need, sudden temptation, a covetous desire to get big returns for a small outlay, or the negative influence of friends or associates. Addiction comes easily, and there is usually a trail of deception, cover-up, broken promises, ruined marriages, loss of jobs, and sometimes criminal charges and suicide.

One man with whom we prayed had been to all the major international gambling dens, and estimated that he had lost over one million dollars through his addiction. After he became a Christian, not only was he freed from his gambling spirit, but from many other associated spirits which had dominated him through his self-indulgent lifestyle.

(6)   Excessive bodily exercise.

Christians are certainly subject to domination by this spirit. Because it is associated with physical fitness and is not linked to anything which compromises Christian living standards, believers are unaware of the potential danger of addiction.

Whenever people feel under compulsion to don track suits and run even late at night, or in atrocious weather conditions, relentlessly pushing themselves beyond their normal endurance levels, they are hooked. What will surprise many is that there is a compulsive spirit of physical exercise.

A young lady used to compulsively run for about 15-18 kilometres over hills, each day. She did not realize she had spirits of addiction until she came for a deliverance session. Suddenly she started stamping on the floor with her feet, banging her knees with her clenched fists, and shouting at the top of her voice, "I won't go, no I won't go." The Lord set her totally free, and the next day she enjoyed a quiet two kilometre jog on flat ground without any desire to continue running.

(7)   Compulsive money spending.

Husbands sometimes laughingly claim that their wives are compulsive spenders! But those men are either trying to be humourous, are mean, or have no idea in the world just how much it costs to keep an average family going.

A dominating spirit of compulsive spending is usually the extension of another addiction such as gluttony. The demonic link between all addictions is evident; when one addiction is overcome, another normally replaces it if all the addictive roots have not been removed. A hypnotist was heralding his 'great discovery' of this principle recently in a local newspaper, blissfully unaware that the Spirit of God had revealed it long ago. Addicts also need to be freed from spirits of false comfort, habit, and compulsiveness. In dealing with addictions to alcohol, cigarettes, or food, spirits of lust of the eyes, taste, and smell also need to be evicted.

5. Sexual lust and the fulfillment of its desires.

When Christians do not fear God, they will no longer fear to sin. When lust is allowed to dominate a Christian's mind, unclean, immoral, and degrading acts soon follow. They turn God's day of grace into their disgrace.

There are very few people who come for help who have not had some defiling sexual experience which troubles, influences, or controls them. Some of these areas are:-

(1) Masturbation by choice, or non-hereditary influence.

The habit of self-stimulation usually begins early in life. It may be triggered by self-examination, the example or influence of others, a desire for self-comfort, or it may follow sexual rape or molestation.

Once it establishes itself as an irresistable habit, masturbation may continue throughout adulthood. Both sexes may become bound and dominated by this lustful spirit. The fall-out is guilt, low self-esteem, spiritual barrenness, and sometimes marriage breakdown. Some Christian doctors, psychologists, psychiatrists, pastors and counsellors advocate the practice. But masturbation is lustful, and is usually associated with lewd fantasies; it is egocentric, often to the point of idolatry to sexual organs; it is in every way contrary to Biblical standards of purity.

We have seen God set many people free from this dominating spirit of self-stimulation and regain their self-image once cleansed from guilt. This has made marriage a realizable objective for those whose self-condemnation had made them introvertive and wary of heterosexual relationships.

Case histories illustrating the release God gives will not be given for obvious reasons, but we have witnessed the Lord free people who have masturbated excessively from early childhood into adulthood.

(2) Sexual problems caused by molestation, incest, or rape.

These experiences are usually totally devastating and cause both immediate and long term problems. The sense of defilement the victims suffer will often make them withdraw and become emotionally cold. Long-term results may include sexual frigidity in marriage. Others become lustful, masturbate, and indulge in promiscuity as they have convinced themselves that no decent person would be attracted to them. Deliverance, cleansing, and renewal are essential for them to regain self-respect, and a healthy attitude to sex and marriage.

(3) Promiscuity by choice.

Five sexual acts which open the life to domination by unclean spirits are:-

(a) **Fornication** or sexual intercourse between unmarried persons.

(b) **Adultery** or sexual intercourse by either party of a marriage with a married or unmarried person other than the marriage partner.

(c) **Technical fornication or adultery** which is the stimulation of sexual organs as an alternative to the carrying out of the full act.

(d) **Oral sex** or the oral stimulation of sexual organs as a lustful act. It is also used as an alternative to the normal sexual act in order to avoid pregnancy and the guilt of fornication or adultery.

(e) **Masochistic sexual practices** introduce violence and the infliction of pain for sexual pleasure. These dishonour the body, pervert the nature of relationships, and offend God.

(4) **Fantasy lust.**

Lustful mental fantasies unless checked, will dominate the mind. At least they cause a sense of defilement. At the most they can precipitate all manner of immoral activities. Jesus Christ warned that sin in the mind is as culpable as the act itself (Matthew 5:28). This is one reason why pornography in any form must be avoided. The believer's mind is the schoolroom of the Spirit, and every seed of defilement should be kept out.

(5) **Homosexuality.**

The perversion of sexual relationships has previously been shown to be the fruit of sin and the deliberate rejection of God and his standards.

Homosexual acts in the Old Testament were punished by death. The Bible provides no court of appeal against the sentence on the grounds of hormonal imbalance, or childhood female domination. The question of minority rights for homosexuals never became an issue under the Law because offenders were punished by death. "If a man lies with a man as one lies with a woman, both of them have done what is detestable. They must be put to death; their blood will be on their own heads" (Leviticus 20:13).

The New Testament is just as clear. No practising homosexual will inherit the kingdom of God.

"Do you not know that the wicked will not inherit the kingdom of God? Do not be deceived: Neither the sexually immoral nor idolators nor adulterers nor male prostitutes nor homosexual offenders . . will inherit the kingdom of God" (1 Corinthians 6:9, 10).

How obnoxious to God must be the actions of those homosexuals who claim to be evangelicals, 'worshipping' in their own churches in order to continue their sin under the 'blessing' of false shepherds. Rather than being denied rights, homosexuals refuse to use their Biblical rights to repent and receive cleansing and freedom. Continual sin makes repentance so difficult to achieve.

But as Paul said, some of the Corinthian homosexual offenders had been washed, sanctified in the name of Jesus Christ and by his Spirit (1 Corinthians 6:11). This means that no homosexual or lesbian is without hope of release.

The writers have had the joy of seeing lesbians and homosexuals totally released from their dominant spirits, and enter into fulfilling marriage relationships. Male, female, and bi-sexual prostitutes have also been released and renewed, to the glory of God.

● A young male prostitute who frequented toilets in search of partners came for deliverance. The homosexual spirits resisted the power and authority of the name of Jesus so vigorously that we required extra male strength to restrain him. The Lord totally released him. He later married and rejoiced in fatherhood.

● A boy who was sexually interfered with at the age of two grew up having sexual relationships with male relatives, friends, and older men. At eleven years of age he was seduced by a man who introduced him to pornographic films. Over the next two years he acted in eleven pornographic films, being involved in sexual intimacy with other boys and adult males. He later worked for the same man in a homosexual club as a teenage prostitute available to professional and business men. He was also deeply addicted to horror movies, and from the age of four had had active demonic experiences which included sexual stimulation.

At the age of nineteen years, this young man was amongst a group of people receiving deliverance. He had been born again twelve months, but was filled with fear and mental torment although he had not been involved in homosexual acts during that time. During prayer for release, his body was constantly twisted into unnatural shapes and he perspired profusely from physical pain. In two further times of prayer, a host of demons contested his release, but finally his whole body and soul was filled with peace. His face lit up with the joy of the Lord, and with his mental torment gone, he was able to sleep peacefully at night.

It has also been our joy to see the Lord free lesbians and give them fulfilment in marriage as wives and mothers.

(6) The defilement of anal sex in heterosexual relationships.

This unnatural act is sometimes used by agreement to avoid pregnancy. It may also be forced by one party, sometimes as an outlet for homosexual fantasy. Some women have felt so degraded by this that they have the greatest difficulty talking about it in counselling sessions. They have needed deliverance from spirits of homosexuality, unnatural lust, defilement, degradation, perversion, guilt, shame, and low self-image. Sometimes spirits of bitterness and hatred towards the person responsible have also needed to be removed.

(7) Bestiality.

This act was punished in the Old Testament by death.

"Anyone who has sexual relations with an animal must be put to death" (Exodus 22:19).

"If a woman approaches an animal to have sexual relationships with it, kill the woman and the animal. They must be put to death, their blood will be on their own heads" (Leviticus 20:16).

The frequency with which bestial fantasy or bestial acts are confessed by believers of both sexes is surprisingly high. While the acts of bestiality were mostly committed before regeneration, fantasy and guilt continue afterwards. Sons of farming fathers who have showed them little affection often succumb to this temptation.

● A man who was a student in a Bible college came to see the writer because of his low self-image, withdrawal, and an inability to communicate or form friendships. One night after lectures, he showed extreme agitation, and urgently asked to see me privately. He then blurted out a confession of bestiality, and shared his guilt for the first time. He was deeply repentant. That night the Lord released him from his unclean demonic spirits, and his personality just seemed to burst out of its forty year old prison. From that time onwards he communicated, loved people, sang continuously, and visibly showed a total change of lifestyle.

(8) Pornography.

The Greek word 'pornographos' comes from 'porne' (prostitute), and 'grapho' (write). The trap is obvious. In the widest sense of the word, photographs, magazines and books, explicit films, videos, triple X-rated sex movies, and live sex shows, are included. They contribute greatly to sexual aggressiveness in communities which permit them. This is reflected in the growing statistics of rape and sex-related crimes. Sexually defiling and pornographic materials brought into the family home can break marriages and introduce children to masturbation and sexual experimentation. Mental pictures remain etched on the mind indefinitely, and resist attempts to dislodge them. Many adults have confessed with shame that they are constantly battling with persistent memories which began in childhood or teenage years. But praise God for the completeness of his cleansing and renewal.

Women who have allowed themselves to be photographed or filmed in the nude for pornographic materials, magazine centrefolds, or X-rated movies, become dominated by many unclean spirits and need deep deliverance. The writers have had the joy of seeing some of them cleansed and renewed. It is not a little awesome to witness what God will do for his children when they repent, and seek him with all their hearts.

(9) Abortions.

Abortion is the forcible removal of a foetus from the womb. The termination of the potential or actual life of a living person can only be termed murder. Women who have had abortions need to be released from spirits of murder, death in the womb, and guilt. If an abortion was forced by a husband or sex-partner, spirits of bitterness and hatred may also need eviction.

Sadly, some women come to us who have undergone abortions before marriage and are unable to bear children in marriage. They are filled with grief and remorse, but we have found that the Lord is able to lift even these burdens.

(10) Sexual activity by demons with women or men.

The matter of the Nephilim and the women of Noah's day has already been mentioned. Throughout the church and secular history there are frequent references to sexual activities known as 'incubacy' and 'succubacy'. An incubus is a male demonic sexual spirit which stimulates and brings women to orgasm. Succubus is the female counterpart acting with men. Over the past several years, some men and many women have received deliverance from sexual stimulation and climax caused by demons.

● A young lady was lying in bed in a caravan, when she heard a voice in her ear asking permission to have sex with her. No-one was with her at the time. She readily agreed, then felt the weight of a body, was stimulated, and came to orgasm without seeing anyone. From then onwards, she was subject to periodic internal stimulation.

● A young man who had been deeply into all forms of sexual perversion and witchcraft, ended up owning two massage parlours. He confessed to having had naked female demons masturbate him frequently at night. He said, "I used to think it was in my mind, until I woke up and found they were really there."

From counselling experience we have learned that unaccountable sexual stimulation which leads to a sexual climax at any hour of the day or night, is demonic. On a number of occasions while these unclean spirits were being cast out of women, they were sexually stimulated and have been repulsed by it.

Pastors and male counsellors who minister to the opposite sex with this problem would be well advised to have a woman or other colleagues present. The evil one will not hesitate to tempt, or cause lying accusations to be made against, the servant of the Lord. An anointed husband-wife team is ideal in such cases.

(11) Involvement in occultism and witchcraft.

This subject is too spiritually devastating to be confined to a paragraph. It will be more fully discussed in the next chapter.

THE SPIRITUAL BATTLE FOR THE MIND.

How true is the maxim: 'Sow a thought and reap an act. Sow an act and reap a habit. Sow a habit, and reap a destiny'.

Sin is conceived in the thought-life when temptation is welcomed by desire. In the list of deliberate sins we have looked at, every one began by a thought, except where a person has been forced to submit to an indecency beyond their ability to resist.

The Scriptures clearly show the two influences which have power to control the mind.

1. God and his purpose for the believer's mind.

"Let this mind be in you, which was also in Christ Jesus" (Philippians 2:5 KJV).

"Let this same attitude and purpose and [humble] mind be in you which was in Christ Jesus . . " (Philippians 2:5 Amp. Bible).

"Do not conform any longer to the pattern of this world, but be transformed by the renewing of your mind" (Romans 12:2).

"But we have the mind of Christ" (1 Corinthians 2:16).

2. Satan and his purpose for the human mind.

Paul speaks to the Corinthian believers about the spiritual weapons for overcoming what Satan is able to do in the mind.

The wording of the King James Version is crystal clear:- "Casting down imaginations, and **every high thing that exalteth itself against the knowledge of God,** and bringing into captivity every thought to the obedience of Christ" (2 Corinthians 10:5, emphasis added).

If spiritual power from God is needed to cast down and capture the anti-God thought life, it can only be because the source and power of it is demonic.

When Christians manifest the same attitudes and actions as the world does, the Holy Spirit is grieved, and demonic powers have energised those areas of soul and body to which they have gained access.

God's directive will for his children is that they keep their minds preserved for his glory. "Finally, brothers, whatever is true, whatever is noble, whatever is right, whatever is pure, whatever is lovely, whatever is admirable - if anything is excellent or praiseworthy - **think about such things**" (Philippians 4:8, emphasis added).

Christians, don't be mental schizophrenics! It is certainly preferable to keep your thought life pure and submissive to God than to have to seek deliverance from demonic domination and defilement. The past can never be re-made.

CHAPTER SUMMARY.

1. Sin is not only an affront to God, it is an open invitation to the evil one to move in, make himself at home, and control the life.

2. The 'pleasures of sin' which demons (unclean spirits) are unable to enjoy because they do not have human bodies, they are able to enjoy when they dominate human activities and cause their victims to defile themselves and dishonour God.

3. The mind is the battleground where victories are won and lost. The Christian has every assurance of victory.

ADDENDUM. Trying to overcome the domination of evil spirits without the power of the Spirit of God is as effective as trying to catch a seven metre shark with a bent pin on a pyjama cord.

"Many of those who believed now came and openly confessed their evil deeds. A number who had practised sorcery brought their scrolls together and burned them publicly . . . In this way the word of the Lord spread widely, and grew in power" (Acts 19:18-20).

CHAPTER 16.

Partnership with the devil through occultism and witchcraft

The words 'occultism' and 'witchcraft' are to demonology what a canopy is to people - a shelter for many separate identities. Some of the Biblical terms which are still most relevant today are defined by the Concise Oxford Dictionary as follows:

(1) **Occult.** "Kept secret, esoteric, recondite, mysterious beyond the range of ordinary knowledge; involving the supernatural, mystical, magical, whence occultism, occultist."

(2) **Witchcraft.** "Sorcery, use of magic."

(3) **Magic.** The "supposed art of influencing courses of events by occult control of nature or of spirits". Egypt was full of magicians in the days of Moses.

(4) **Sorcery.** "Use of magic arts, wizardry, enchanting."

(5) **Astrology.** "Art of judging reputed occult influence of stars, planets, etc. on human affairs."

(6) **Divination.** "Divining, insight into or discovery of the unknown future by supernatural means."

(7) **Necromancy.** "Art of predicting by means of communicating with the dead; magic, enchantment. (From the Latin 'nigramantia' - niger, nigri, meaning black)."

(8) **Idolatry.** "Worshipping idols (images or deities used as objects of worship; false gods)."

(9) **Spiritism (spiritualism).** "Belief that departed spirits communicate with and show themselves to men, especially through mediums, or at seances by means of spirit rapping, handwriting, etc."

(10) **Seance.** "Meeting for exhibition or investigation of spiritualistic phenomena."

God's attitude to these, and all similar activities is unequivocal: "Do not practise divination or sorcery" (Leviticus 19:26).

"Do not turn to mediums or seek out spiritists, for you will be defiled by them. I am the LORD your God" (Leviticus 19:31).

"I will set my face against the person who turns to mediums and spiritists to prostitute himself by following them, and I will cut him off from his people" (Leviticus 20:6).

"Let no-one be found among you who sacrifices his son or daughter in the fire, who practises divination or sorcery, interprets omens, engages in witchcraft, or casts spells, or who is a medium or spiritist or who consults the dead. Anyone who does these things is detestable to the LORD .. " (Deuteronomy 18:10-112).

"If a man or a woman .. is found doing evil in the eyes of the LORD your God in violation of his covenant, and contrary to my command has worshipped other gods, bowing down to them, or to the sun or moon or the stars of the sky .. if it is true and has been proved that this detestable thing has been done in Israel, take the man or woman who has done this evil deed to your city gate and stone that person to death" (Deuteronomy 17:2-5).

"Therefore my dear friends flee idolatry .. the sacrifices of pagans are offered to demons not to God and I do not want you to be participants with demons. You cannot drink the cup of the Lord and the cup of demons too; you cannot have a part in both the Lord's table and the table of demons" (1 Corinthians 10:14, 20, 21).

Satan has never taken a holiday since the events of Genesis chapter three. He still works in disguise, but his insidious work comes to the surface during deliverance sessions. Most believers who seek help have become his slaves before they came to Christ, but some have become trapped as Christians. The problem with each of them was that the evil one maintained his bondages and dominations over them despite their faith in Jesus Christ. Without special freedom from Satanic oppression, Christians are unable to glorify Jesus Christ as Lord.

1. Examples of the continuing Satanic influence in Christians after they have been born again.

● A young man who had just come to Christ asked that all demonic power over him should be broken. He had used voodoo practices on a policeman against whom he held a grudge by sticking pins into a doll and pronouncing curses on him. And the policeman had in fact become sick. During prayer the writer was unaware that this young man was carrying a flick knife. He confessed it afterwards when he realized God was changing him into a new person.

● An Irishman who had dabbled in occultism and witchcraft came to know Christ as Saviour. He witnessed about Jesus to a wizard and was immediately challenged about the powerlessness of the Gospel. To prove his point, the wizard said he could cause lightning to flash whenever he wanted to. Not only did he do so by clapping his hands, but he foretold an accident which later happened to the Irish Christian. Because this man continually suffered health problems he came to the writer asking for deliverance from any demonic curse or oppression. The Lord set him free.

● A national of Belize (formerly British Honduras), was released from cultural bondages and personal problems. He afterwards testified to the power of voodoo. He had personally seen a mango on a tree develop a human face and weep tears. He had also seen frogs move around under the skins of voodoo victims. He said that if the skin was cut, the frogs would jump out, continue jumping around on the ground for a short time, then die.

● Some believers have experienced the activities of a spirit of poltergeist both before and after being born again. These demonic powers have turned on taps, moved furniture, made pictures fall, opened drawers and even pulled out articles of female underwear.

• A lady who had been receiving psychiatric treatment for some time and who suffered from agoraphobia, suddenly found an important religious medallion in a drawer which was in constant use. She knew that nothing of that nature had been in that drawer for years. She felt a twinge of the old superstition and fear and had to be freed from the influence of that spirit of poltergeist.

• Some adults set free have told us that during childhood they were able to move heavy furniture without help, and open locked doors without keys. One young lady was able to open and close doors, and alter the hands of a clock, using only her eyes.

• Another believer who had been a psychic medium was still able to read the thoughts of people and influence them by thought control. He strongly denied my suggestion that he used mind dynamics to control his sexual urges, but when the Lord freed him from a spirit of lust, he realized he had been deceived, and confessed it openly.

• The husband of a certain woman had been, among other things, a hypnotist. He had his own travelling show which included his daughter who had hypnotic power in her eyes. When the girl later became a Christian (through her mother's influence) she asked to be released from the power of hypnosis. After she came to Christ, the mother herself found that she was oppressed and terrorised by a particularly evil and destructive spirit from her husband. The marriage broke up but the husband visited the property occasionally. One night as he was leaving a spirit seized her and she destroyed furnishings in her home. Finally in the early hours of the morning when totally distraught, she bundled her children into the car and drove to some Christian friends in another city. After they had prayed for some time, around 3 a.m. she was freed from the terrorising spirits and slept peacefully. She returned home later in the day to find that the entire aluminium canopy on the side of her house, plus the pipe supports which had been anchored in concrete, had been ripped out. The canopy was compressed like a concertina and the pipe supports had penetrated the side of the house. She told her neighbours that it must have been a fierce storm to have done so much damage. They assured her that there had been no storm. They said that around 3 a.m. they had heard the most fearful crashing sounds, and on investigation, found the house extensively damaged. They had no explanation to offer. It was then that the woman remembered that she had been set free from those evil spirits at that very time. The woman explained that she had been waiting six years for further deliverance, and the Lord did not disappoint her, or her daughter.

2. A few examples of satanic influences.

• Psychic healers are 'healing' psychosomatic and pathogenic illnesses around the world today. For example, there are Filipinos who are regarded as 'faith healers' but who use sleight of hand and demonic trickery to convince sufferers that 'miracles' have happened. Thousands flock to them.

• A number of Christians who have had spirit-caused healings have needed release from demons which have inflicted mental confusion, fears, and other manifestations as the spiritual price for services rendered.

• One Australian state police force was recently reported as having set up a 'Satan Squad' to tackle crime suspected of originating from black magic rites and demon worship.

- As recently as 1986, witch doctors in a Northern Transvaal province in South Africa have been sentenced to burning at the stake for killing people by calling down lightning strikes. Seven witches have been reported to have died this way.

- Several years ago, an Australian acupuncturist visited Tibetans living in India. To his amazement, he was unable to penetrate the skin of an old exile. He was both confused and apologetic. Then the Tibetan apologized, saying he had forgotten to take off his amulet. When the charm was removed, the needles penetrated his skin easily. The charm had been given him by a Lama as protection against the bullets of the Chinese.

- On the 27th June 1980, the West German Chancellor, Herr Schmidt, held a political rally in Bonn. The writer has been given copies of the official invitations which were covered with drawings of cloven-hooved demons, naked women, and naked witches on broomsticks. The pages were liberally decorated with demonic and astrological symbols. Christians interceded, and greatly hindered the intended witchcraft content of that rally.

- The enormously profitable business of astrological predictions sways millions today; nearly all magazines and newspapers carry syndicated columns.

- There has been a considerable upsurge in films dealing with the supernatural, outer space, violence and horror. Patrons have experienced fear, demonic visitations and sexual molestation after viewing them, and some have committed suicide. One believer told us she came under the control of an evil spirit when she watched a film on a home video. The Lord freed her.

- Books with veiled and explicit occult content are freely available in bookstores. Richard Bach claims to have written 'Jonathan Livingstone Seagull' as a result of visions and direct dictation from 'disembodied' spirits. Christian bookstores sold it and many Christians were deceived by its philosophy. The Satanist '5th and 6th books of Moses' have a particularly evil effect upon readers. Satan worship and Satanist churches abound with black alternatives to Jesus Christ. Anton Le Vay's Church of San Francisco uses his Satanic Bible. Its priests all dress in black. Le Vay himself wears pink horns projecting from a black cap which covers his head and surrounds his face. Black rites are used, prayers are made to Satan, and demonic tongues and prophecies counterfeit gifts of the Holy Spirit. In a film shown on a Sydney television station, a naked woman was seen sitting crosslegged on a Satanic altar with only a skull between her legs. The figures 666 were prominently written in black across her breasts and chest, and she handled a snake above her head while the camera was focused on her.

- Past devotees to Satan-worship speak of human sacrifices, and suggest that at least some of the huge numbers of missing persons of this world have ended their days in this way. A beloved colleague now with the Lord told me the following story concerning a woman whom he had helped set free. She had become trapped in a circle of professional men who were involved in Satan worship. As a result of sexual rites performed on her she became pregnant. When the child was born it was sacrificed alive to Satan. Even after the young lady married, she was blackmailed into continuing her sexual submission in coven activities. Finally, she moved across the world to another country to break the evil association and commence life again. While there she became a born again believer in Jesus Christ and her life was transformed. She became deeply repentant for allowing her baby to be murdered, and decided to return to her country of birth intent on making a full confession of her past to the police. Undoubtedly it would have caused a scandal of great proportions because of the involvement of well-known identities. Shortly before she was due to fly home she was killed in an automobile accident.

• From time to time stories appear in the press about houses which are bombarded with rocks at night time. Many countries, including Australia, have reported such incidents. Despite floodlights and intensive police investigation, the showers of missiles continue unabated. Although novel and rational explanations are offered, no person or persons are ever charged with the offences. Demonic activities are not a normal part of police investigations!

In the writings of Ms. Marilyn Ferguson already referred to, she states: "Whether or not it was written in the stars, a different age seems to be upon us; and Aquarius the waterbearer in the ancient zodiac, symbolizing the flow and the quenching of an ancient thirst, is an appropriate symbol" (page 19 'The Aquarian Conspiracy' - Paladin).

In the Age of Aquarius, acclaimed by The New Age Movement, the zodiacal waterbearer's pitcher can only offer deception to a spiritually thirsty world. It is Satan's alternative to the true water of life which only Jesus Christ can supply (John 7:38). Linked with the thrust of the New Age Movement's so-called spiritual enlightenment is an international undercurrent aimed at bringing monetary currencies, religions, trade, and governments under one world head. The manipulation of human resources by a spiritual and material federation of demonic power is clearly set out in the book of Revelation and is truly beginning to operate in full view of believers today. Daniel foresaw this and said "those who are wise will understand" (Daniel 12:10). Who among us is wise?

3. Areas of involvement in occultism and witchcraft from which believers need release and subsequent renewal.

(1) Astrology.

(a) Horoscopes.

A horoscope is a written astrological prediction about a person's life, charted from the position of the stars at the time of birth and based on the supposed influence of stars over the affairs of mankind.

Mothers frequently have horoscopes prepared for their children without their knowledge. If they are known to be in existence after the child comes to Christ they should be destroyed and the power of their prognostications broken. Until then Satan will see to it that predictions do come to pass. Christians have been known to be fearful of their fulfilment, especially when sickness, death, divorce, and other negative or harmful things are said to lie ahead.

(b) Weekly star sign predictions.

Some people mistake the weekly astrological column for a horoscope. Ancient astrologers divided the year into twelve equal portions, corresponding to the position of the sun, moon and stars. They are Aries, Taurus, Gemini, Cancer, Leo, Virgo, Libra, Scorpio, Sagittarius, Capricorn, Aquarius, and Pisces. Each has an identifying sign, and is matched with a gemstone and flower. Christians who wear jewelry with any of these identifications should destroy them, and be cleansed from all evil influence.

(c) Chinese astrology.

Every child born to Chinese parents receives its birth sign from one of the following in a twelve year cycle:- ox, rat, pig, dog, rooster, monkey, ram, horse, snake, dragon, rabbit, and tiger. It is believed that people inherit the characteristics of the sign of their year of birth, and should marry a person born in one of several designated compatible years, for the best results. Caucasians who become involved in Chinese astrology become very bound by its classification of personalities. One young lady needed several periods of prayer for release and renewal before being set free.

4. Non-Biblical methods of meditation for inner peace.
(1) Transcendental meditation.

Indian gurus, swamis, holy men, and their proselytes have always been eager to exchange their philosophies for the Western dollar. The volume of exchange is high. The teachings are basically from Hinduism and its 5th century B.C. refinement, Buddhism. One of the high priests of the trade, who popularized T.M. is the Maharishi Mahesh Yogi. He now has his headquarters for "The World Government for the Age of Enlightenment", in Switzerland, and a number of related universities are scattered worldwide. His deceptively seraphic smile, searching eyes, and enigmatic speech has swept academics, intellectuals, and peace lovers into his fold. His invisible co-sponsor is the evil one.

(2) Yoga.

The word means 'to yoke' in Sanskrit. It involves a system of physical exercise designed to control the internal organs and metabolism of the body. Yoga is a Hindu system of philosophy with at least six schools of thought. The supposed aim is to reach a state of superconsciousness through eight stages of physical and mental preparation. It is claimed that miraculous powers such as levitation and invisibility may be reached when in the higher levels.

Many Christian women have attended Yoga exercise classes not realizing that the whole system is associated with the worship of eastern deities. Hatha yoga involves the massage of the internal organs as an aid to relaxation and meditation. Any believer who has been involved in Yoga classes should be cleansed from its Hindu spirit influences.

Common features of meditation are:

(a) The lotus position.

This is the human equivalent of the large flower of the Indian water plant.

(b) Mantras.

Meditation normally commences with the droning sound of incantation. Names of Hindu demonic deities and words of worship are then added. The Biblical word for this exercise is idolatry.

Christians who have been involved in any form of transcendental meditation before being saved need to be freed from all demonic deception. Satan loves to see Christians operating under the power of his spirit, rather than the Holy Spirit.

The writer had preached at a charismatic fellowship and prayed for believers at the close of the service. After nearly everyone had left, the treasurer came up and said, "I have just realized that I have never received deliverance from deep involvement in T.M.". He coughed vigorously during ministry, showing us what a grip those spirits still had. He was completely released.

A friend of ours is a high ranking officer in the Australian Armed Forces. He represented his branch of the services at the Australian embassy in Jakarta, Indonesia. One of his regular contacts, a senior officer of the Indonesian Air Force, said to him on one occasion, "We Indonesians don't need aeroplanes in oder to fly!" When pressed for an explanation, he said that his brother who lived well over a hundred miles from him would seometimes embarrass him by materializing in his lounge in front of guests. When told to go home immediately, the brother would disappear as quickly as he had arrived. The officer said he had often telephoned his brother's home to make sure he really had gone, and his brother had personally answered the phone each time. Our friend asked about the source of his ability to do this and was given the name of a street in Bali - JALAN SE SATAN. The meaning of this was given as "Friend or buddy of Satan Street'. No wonder walking on water is another demonic possibility in Indonesia!

5. Practices of occultism and witchcraft known as the 'black arts'.
(1) Fortune telling.

Christians are forbidden to use any form of prognostication. Our lives are in God's hands, and he expects us to trust him with the future. When people go to fortune tellers, there will be spirits of deception, superstition, and fear or dread of predictions. Spirits need to be evicted, and cleansing received.

Regrettably, some immature Christians indulge in a practice which is a form of fortune telling. They constantly ask people to prophesy over them so that they can get spiritual guidance for the future instead of searching God's Word, and allowing prophecy to confirm it. Often what they receive comes from a human or demonic source rather than from the Holy Spirit (Ezekiel 13:3), and they end up with pride, confusion, and bondage to spirits of deception.

A confused young man came to me after a service. He said, with obvious pride, "God has told me by prophecy that I am going to startle the music industry!" I asked him if he could sing or play a musical instrument. He answered 'No' to both questions, but added hopefully, "I did have one semester at the piano!" I told the young man the obvious, that that prophecy certainly had not come from God. He then admitted to having openly boasted about it for years. He was very clearly wrapped in his own euphoria, encouraged no little I suspect, by the medication of the psychiatrist he then confessed to be consulting.

(2) Seances.

Demonic delusion reigns supreme when mediums try to consult the spirits of the dead. God says that in death the spirit returns to its maker (Ecclesiastes 12:7). The voice the clairvoyant claims to hear, or which expresses itself through his or her lips, is a demonic spirit who has had intimate dealings with the deceased during their lifetime. The demon knows the personal details of the dead person, and the making up of faked messages is no problem. The witch of Endor was greatly shocked when her deception failed, and God allowed Samuel to return in person and speak his message of judgment to King Saul (1 Samuel 28).

(3) Ouija boards.

When direction is from this demonic 'game' or from the use of tumblers and letters, direct communication is set up with spirits. Many Christians have played with ouija boards, some innocently, and they all need release from the powers who control the messages.

The Japanese equivalent is called 'kokkri-san'. The user bows in respect to the 'spirit of the fox'. A Japanese young lady in a school of discipleship asked for release from the influence of this spirit. Her closest friend at school had been taken over by it and it had refused to leave when she had finished the fortune-telling. The friend had been very popular amongst fellow students because of her special ability. Then she began to pour out a stream of blasphemies and obscenities during lessons, and finally had to be kept at home. She ended up by being committed to a mental institution. As I prayed for this student to be released, a man on the other side of the room saw a black shape leave her. Immediately another girl cried out, 'It has hit me'. The Lord freed her too. A Presbyterian minister, his wife, and mother-in-law who were present asked for prayer when they saw the power of God setting people free.

An Australian grandmother, a nominal Christian, was a frequent user of the ouija board. One day a voice told her that she could forget the board, and that he would speak through her lips. Many years later, after she had been filled with the Spirit she became troubled about this 'gift' and contacted the writers. She was then suffering from an incurable disease. The Lord certainly released her from the spirits of deception, but to our knowledge the sickness remained.

6. Other means of seeking knowledge of future events.

(1) **Parts of the human body** are commonly used as a basis for divination. Firstly, palmistry is based on the lines of the hand. Secondly, phrenology is based on the shape of the head. Thirdly, iridology is based on the iris of the eye. Medical use of the last two for diagnostic purposes is of course legitimate. However their prostitution for the purpose of fortune-telling is contrary to the Word of God.

(2) **Tea leaves or coffee grounds** are sometimes used for predictive purposes. Tea or coffee cup reading may be done 'in fun' or by professional charlatan. Either way it is dangerous, and may commence a chain of events which can only be terminated by the power of God.

(3) **Numerology.** Practitioners give a number to each letter of a name in accordance with a mysterious formula. After certain calculations, the numerologist comes up with a final number which is used to select the appropriate information from a standard personality chart. Numerologists, like astrologers, often operate in shopping plazas.

7. Spirit based manipulative methods of mental control over people and situations.

(1) E.S.P. (Extra Sensory Perception), systems of mind dynamics such as Silva Mind Control, E.S.T. (Erhard Seminars Training), Actualisations, Lifespring, and processes of re-birthing all fit this category. The New Age Movement calls these and similar processes, 'psychotechnologies'. No 'mind bending' technique should be used by Christians, even if the operator claims to use Christian principles and believes in God. There is a very strong possibility of the patient's coming under demonic domination.

(2) **Hypnotism.** Believers are well advised not to allow their minds to be taken over by another person or power for medical or entertainment purposes. The

practice was first named Mesmerism, after a medical doctor who experimented with magnets to influence people's actions. He later found that by using his hands he could achieve the same results.

There are two common forms of self-imposed mind control which can have long-lasting and sometimes drastic results:

Firstly, intellectuals sometimes edit out their emotional feelings so that their minds can be more finely tuned for study and examinations. Unless this process is deliberately reversed (and this seldom appears to happen) the individual becomes emotionally cold and is unable to express feelings when he later so desires. This has been found to be the cause of many problems between marriage partners, and between parents and children.

Secondly, children who have been deeply rejected will sometimes shut off their emotions for fear of being hurt again.

All influences of mind control, whether of a demonic or self-imposed nature must be dealt with thoroughly. Bondages need to be broken, deceptive spirits cast out, and the mind cleansed from habit patterns. In fact, the whole personality needs to be liberated so that each portion of the soul is able to carry out its function as God intended in harmony with the whole.

8. Demonic art forms.

Many Christians have innocently permitted a demonic invasion of their homes and personalities by their selection of art or artefacts which the evil one has initiated or influenced. This short list does not come from personal prejudice, but from experience in helping people to find release:
(1) Abstract, psychedelic, or surrealistic art.

These are overt or covert demonic art expressions. These often feature snakes, dragons, witches and unicorns.
(2) Music with a heavy beat, or when flashing coloured lights pulsate in time with the music. Rock and roll and punk rock music have been proved to possess a psychological 'power' to stir up anti-social conduct including illicit sex and violence. Many Christians are 'hooked' on to this class of music, and even though they may deny it, are unable to live in genuine spiritual victory.

The dangers of backward 'masking' are also very real. Heavy rock groups sometimes impose words such as 'Satan, Satan, he is god' and similar blasphemies over their music by having them recorded backwards. Although the words can only be distinguished clearly by playing the tapes backwards, psychologists assured an American committee of enquiry that the human brain is able to decipher such messages despite their backward masking. It is claimed that the Beatles were the first to record a subliminal message. They experimented with a brief message about one of their number leaving the group and their record sales soared dramatically.

Some heavy rock groups are known to give their tape masters to Satanists who perform rites over them before they are released to the market.
(3) Sensuous classical music is able to induce fantasy experiences in devotees, and anything which restricts the Holy Spirit's ministry to believers grieves him.
(4) Forms of sensuous dancing. A Christian previously involved in 'belly dancing' realized it still had a demonic hold, and was released.

9. Other demonic activities.
(1) Pendulum diagnosis.

This traditional test for pregnancy involves suspending a wedding ring (or band) over a pregnant woman by a hair of her head, or by a piece of cotton. The clockwise or anti-clockwise swing of the ring is supposed to indicate the sex of the expected child. It is a witchcraft practice and no matter how innocently it may have been used, it gives Satan an opportunity to oppress both mother and child.

(2) Colour therapy.

Therapists use a form of pendulum diagnosis to find the distinctive colour of the patient's 'aura', then use a copper coil and strands of cotton to 'heal'. Christians who practise this art are usually legalistic, emotionally hard, and antagonistic to the fulness of the Holy Spirit and the use of spiritual gifts. Colour therapy is a holistic means of healing.

A New Zealand Christian farmer once told me that he had proved the effectiveness of colour therapy on his cattle and sheep. Sheep were freed from what he described as 'pulpy kidney', and sickly cattle became fat and well nourished. This certainly disproves any thought of the treatment being a psychological trick. But as a copper coil and a piece of coloured material have no scientifically proven healing qualities, the only other power source is demonic.

A young lady asked for deliverance from the demonic influence of colour therapy. Her father, an ordained minister, had practised it for twenty years. The daughter said her father was hard, legalistic, and very opposed to teachings on the fulness of the Holy Spirit. The Lord released her from all these oppressions.

(3) Charms and amulets.

Practitioners of psychic and spirit-based healing often give their patients items to wear. They can be worn around the neck or arm or sewn to clothing. They are usually warned not to open them under threat of losing the healing. The charm places that individual under demonic control. Chinese Buddhist parents often have their children's clothing dedicated by the priest at the temple. They are then stamped with the personal chop (kanji seal) of the priest. Chinese nationals who have worn dedicated clothing as children, and who have been saved subsequently have shown demonic resistance to deliverance. When I prayed for young Christians in Taiwan, Taoist spirits caused their eyes to become glazed. They also became so confused that they were unable to understand what was being said. Release took a little longer than usual, but victory was always assured.

(4) Curses placed on families.

Disgruntled witches, gypsies, and practitioners of the black arts sometimes curse families. The results continue for generations, some for more than a century. Mental and health problems, accidents, death, and mysterious tragedies have occurred at consistent intervals. When curses are known to have been pronounced, or the Lord reveals this, deliverance and cleansing will break the chain of events.

An interesting case of a personal curse came to light during ministry to a young lady who had been involved with the Ragneeshis. After the teaching phase she was faced with a sexual initiation which she refused. The leader gave her a black eye, and over a period of two hours tried to choke her, demanding sex. Finally he raped her. For six months after this the woman was unable to swallow properly, and developed a scabies type of rash around her neck which gradually spread to other parts of her body. After becoming a Christian, she heard from friends that the rapist was serving a prison term for committing similar offences against other women. She went to see him, and through a separating glass partition, asked him to remove the curse he had placed on her. He wept, and asked for forgiveness which she freely gave him. The rash immediately cleared up. Phyl prayed with her and the Lord freed her from other dominating spirits she received when attacked, such as rape, lust of man, rejection, self-rejection, low self-image, worthlessness, and a spirit of grief.

(5) Superstitions, deja vu, premonitions, and psychic sight.

In addition to hereditary spirits, the reading of Satanic books, and involvement in witchcraft practices can produce bondages and dominations which will only be terminated by spiritual release.

In praying with people dominated by these and other spirits of witchcraft, we find that they are often attacked by severe bouts of pain in various parts of the body, particularly in the back and head. We have seen the skin on the surface of arms, legs, and stomach 'ripple' as pain producing spirits have moved around in attempting to avoid eviction. When authority is taken over them and they are cast out in the name of Jesus, all pain ceases immediately. On numerous occasions blinding headaches which have commenced as soon as a particularly troublesome spirit has been named, stopped completely when the oppressing spirit was evicted. The counsellee's normal response is "No-one will ever convince me now that deliverance from evil spirits is not very real and powerful".

(6) Parlour games of a demonic nature.

The games are addictive, emotionally harmful, and expose the players to demonic domination. They include: Dungeons and Dragons; Cults and Prax; Sorceror's Apprentice; Chivalry and Sorcery; Hellpits of Nightfang; Rune Quest; Arduin Grimoire; Tunnels and Trolls; and The Illuminati, a game of taking the world by stealth. These are not for the child of God.

Newspaper articles have stated that over sixty people are known to have committed suicide after their favourite game personality has been eliminated from the ongoing play. Their suicide notes explain that they feel emotionally unable to face life alone. When it is realized that these games are able to dominate the players' minds totally in fantasy roles for years, the demonic cause of such tragedies becomes obvious. The teenage High Schooler who came of his own accord for deliverance claimed to have been addicted to Dungeons and Dragons for five years. The levels of demonic power, cruelty, horror and sexual perversion through which players move in D and D is evident to anyone who takes time to scan the materials so freely available in bookstores.

(7) Demonic symbols.

(a) **Frogs.** They were worshipped in Egypt. 'Heqt', the frog goddess, was one of the demonic powers which God judged (Exodus 12:12). John the apostle wrote that demonic spirits that look like frogs will come directly from the trinity of evil to stir up the nations against God in the last days (Revelation 16:13).

● A woman who withdrew from communicating with others except by writing, used to lie in bed hugging a large stuffed green frog. The Lord revealed to Phyl that she had a spirit of death. This was cast out. The woman immediately got up, dressed, and quite spontaneously went out and burned the frog. Her joy in the Lord, and communication with others was immediately evident to all.

• In Lausanne, Switzerland, the writer was praying for a woman to be delivered from dominating spirits of witchcraft, mind control, and aggressive sexuality with men. She began to make spitting sounds during this time. I asked her why she was doing this, and she replied, "I am spitting out little frogs". I couldn't see them, but they were real to her.

• A friend of ours removed five frogs of various types from her daughter's room without the child realizing they had been taken away. The following night the mother was awakened by her daughter's screams. She rushed into her room asking what the problem was and received this reply: "Mummy, would you please get that 'frog-person' out of my room". After prayer for the cleansing of the room, peace and sleep returned to daughter and mother.

(b) **Owls.** The owl is an unclean bird (Leviticus 11:13-18; Deuteronomy 14:15, 16). It is associated with demon satyrs in the judgment of Babylon (Revelation 18:2; Isaiah 13:21; 14:23; Jeremiah 50:39). The owl is usually associated with pictures of witches and their cauldrons.

(c) **Snakes.** God cursed the snake because Satan used it to deceive Adam and Eve in the garden of Eden. Since then the snake has been a spiritual symbol of Satan (Genesis 3:1; Isaiah 27:1; Revelation 12:3, 9). A young lady who came for release from spirits of witchcraft explained that she used to have a fixation for breeding frogs, insects, and snakes.

(d) **Dragons.** The dragon is a mythological creature often used in demonic art. It is a Biblical symbol for Satan used thirteen times in the book of Revelation (Revelation 12:3-17 etc.).

(e) **Unicorns.** This is another mythical creature used in demonic art and in Freemasonry symbolism.

(8) Artifacts and souvenir articles representing forms of spirit worship.

Buddhas, totem poles, spirit face-masks, joss sticks, and all items venerated or used in countries where animism or spirit worship is practised should be destroyed and the home where they have been located, cleansed. Dramatic changes in the atmosphere of homes and the health of those living in them have resulted when this has been carried out.

(9) Demonic jewelry.

(a) **The ankh.** This is the cross with a loop [☥]. It is an Egyptian symbol of the re-incarnation of Ra, the sun god, and is associated with sexual rites. It is also called the Sceptre of Pharaoh.

(b) **The unicorn horn** was created by Druid priests in Scotland and Ireland. It represents an appeal to Satan for financial assistance. It is also known as the Italian Horn, the Fairy Wand, and leprechaun's staff.

(c) **The Pentagram** is the witchcraft sign which represents Lucifer as the bright and morning star.

(d) **The Horned Star** is the symbol of Satanist churches.

(e) **The Hexagram.** This is the most evil occult sign and is used in Satanic ceremonial rites. The basis of the word 'hex' means to place a curse on someone.

(10) Demonic activities.

(a) **Levitation.** This is a consciousness of being separated from the body, and a person may look down on his or her form from nearby or at a distance. Levitation may also take the form of a consciousness of one's body being in suspension.

(b) **Astral travel** involves conscious travel without the body, oftentimes to places in space. It is a delusive demonic experience which may be induced by drugs, meditation or spirit control. It is much more realistic and often more terrifying than dreams.

● One young man who asked for prayer had had frequent experiences of astral travel under the influence of drugs. On one such occasion he claimed to have met and had a bizarre sexual experience with, a female spirit being. Demon powers were certainly very active in his body during deliverance.

● A young lady being prayed for suddenly said, "I am on another planet." The demons had forced her into fantasy and unreality as a delaying tactic, but the Lord totally freed her.

People who claim to have had a death experience but return to life also speak of having travelled spatially while out of the body. Many of them testify to having viewed their own bodies from a distance before 'coming alive' again. This experience is quite different from those caused by occultism or witchcraft.

● The writers have prayed for a young lady who claimed to have died in hospital after starving herself for four weeks while bingeing on alcohol. She remembers going upwards for a long time then coming to a place of light. There she heard voices and saw shadowy outlines of people, but was unable to enter. Finally she heard a special voice telling her to return to earth as she had a work to do. She said she asked to be allowed to enter, but found herself falling again. The hospital later came into view and she clearly saw the outline of her body covered by a sheet still on a bed in a private room. She spoke of the real shock of re-entering her body. Throwing off the sheet, she ran into the corridor where she met a nurse who screamed, thinking she was seeing an apparition. Twenty minutes had elapsed since the entry in the hospital record reporting that she had died.

Shortly afterwards, a person 'clothed with light' came into her hospital room and putting his arms around her told her to go to Los Angeles. As a result she was born again. The Lord then led her to the place where we were ministering God's Word and praying for needy people. The Lord had previously promised he would bring her into full deliverance, and confirmed that this was his purpose for her the day we prayed together. She was freed from deep rejection, the spirit of death, and many other dominating spirits from her past life. The releases she received soon became evident in her lifestyle.

(11) **Automatic writing.** This is a demon-controlled experience whereby a person may write or type extensive materials without any mental effort or conscious thought. The results are overtly anti-Christ. Many false doctrines and schemes for establishing demon-controlled churches have been received this way.

Counsellees have told us that when such materials have been burnt in a fire, faces have appeared in the flames and screams have been heard.

(12) **Demonic philosophies.**

Metaphysics and Anthroposophy both owe their origin to one Adolph Steiner who refined some of the teaching of Theosophy. Both have a deceptive religious appeal to the unregenerate, and to weak Christians.

(13) **Martial arts of all descriptions.**

The martial arts are forms of self-defence, inextricably linked with Buddhism. They came into being when a Buddhist monk and a number of novitiates were travelling from India to China. The group was attacked and robbed so many times that the senior monk devised a system of self-defence after studying the manner in which animals attacked their prey. When the group disbanded the monks went to different Eastern countries where they developed their own styles of self-defence patterned on their studies of animals and birds. A few examples are 'Win Chung' (Snake-crane); 'Hung Gar' (Tiger-crane); and 'Karati' (White crane from Okinawa). Others include 'Te Kwon Do', 'Kung Foo', 'Hap Ki Do', 'Judo', 'Ai Ki Do', 'Jujitsu', 'Sei Ku Kan', 'Perisai Diri' (known in Indonesia), and many more.

In ministering deliverance to those who have been involved in martial arts, the writers have witnessed manifestations of aggressive strength. Proponents of the arts will stress their peaceful objectives, but we have found spirits of anger, violence, revenge, and murder will sometimes try to resist the freedom offered by Jesus Christ. One ex-Karati expert expelled his breath in the typical fashion used in preparing for combat. He then shouted, and struck the carpeted floor violently a number of times with the clenched fist of his right hand. After he had been set free from those dominating spirits, we found that large strawberry-red, and strawberry-sized lumps had appeared between the knuckles of his hand.

CHAPTER SUMMARY.

Because of the extent of the beliefs of occultism and the practices of witchcraft which bring participants into partnership with Satan and his evil forces, principles only can be stated in a summary:

1. Any form of involvement in the activities sponsored by the kingdom of darkness is contrary to the express command of God. It invites domination by evil spirits and God's judgment.

2. Christians need deliverance and cleansing from any form of innocent or deliberate involvement at any stage in their lives. Any cursed possession needs to be burnt or destroyed, and homes cleansed.

3. Christians need a revival of the fear of God so that the Body of Christ is cleansed from idolatry regarding anything that does not glorify God and his son Jesus Christ.

"Therefore my dear friends, flee from idolatry . . . You cannot drink of the cup of the Lord and the cup of demons too; you cannot have a part in both the Lord's table and the table of demons" (1 Corinthians 10:14, 21).

"Lo, children are an heritage from the Lord" (Psalm 127:3).

CHAPTER 17.

Satan's greatest infamy - oppressing our children

I have invited my wife Phyl to write two chapters sharing lessons the Lord has taught us about Satan's activities in, and with children. She is a qualified general and obstetrics nurse by profession, having given over sixteen years in ministering to others.

The mother of three beautiful daughters, a devoted grandmother to nine grandchildren, and the spiritual mother and grandmother of countless more, she writes from practical experience as well as from over thirty years of ministry. As you would expect, and maybe even hope, her style is different from mine. We share one Lord, and one heart as two personalities whom God has finely tuned together. She writes as she speaks, and already her teachings have blessed many mothers and their families. This is what she wishes to share:

You may not want to agree with the verse of Scripture which heads this page because of some of the mental, emotional, spiritual, and physical difficulties you have experienced with your children. Perhaps you have difficulty in believing that this or that child is really a gift from God.

Having read the previous chapters, you will probably already have new insights into some of the causes of problems in children. Heredity plays a major role in forming the lifestyle of a child, and the power of example exerts tremendous influence. You will easily recall the effects that your parents, friends, and school teachers had in your life.

Some parents feel the burden is too heavy, and are perplexed as to what to do for the best. Others feel guilty about their failures. But no-one has yet come up with anything better for children than parents!

If you recall your childhood memories, and remember some of your own conduct and needs, you will realize that some of your children's actions and reactions come from you yourself, either by heredity, or from example. A problem child usually means a problem parent, or parents. Here is a suggestion. Make a list of your own childhood problems such as fears, loneliness, rejection, anger, rebellion, jealousy, etc. Have you seen those problems in your own parents and grandparents? Then remember that sin creates a problem to the third and fourth generation (Exodus 20:4-6).

In dealing with children we constantly prove the reality of the hereditary curse. When a child is cleansed from every hereditary bondage, this means a life is freed to live as Jesus intended.

How do you inwardly react to your children? Run a cross check on yourself. Which attitude best describes yours? Is your child:

1. A blessing or a brat?
2. Someone to love, or someone to love you?
3. A nuisance?
4. An endurance test?
5. A means of holding a marriage together?
6. A gift from God?

How we evaluate our children will determine our reactions to them, and consequently their reactions to us. They are more perceptive than we think and are not fooled with sweet words.

Jesus stressed the importance of children, and always gave them time and love. "And they were bringing young children to Him that He might touch them; and the disciples were reproving them [for it]. But when Jesus saw [it], He was indignant and pained, and said to them, 'Allow the children to come to Me - do not forbid or prevent or hinder them - for to such belongs the kingdom of God. Truly I tell you, whoever does not receive and accept and welcome the kingdom of God as a little child [does], positively shall not enter it at all.' And He took [the children up one by one] in His arms and (fervently invoked a) blessing, placing His hands on them" (Mark 10:14-16 Amp.). On the other end of the scale, Satan has no respect for the handiwork of God, and is totally dedicated to the corruption of our children.

God's word is very specific in stressing the importance of bringing release to children.

In Mark 7:25, we see a little girl dominated by a spirit of lust. This child was too small to have committed a lustful act. Where could this spirit have come from? Obviously, it was an hereditary spirit of lust from her parentage.

In Mark 9:17-26, a little boy is brought to Jesus for help. The Amplified Bible names four spirits which were troubling the boy. They were: deafness, dumbness, uncleanness, and epilepsy. Once again these spirits were from heredity. All epilepsy does not come from Satanic domination. There are numerous causes of this malady, but Satan certainly is one.

From the basis of Scriptural case histories, my husband and I began to enquire more closely into the hereditary background of children whom we were asked to help. The Holy Spirit revealed many things, then confirmed them in a practical way with many wonderful results. Praise God Satan is a defeated foe!

The following problems in children we have proved as having come from heredity:

> Rejection
> Witchcraft and occultism
> Abnormal fears
> The curse of Freemasonry
> Sexual lust
> Cultural problems
> Addictions
> Schizophrenia
> Rebellion and anger

1. Rejection.

We have all been rejected at some time by one source or another. It is what we do with it, or how it rules us, that produces victory or defeat. Children are victims of their circumstances, and cannot choose their parents, so let us take the victory Jesus Christ purchased for us, and free them from these bondages and dominations.

If a parent is suffering rejection (which always has active and passive manifestations), then regardless of how much a babe is desired, that rejection will be passed to the child. Some common causes of rejection in children are:

(1)   hereditary rejection
(2)   an unwanted pregnancy
(3)   an attempted abortion during pregnancy
(4)   hospitalisation as a baby, or as a child
(5)   a difficult, protracted, or instrumental birth
(6)   the separation or divorce of the parents
(7)   a parent spending long periods away from the family, or both parents working
(8)   boarding school
(9)   lack of physical love or discipline
(10)   the death of a family member or close friend
(11)   the middle child syndrome (e.g. no. 2 in a family of three children)
(12)   competition from clever siblings
(13)   adoption.

In 'The Secret Life of the Unborn Child', Dr. Thomas Verny goes into considerable detail about how a mother affects her child in utero. Mothers, I don't want you to be disturbed or feel guilty about all the little problems that may have happened in your pregnancies. Only the major things affect the baby. Even then, Jesus Christ has given us his power to reverse any traumas which may have occurred during the lives of our children in utero.

Some of the symptoms of rejection are:

(a)   A baby may reject the mother by refusing to breast feed.
(b)   A child does not show love or respond to being loved. Affection may be resisted.
(c)   Rebellion or disobedience which resists discipline.
(d)   Being quick to get angry, often with little outward cause.
(e)   Showing anxiety over little things, and being fearful of being left alone.
(f)   Insecurity, and lack of self-confidence.
(g)   Always looking for acceptance.
(h)   Adopted children often display these symptoms:-
    (i)   Fear.
    (ii)   A lack of identity. They often ask, "Who am I?"
    (iii)   Rebellion and anger.
    (iv)   Scepticism, when told they are loved. They constantly look for acceptance.

2. The special case of adoption.

Most children who are put up for adoption are unwanted, otherwise they would have been kept. So adoption is a special source of rejection. We have seen heartbroken parents bring their 'specially chosen children' to us saying, "We have always loved him, and spent unlimited time with him. Why all this anger and resistance to our love?"

The history of an adopted child's parents is usually very sketchy. For children born out of wedlock, this is particularly so. When a child is conceived in lust, it not only picks this up, but also the mother's fear of pregnancy, and the hate, anger, and rejection of a father, if this follows. Evidences of other hereditary problems can also be discerned from listening to the parents, or through asking leading questions. Unless these are dealt with thoroughly, there will continue to be some strain between the parents and child. Teaching and love will never replace the freedom which Jesus Christ gives.

3. Influences of occultism or witchcraft.

If this curse is in the family, it will produce:-

(1)   abnormal fears, particularly in the dark. The imagination tends to run riot concerning what can be seen in the dark, but it can be a real experience.

(2)   very disturbing dreams.

(3)   a hatred of being left alone.

(4)   spirits of anti-Christ which may cause a child to become very antagonistic to Christian music, church attendance, and Bible reading or prayer in the home.

● A little girl of seven was distressed about going to bed. She said she saw shadows, even with the light on. Everything she drew had a black face, even trees, stars, and the sun. When asked why she drew that way, she replied, "That is the way I see them, black faces looking at me." The mother confessed to having been heavily involved in occultism and witchcraft both before and during her pregnancy. Although the mother became a Christian when her little girl was only three years of age, the child was troubled until she was specifically prayed for. From that time she was never bothered again.

● A six-year-old boy was disturbed in his sleep, often screaming. He said he could see dark things over his head. We learned from the boy's mother that he spent a lot of time with his grandmother who was involved with witchcraft practices. The bondage and influences were broken and the boy was freed.

4. Freemasonry.

The curse of this Luciferan doctrine has been detailed in chapter ten. Hereditary Freemasonry spirits affect children particularly in health, emotional imbalance, mental confusion and lack of concentration.

A three-month old baby was brought for prayer, because his grandfather had been a Freemason. The babe was asleep when prayer began, but when the masonic curse was broken, the baby almost jumped out of the carry-cot.

Some children brought to us have showed strong disinterest in their school work, and in fact, have been generally apathetic about most things in life. Allergies and sicknesses in children can often be traced back to the curse of Freemasonry.

5. Addictions.

These spirits do not usually manifest themselves until the teenage years or later, but when they become excessive, deliverance is the only answer. This coterie of spirits stick closely together, and when one is defeated another is happy to take its place. They include alcohol, nicotine, drugs, gluttony causing obesity, gambling, and excessive exercise. Not only does a specific spirit need to be cast out, but also the hereditary spirit of addiction.

6. Lust.

All children are curious about their bodies, and normal exploration is generally not harmful. When excessive interest in sex is being shown, it should be investigated. Masturbation at an early age is a warning symptom of hereditary lust, or it may indicate that the child has been sexually molested.

A child of three years was stimulating himself excessively. Inquiries revealed that both parents had been masturbators prior to marriage. Their little boy was released from an hereditary spirit of lust, and things returned to normal.

Promiscuity in teenagers.

When young people are strongly attracted to pornography, it is usually an hereditary spirit of lust that drives them.

Ned was a ten-year-old. He was found under a bridge, surrounded by pornographic magazines. He looked guilty when discovered, and said, "Something inside me is hungry for it." The boy had come from a family of ten children. They had a common mother, but each had a different father.

7. Schizophrenia.

This is a frightening word, because people generally think it means insanity. The word actually means 'a disconnection between the mind, emotions, and actions'. We have found many children and adults who think one thing and do another. This produces a swinging personality. We often see children who change in a flash from excessive disobedience to angelic sweetness. Don't blame the child - look for the cause.

God has privileged us to see some spectacular results arising from the driving out of a schizophrenic spirit, and then seeing the Holy Spirit bind together the functions of mind, emotion, personality, and will.

Billy was brought for prayer at the age of seven. He was disruptive at school, and had poor learning ability. He swung between being aggressive and sweet. His parents were divorced, and he lived with his mother. She told us that the father was a schizophrenic. We had two half-hour sessions with Billy, ministering release and healing. That was some three years ago, and the boy is going from strength to strength in all-round development. His latest school report is a triumph of victory for Jesus Christ, the Deliverer from Zion (Romans 11:26).

8. Cultural bondages and dominations.

These really affect children. Little Neville was a Samoan boy of twenty-two months. He seemed to possess a 'supernatural' power of destruction. Even solid steel toys would break in his hands. He was also rebellious, and very aggressive towards other children. He used to wake up screaming six to eight times a night. When his cultural bondages were broken, he became a normal child and never regressed. At first his child-minder thought he was sick, because there were no tantrums or broken toys, but when she learned that he had been set free, she gave glory to God.

9. Rebellion and anger.

Hereditary rejection will produce anger. But we have learned that hereditary anger can also come from a father, and rebellion from a mother who has been violently rebellious as a teenager.

Children may also try disobedience until they learn that it does not pay, but when there is defiance which cannot be controlled by normal discipline, then special help is needed. What children need, is to be freed from that dominating spirit. Psychology and drug treatment do not deal with the roots of the problem.

Do not despair if you discover that some of these truths apply to your children. Read Hebrews chapter two, verses fourteen and fifteen, particularly in the Amplified version, and take the help available for them.

CHAPTER SUMMARY.

1. Children are gifts from God, but need to be set free from hereditary dominating spirits.
2. Children are very susceptible to rejection, particularly those who are adopted, and this is usually evident in behavioural problems.
3. Unusual fears, disturbed sleep patterns, and unexplained changes in behaviour need investigation because they often have demonic causes.

PART THREE

The processes of setting people free and maintaining their freedom

"We are therefore Christ's ambassadors, as though God were making his appeal through us - we implore you in Christ's behalf: Be reconciled to God"
(2 Corinthians 5:16).

CHAPTER 18.

Check your credentials first

When a new representative of a foreign government arrives in a country, he is obligated to present his credentials and terms of appointment to the appropriate authority. As soon as he has been accredited he may speak and act for those whom he represents. Christians have the full diplomatic rights of the kingdom of God wherever they go. The king of darkness may not want to acknowledge it, but when it comes to a showdown, the servant of the Lord has all the power and authority of the blood and name of Jesus Christ.

Unlike diplomats, Christians do not require accreditation in God's world, but their authority doesn't concern Satan until it is used against his kingdom. Then the world's greatest expert in bluff threatens, blusters, delays, and argues. But he is a defeated foe, and knows it. He and his demonic hordes cannot resist a Spirit-filled believer operating with divine authority. Before proceeding to outline methods of setting people free, a review of our ambassadorial credentials is essential:

Firstly, our PROMISE in Jesus Christ (Mark 16:17).
"And these signs will accompany those who believe: In my name they will drive out demons; . . . "

Matthew concludes his Gospel with details of the Great Commission (Matthew 28:19, 20). Mark concludes his Gospel, doubtless under Petrine influence, by highlighting the power by which the Great Commission would be fulfilled and by indicating some of the confirmatory signs which could be expected.

The twelve disciples had of course been exercising this power and authority since their appointment to apostleship (Luke 9:1). And the seventy were given the same privilege for their brief ministry (Luke 10:17).

It is obvious that Jesus Christ expected his church to be as dynamic after the resurrection as the disciples had been during his earthly ministry. The leaders of the early church certainly had no doubt that they had received power and authority.

The following story illustrates the extent to which some people are willing to trust the Lord to fulfil his word. It was given to me first hand by a pastor attending a refresher course at a college for training Christian leaders in South East Asia.

An expatriate missionary had left an indigenous pastor in charge of his mission complex during a short absence. Not being conversant with machinery the pastor filled the portable generator with gasoline without any oil additive. In a short time the generator overheated, caught fire, and finally seized up. It was ruined beyond repair. When the missionary returned, he was very angry to find what had happened; the pastor was ashamed; and neither of them had the finance to purchase a new generator.

After praying about the situation for several days, the pastor decided it was time to put his faith into action. He had the ruined generator carried into the open, and impressively applied a large spanner to every visible bolt. As he refilled the generator's petrol tank with the correct two stroke mixture, his faith was further challenged by the small but curious crowd which had gathered. Having done what he could, he felt it was over to God, so he lifted up his hands and eyes to heaven and loudly paised God, and defied the devil in particular and his works in general. When he finished he just wound the rope around the starter pulley and pulled with all his might. With a big smile, he told me, "It went vroomm and didn't stop." At the time of our conversation the burnt out generator had continued to generate power for at least three months without once faltering or showing any sign of damage! James says "You see that a person is justified by what he does and not by faith alone" (James 2:24).

Secondly, our POSITION in Jesus Christ (Ephesians 2:6).

"And God raised us up with Christ and seated us with him in the heavenly realms in Christ Jesus . . . Far above all rule and authority, power and dominion, and every title that can be given, not only in the present age but also in the one to come. And God placed all things under his feet and appointed him to be head over everything for the Church which is his body, the fulness of him who fills everything in every way" (Ephesians 1:21-23).

Satan and his demon hordes are now under the feet of a triumphant church. Every sanctified, Spirit-filled, Bible-believing child of God has all the power and authority needed to free people from the clutches of the evil one.

A Christian lady agreed to foster a five or six year old girl from a broken marriage, and put her in the same room as her son of the same age. Their beds were separated by a large piece of furniture. The girl visited her natural mother from time to time, and whenever she returned her foster parents were disturbed by a sense of evil, and found it difficult to control her.

One day, the woman's son quite casually told her that every time his 'sister' came back home, an evil presence would move around his bedroom and come to him in the dark. The mother was alarmed, but the boy was quite calm about it. "It's all right Mum," he said, "I just know that Jesus is stronger, so every time it comes I just tell it to go because Jesus is with me, and it can't hurt me. It goes away every time."

The mother assured me she had never told the boy what to do as she was unaware of what was going on. The Lord himself had obviously taught that little boy who loved him just what to do. The lad repeated the story to me without the slightest evidence of fear.

Thirdly, our PERSONALITIES in Jesus Christ (Colossians 2:9, 10).

"For in Christ all the fulness of the Deity lives in bodily form, and you have been given fulness in Christ who is the head over every power and authority."

Not only does every believer spiritually reign with Christ, but Christ expects to live and reign through every believer in daily life. That includes being victorious over every demonic power that might be encountered in daily life or service. In real terms, he desires to clothe himself with us.

154

Fourthly, our POWER in Jesus Christ (Ephesians 1:19, 20).
(1) The Spirit of Jesus desires to fulfil his ministry through us.
"I will build My Church, and the gates of Hades (the powers of the infernal region); shall not overpower it - or be strong to its detriment, or hold out against it" (Matthew 16:18 The Amplified Bible).

Praise God, Jesus Christ has accepted the responsibility for building his Church. If the 'divine builder' and his supervising 'clerk of works' were to be given more 'on-site' freedom to operate in accordance with the master plan, very much more would be done, in much less time, and at a fraction of the cost in terms of energy and finance.

God has given his Church divine power and enablement for world evangelism, for setting people free from all the devil's works, and for growth and maturity to his glory. The nine charismata listed in 1 Corinthians chapter twelve verses eight to ten, cover the need the Church faces in this task (see Schedule "B" in the resources section for details). They are indeed some of 'the keys' Jesus promised his disciples in building his church (Matthew 16:19; 18:18, 19).

Of course this comparison between the 'keys of the kingdom' and the 'charismata' is only one aspect of the use of the gifts of the Spirit which are invaluable in deliverance. This does not imply that people who do not accept or use the charismata are unable to free people from Satan's grip. All believers have the right to use the power of the name and blood of Jesus Christ in faith. But Paul says, "The weapons we fight with are not the weapons of the world. On the contrary, they have divine power to demolish strongholds" (2 Corinthians 10:4). From experience, I have learned that the gates of hell will only yield to those through whom God is able to manifest the power of his Holy Spirit.

(2) Biblical evidence for the authority of Christ's name.
The early Church recognized, used, and submitted to the lordship of Christ, represented by his name.
(a) Salvation came through his name (Acts 2:21; 4:12; 10:43).
(b) Baptism was in his name (Acts 2:38; 8:16; 10:48).
(c) Miracles were performed in his name (Acts 3:6; 4:30).
(d) Bans were placed on the use of his name by the Sanhedrin (Acts 4:17, 18; 5:28).
(e) Disciples rejoiced at suffering shame for his name (Acts 5:41).
(f) Paul was chosen to represent his name, and preached fearlessly in his name (Acts 9:15, 16, 27, 28; Romans 1:5).
(g) Paul and Barnabas risked their lives for his name (Acts 15:25,26).
(h) Deliverance was ministered in his name (Acts 16:18).
(i) The name of Jesus was held in high honour amongst the Ephesian Jews and Greeks because unbelieving exorcists had tried to use his name without authority (Acts 19:17).
(j) The name of Jesus will one day require the obeisance of every created spirit personality, whether angelic, or human (Philippians 2:10).

What the world treats with disdain is the believer's key to power and authority. One night when my wife, Phyl, was sister-in-charge of a ward in one of Sydney's large hospitals, a patient showed sexual aggressiveness to one of the nurses and followed her around the ward. When Phyl asked the man to return to bed, he grabbed her by the wrists and began to drag her towards the toilet cubicles. A call for help resulted in a doctor and two orderlies joining Phyl and the nurse in endeavouring to restrain the man who was acting violently and irrationally. While the five of them were struggling to gain control, Phyl quite spontaneously said to him, "In the name of Jesus, sit down." The violence ceased immediately, and the man said in a quiet voice, "I'll be good." The staff were astonished at the sudden change. One of the nurses who was totally irreligious said later that night, "Sister, I have never believed in demons, but I do now!"

Fifthly, our PROTECTION in Jesus Christ (Luke 10:19 emphasis added).

"I have given you authority to trample on snakes and scorpions and TO OVERCOME ALL THE POWERS OF THE ENEMY; NOTHING WILL HARM YOU."

Both writers have found this promise true, time and time again. A young lady who was being freed from spirits of occultism and witchcraft tried to choke us. She confessed afterwards that we both had special protection around our throats, and no matter how hard the spirits had tried, they were unable to get through the protection.

On other occasions when the demonic powers have become aggressive, counsellees have become exhausted while we have been physically strengthened.

The armour of God, which Paul lists in Ephesians chapter six, verses ten to eighteen, carries three specific guarantees to the wearer:

(1) Confidence to stand up to the devil, no matter what scheme of attack he may use (v. 11).

(2) Assurance that when the day of attack arrives, the bearer will be able to stand his ground (vv. 13, 14).

(3) Victory in battle for the person who wears the spiritual armour, not for the devil (v. 13).

An old fable tells about the devil's auction sale. He was supposed to be selling off some of his old equipment and kept his most highly prized possession under cover until the last. Then to the surprise of the potential buyers, it was seen to be just an old wedge. On it was written one word DISCOURAGEMENT. According to the old fable, the bidding did not reach the exorbitant reserve price, so the devil kept it, and is still using it. Perhaps to keep the Lord's servants from becoming involved in a ministry of deliverance?

Sixthly, PURPOSE in Jesus Christ (Ephesians 3:10).

"His intent was that now, through the church, the manifold wisdom of God should be known to the rulers and authorities in the heavenly realms."

In terms of the modern idiom, it should 'blow our minds' to think that God is using the church as an example of his unfathomable wisdom to all spiritual powers. How galling it must be to Satan and his hordes to see the finger of God pointing to you and me and those around us as examples of his wisdom and love. Every time a believer is released from any form of demonic oppression, or any unbeliever freed to trust in Jesus Christ as Saviour, the powers and authorities must be reminded of their fallen state and future judgment. The redeemed, who will judge angels in their future state (1 Corinthians 6:3), are preparing now by controlling fallen angels while still in their present state. It certainly is a mystery as Paul indicated (Ephesians 3:9), but it is nevertheless very real.

Setting people free in the name of Jesus Christ not only brings glory to God, it justifies his wisdom and reveals the confidence he has in his people as representatives of his kingdom here on earth.

CHAPTER SUMMARY.

1. Ministering freedom to the oppressed is to continue the liberation process Jesus passed on to his disciples. "As my Father has sent me, I am sending you" (John 20:21).
2. God has given his people all they need to overcome the enemy. All he requires of us is obedience.
3. Great honour was brought to the name of Jesus Christ by the early Church through all that was done through its power and authority. It is not God's will this to cease.

Question.

Could it be the fear of losing our reputations, or the fear of what people may think of us, which prevents our obedience, and condemns our fellow believers to continue their servitude to the forces of darkness?

"From the LORD comes deliverance. May your blessing be on your people" (Psalm 3:8).

CHAPTER 19.

Don't limit God to your methods

God alone is the deliverer. Counsellors are only directors of human operations, therefore they should be open-minded about methods. God is sovereign in both the timing and means of bringing release. Phyl and I are constantly open to learn from the experience of others.

Some of the means God has been pleased to use include:

1. His own clear word of instruction.

A colleague shared his experience of hearing a clear word from God instructing him to destroy a small painting given him by a friend who was involved in occultism. As soon as he did so, he said he felt strong churnings in his stomach causing him to vomit freely, and he felt cleansed afterwards.

The writer has at times been led by God to initiate bonfires for the destruction of articles which have been symbols of past domination in sex, occultism, witchcraft, Freemasonry, and other demonic bondages. People have expressed freedom from bondages, dominations, fears, taunting memories, and idolatry when they have burned artifacts, witchcraft items, music tapes, regalia, paintings, photographs, even jewelry and other gifts from persons with whom they had emotional ties.

2. A believer's growth to spiritual maturity.

By submission to the twin ministries of the Holy Spirit (Ephesians 5:18), and the Word of God (Colossians 3:16), some believers find themselves being freed from bondages and lifted to new levels of victorious living.

Prayer and fasting may or may not feature in this process. But letting the oppressed go free and breaking the yoke are certainly approved objectives in the fast which God honours (Isaiah 58:6).

The more Jesus Christ is given Lordship in the whole personality, the less effective some forms of demonic oppression will become; bondages can be broken, and dominating powers will be muted. But with stronger bondages and dominations, and particularly those which afflict the mind with temptation, accusation, and fantasy, a deeper release is generally needed.

3. The power of love.

Some fears (Gr. 'phobos'), are deeply rooted and may even cause terror and panic. These need to be cast out for the oppressed person to have relief, but there are many lesser fears which love and affirmation may remove. Uncertainties, over-sensitivity to noises, a tendency to jump at shadows or when touched unexpectedly, or a constant fear of punishment, are all in this category. "Perfect love drives out fear because fear has to do with punishment" (1 John 4:18). Love is a divine emotion, and when fear-prone people in the Body of Christ are surrounded with love, tenderness, acceptance, and affirmation, many find release.

4. The effect of praise and worship.

Paul says: "Where Jesus is LORD, there is freedom" (2 Corinthians 3:17). It is no wonder then, that in an atmosphere of worship, praise, and thanksgiving, the Spirit of Jesus sometimes releases people without human ministry. Many testify to a sovereign work of God under these circumstances.

5. The observant pastor or counsellor use deliverance when seeing a need for it.

Some of the sure signs which indicate a need are:

(1)   Compulsive behaviour.

(2)   Unusual involuntary muscular movement in any part of the body, other than a normal nerve twitch.

(3)   The wearing of occult or astrological jewelry.

(4)   An unending and irrepressible volume of religious small talk. Conversations tend to be spiritually irrational. The counsellee usually agrees with everything said, and when asked questions, may give wordy or mystical answers which generally evade the point at issue.

(5)   A counsellee confesses to be unable to live in victory, is always falling into sin, and has no sense of joy in the Christian life.

(6)   The casual mention of books read or possessed that are known to be orientated toward occultism or the practice of witchcraft.

(7)   Reference to past involvement in the black arts or psychic experiences.

(8)   A confession of involvement in cults or spiritistic church activities.

6. Deep needs surfacing in altar-call counselling.

Amongst those who respond to altar calls there are usually some whose problems are too deep or complicated to be satisfactorily dealt with in a short space of time. Because of numbers responding, restriction of available time, or the lack of knowledge and inexperience of the person who made the altar call, there is a tendency for these needy people to be passed over quickly or be grouped with others for a "bulk blessing". In some cases this may have a devastating effect on desperate people, and careful thought should be given to obviate this.

Others who respond will have problems which should be dealt with privately rather than publicly. People with psychiatric problems, addictions, spirits of occultism or witchcraft, deep phobias, and those with strong lustful spirits, are much better prayed for in private. Then if they show physical symptoms, scream, or otherwise act strangely they are less likely to affect other people. The availability of counselling rooms and qualified assistance needs prior consideration.

In other words, a clear-cut altar call for specific purposes such as salvation, healing, or the filling of the Holy Spirit, may reveal deep and time-consuming problems which if ignored, lead to needs being unmet.

7. Deliverance is not necessarily an indication of inspiration!

Those who scream and shout at demons when casting them out of the oppressed would do well to remember that in the New Testament accounts of deliverance, only the demons made the noise (Acts 8:7).

(a) **Luke 4:33-37.** When a demon-possessed man shouted at the top of his voice in the synagogue, Jesus sternly said, "Be quiet - come out of him" (vv. 33, 35).

(b) **Luke 4:41.** "Moreover demons came out of people shouting, 'You are the Son of God.' But he rebuked them and would not let them speak because they knew he was the Christ."

(c) **Luke 8:28.** "When he (the Gadarene demoniac) saw Jesus, he cried out and fell at his feet shouting."

(d) **Luke 9:38,39**. A man in the crowd called out to Jesus, asking him to do something for his son, saying "A spirit seizes him and he suddenly screams."

Manifestations and noise can be controlled, and need controlling.

Demons like to be centre stage and will attempt to dominate and discredit the ministry where possible. This should not be tolerated. Demons should be forbidden to speak, silence can be enforced on them. Should it be necessary to ask a demon a diagnostic question, it should be remembered that they are liars by nature and are out to deceive. Conversation and dialogue should be avoided at all times. The only noise the servant of the Lord should want to hear is what Philip the evangelist heard in Samaria: "With shrieks, evil spirits came out of many" (Acts 8:7).

8. Bringing release by proxy.

Persons who are spiritually and emotionally close to those under oppression, particularly close relatives, may take their place during a prayer for deliverance. The writer has followed this course on several occasions. A mother, whom the Lord had freed from a very immoral past, asked for prayer for her son thousands of miles distant in Europe. Although she had been totally cleansed and renewed, she coughed strongly and spontaneously when hands were laid upon her, and specific spirits in her distant son were bound and released. At the same time she had a vision of her son responding to the prayer for deliverance.

9. Deliverance from a distance.

Both writers have known God move in this way. On one occasion a teenager was about eight kilometres from the centre of spiritual warfare. The demonic problem ceased after a time of earnest prayer.

On another occasion, while Phyl prayed for a woman, her husband was also set free while lying on his bed about one hundred yards away. At other times a spouse has been freed in another part of the same building where the husband or wife has been delivered. People frequently receive release when prayed for over the telephone. The distance between the counsellor and the counsellee is unimportant. The Lord has freed people at distances of ten and twelve thousand miles (16,000 to over 19,000 kilometres).

10. Open deliverance sessions.

God is never restricted to individual ministry. Just as the 'power of the Lord was present' in the first century (Luke 5:17), so we have seen the Lord sovereignly move amongst small and large groups setting people free and healing many.

Those who have had experience in this specialized area of deliverance will have rejoiced to see the Lord free needy people as demonic influences, bondages, dominations, afflictions, and infirmities, are bound, broken and loosed. Those who have been freed are later led into receiving cleansing, healing and renewal.

One lady who had convinced herself that none of her immediate family had been Freemasons, was unable to resist being released from those same spirits of Freemasonry when authority was taken over them in open deliverance.

Others have similarly testified to being surprised at some of the spirits which left them during open sessions.

11. Self-deliverance.

A colleague of the writers, Mr. J. Graham Powell, has written an excellent book entitled 'Christian Set Yourself Free', containing much excellent advice on this subject. We certainly agree with the principles set out, but have found in practice, that those who have strong bondages, or powerful dominations, first need major release through the help of others. Only then are they able to deal effectively with any root which may have been missed in earlier prayer. Persons who have first received major release certainly have testified to having been able to set themselves free on later occasions by using the principles in the book.

12. Ministry to the whole person.

Years ago, the writers were faced with the need to find the root causes of people-problems, so that help would be more than just temporary. After seeking God's will, a detailed questionnaire was developed covering the major areas of a believer's life most open to attack by the evil one. By giving careful attention to the answers, observing the counsellee's actions and reactions, and being sensitive to the Holy Spirit, a body of comprehensive information is assembled as a basis for ministry. The average time needed to deal with each counsellee varies from between one and a half to two hours.

Because the Lord has so clearly blessed this kind of ministry, and as so many pastors and counsellors have requested full details, the basic questions are given below. We have found that by naming the spirit of each problem we have been able to exercise divine authority and people have been set free. The questionnaire contains:

1. Questions concerning the rejection syndrome.
(1)   Was your childhood relationship with your parents good, bad, or indifferent? (If the answer is 'bad' or 'indifferent', there will be a rejection problem. More questions about parental attitude or treatment will open up further areas for ministry.)
(2)   Do you have a low self-image?
(3)   Were your teenage years lonely or unhappy?
(4)   Do you have difficulty in giving or receiving love?
(5)   Do you find it difficult to communicate to persons near you?
(6)   Are you a perfectionist? Is it hereditary?
(7)   Do you come from a proud family? Are you a proud person?
(8)   Have you been, or are you now, a rebellious or angry person? Stubborn?
(9)   Do you harbour unforgiveness, resentment, bitterness, or hatred to any person? Who is that person?
Each question opens up specific areas for which deliverance is needed. For a more detailed list, see the rejection-tree diagram.

2. Questions dealing with mental and emotional problems.
(1)   Are you an anxious or worrying person? Do you get depressed? Did either of your parents suffer from these problems?
(2)   Has anyone in your family had a nervous or mental breakdown? Who was it?

(3)   Have you ever had psychiatric counselling? Hospitalisation? Shock treatment?
(4)   Have you ever been hypnotised?
(5)   Have you had an advanced (or tertiary level) education? (For intellectualism, humanism, rationalism, etc.)
(6)   Has anyone in your family ever been a Freemason?
(7)   Do you ever feel mentally confused?
(8)   Do you day-dream, or have mental fantasies? Do you suffer from bad dreams or nightmares?
(9)   Have you ever been tempted to commit suicide? Have you ever attempted to do so? Has anyone in your family?
(10) What fears or phobias do you have?

3. Questions concerning involvement with occultism, or witchcraft practices.
(1)   To your knowledge, have your parents or grandparents ever been involved in occultism or witchcraft practices? To what extent?
(2)   In what areas have you personally been involved?
(3)   Have you been involved in Eastern religions? Have you visited temples?
(4)   Have you done any kind of yoga? Which one?
(5)   Have you been involved in transcendental meditation? Did you have a mantra? What was it?
(6)   Have you ever used mind control for any purpose?
(7)   Are you superstitious? Were your parents or grandparents?
(8)   Do you wear, or have you worn, lucky charms or signs of the zodiac?
(9)   Do you have spirit or idol souvenirs in your home?
(10) Does abstract art, synthesized music, rock and roll, or punk rock 'turn you on'?
(11) Have you learned the martial arts? Which one?
(12) Do you have psychic sensitivity, such as premonitions, deja vu, or psychic sight?

4. Questions concerning addictions.
(1)   To the best of your knowledge, have your parents or grandparents had any addictions? To what?
(2)   Have you inherited any? Have you ever become addicted? If so, to what?

5. Questions concerning sexual problems.
(1)   Do you have lustful thoughts? Fantasy lust?
(2)   Have you been, or are you, a masturbator?
(3)   Have you ever been sexually molested or raped? At what age?
(4)   Have you ever been involved in incest? Committed fornication, or adultery?   (If there has been handling of genital areas, it should be treated as 'technical' fornication.)
(5)   Have you ever had homosexual-lesbian desires, or relationships?
(6)   Have you ever sexually fantasized about, or committed a sexual act with an animal?
(7)   Has pornography ever attracted you?
(8)   Have you been involved in oral sex in fornication or adultery?
(9)   Have you ever had anal sex?
(10) Have you ever had an abortion?
(11) Have you ever had sexual stimulation from an unknown source at any time?

6. Questions concerning cultural, church, and spiritual problems.

(1)   What is your country of birth? Country of parents' birth?
(2)   What other countries have you lived in?
(3)   What is your church background?
(4)   Have you, your parents, or grandparents ever been in a false religious cult? Which one?
(5)   In one word, who is Jesus Christ to you?
(6)   What does the blood of Calvary mean to you?
(7)   Is repentance part of your Christian life?
(8)   Do you have the assurance of salvation?
(9)   Do you have a problem with doubt and unbelief in everyday Christian living?
(10)   Do you suffer from any chronic sicknesses, infirmities, or allergies?
(11)   Do you have any other specific problems not raised by these questions?
(This section will show whether the counsellee is truly born again, and whether there are roots of religious deception which need to be removed. Healings often follow releases from hereditary and other strong spirits of domination. It is quite customary for people with rejection to lack assurance of salvation.)

Each section should be checked against the fruit of the 'rejection tree', for a full list of matters which may need attention.

The completed questionnaire with your own comments added should become the basis of your deliverance prayer. This will ensure that you will be methodical and comprehensive.

Through years of use in many countries, the questionnaire has been the basis for countless people being brought into total freedom in Christ. Because so much deliverance is based only upon the confession of a counsellee's specific need, associated root-fruit systems are mostly missed. As a result, many people are only partially freed.

The most exciting thing we have learned in the deliverance ministry, is the need to wait upon the Lord. He constantly delights us with fresh insights, in-depth understanding of personal problems, and new and exciting revelations of his ways.

CHAPTER SUMMARY.

1. As servants of God we need to be sensitive to what God wants us to do, and not minister out of habit or routine. The sovereignty of God must never be limited by our human reasoning and experience. Eli was not a good father to his children, but his advice to the boy Samuel was sound. " . . if he calls you, say, 'Speak LORD, for your servant is listening' " (1 Samuel 3:9).

2. Waiting upon God brings revelation, and revelation brings responsibility to obey him implicitly. Responsive, responsible obedience puts God in the centre of the action. That is where he needs to be.

3. Always be expectantly watching for God to do something new. Spiritual miracles happen when faith obeys without question. Make room for a sovereign God to work out his sovereign purpose without 'prior notice'.

"When the sun was setting, the people brought to Jesus all who had various kinds of sicknesses, and laying his hands on each one, he healed them. Moreover, demons came out of many people, shouting, 'You are the Son of God!' But he rebuked them and would not allow them to speak, because they knew he was the Christ" (Luke 4:40, 41).

CHAPTER 20.

Guidelines, warnings and other suggestions

Jesus Christ spent a lot of time dealing with individual needs, "and laying his hands on each one, he healed them" (Luke 4:40). No one who went to Jesus in need ever came away disappointed. I am sure it is the desire of every true servant of God that those they counsel will be similarly blessed.

In considering the great variety of needs which may be met through deliverance and renewal, some important principles should be kept in mind:

1. **The experience and discernment of a counsellor will influence the extent of deliverance, and its lasting effects.**

This is no party game. Neither is it a short-cut to prominence and power for a novice. Spiritual forces are involved, and some people have been hurt and discouraged through acting in zeal without sufficient knowledge.

Knowledge is gathered information. This may come from a confession by the counsellee, a casual statement dropped in conversation, or the supply of answers to questions. Observant counsellors will also gain information from a counsellee's attitudes, actions, or reactions during conversation. When put together, these details will determine the scope and type of deliverance needed.

Discernment on the other hand, is what the Holy Spirit reveals to you about the person who needs deliverance. While training can be given in methods and procedures, discernment is receiving what the Spirit of God tells you about the counsellee. Discernment is directly proportionate to our individual level of faith, spiritual maturity, and sensitivity to the voice of the Holy Spirit. Discernment is a God-given understanding, not the conclusions arrived at by mental effort. Jesus Christ showed his intimate knowledge of the unexpressed thoughts of the Pharisees and of his disciples, on numerous occasions e.g. (Luke 5:21, 22; 9:46, 47). Similarly, Peter was given revelation concerning the deception and lies of Ananias and Sapphira his wife, in presenting the alleged full price for the sale of land to the apostles (Acts 5:1-10).

Speaking out the word of the Lord to a counsellee, or praying specifically for a demonic problem of which the counsellee is either unaware (or to which he may have objected prior to prayer) is indeed like walking a tight-rope of faith. But when God holds the other end, results are assured, and valuable lessons are learned. Should fear, or unbelief prevent those steps of faith, lessons are lost, and the counsellee does not receive all that God intends for him.

From experience, I have learned to trust the discernment given by the Holy Spirit, regardless of my own feelings or judgment. Apart from special revelational understanding of counsellees, God has used a second method of instruction. He plants seeds of understanding in my mind, usually about the root causes of problems, or about the relationship of the problems to each other. When I respond in faith by praying for people to be freed from the root causes he reveals, or by teaching those principles to others, God then gives special confirmation. Usually it is by having to deal with a succession of people whose freedom depends on following the pattern he has revealed. This is a great confirmation to having heard the voice of God, and a stimulus to faith. It is most difficult to isolate a single example of this, as all these deliverances principles have been received from the Lord, not man.

It is exciting to continue to be a pupil in God's school! The constant challenge is to personal obedience, holiness, and righteous living. Satan certainly does not have omniscience, but he knows those who are caught in his web, and his demons will delight in mocking any counsellor who tries to exercise spiritual authority in an area where he himself does not have personal victory.

2. For some, a deliverance session may be worse than going to the dentist, so be compassionate and thoughtful.

People who need help come with a wide variety of attitudes and emotions. They need to be set at ease as much as possible and be treated sensitively.

(1) Some have a real fear of the unknown, needing gentle assurance of the Father's love, and his desire to free them from all the devil's works. Should they be frightened away by insensitive approaches, they may never have confidence to ask for help again, which could mean a life sentence of hopelessness and misery.

(2) Some are so discouraged by defeat, failure, and unanswered prayer, that they believe they are beyond help. They not only need to be assured, but the spirits of unbelief, discouragement, and rejection need to be removed before real progress can be made.

(3) Some come openly sceptical about the effectiveness of deliverance. The causes could be intellectualism, rationalism, humanism, pride, fear, religious legalism, or opposition to the use of the gifts of the Holy Spirit. The demonic spirits responsible for these attitudes will need to be dealt with before dealing with the other problems. When open mockery and laughter occurs during ministry, spirits of Freemasonry or occultism and witchcraft need to be bound, their power broken over the life, then cast out before proceeding further.

There is always the possibility of a person refusing to allow the laying on of hands, or prayer for deliverance. A university student came to see us at the request of his mother who was deeply concerned about his behaviour. Depression, introversion, apathy and lack of motivation had brought his studies to a temporary halt. He answered our questions well, but when we explained how we wanted to pray for him he would have none of it, and rose to go, thanking us for listening and talking to him.

I suggested that it would be nice to ask God to bless him before he left, and he was quite agreeable. We both remained seated about three metres from each other. During prayer, by faith, and by memory of the problems the questionnaire had highlighted, I bound, broke, and loosed the demonic powers I believed were oppressing him. We then shook hands, and he left. I remember clearly that the Lord had given me the faith to believe that the prayer would be effective.

Quite some time afterwards, the mother phoned to thank us for the time spent with her son. She said, "He is much better, and looking for a temporary job. He told me your prayer was a great blessing to him."

(4) Some people come excited at the thought of release; they have been so fed up with their problems. They are always most co-operative.

(5) Some are depressed, confused, dull of mind, and feel hopeless about ministry. They are often bound by strong hereditary spirits causing mental problems which will probably have been re-inforced by other spirits received during their time in mental hospitals, particularly through shock treatment, and primal therapy. These people need compassion, but the responsible spirits must be treated without mercy, and evicted.

(6) Some come for what they consider is a 'minor adjustment', and instead receive a 'major overhaul'. It can have a devastating effect. They need encouragement particularly if they are startled by the types of spirits which are cast out. Their sources are usually from heredity and the counsellee may never have had any personal awareness in the problem. Homosexuality frequently manifests itself this way.

3. A few simple guidelines, from personal experience.

(1) Ideally, deliverance should be ministered by male to male, or by female to female. But if a man prays for a woman, another woman or other men should be present. In fact, a ministering team of two or three is ideal. Women counsellees will feel more secure if a male counsellor is ministering in the presence of others. The possibility of false accusations against a counsellor is also removed, assistance is available if there are strong physical manifestations which need to be restrained, and the prayer and discernment base is widened. The ideal team is a husband and wife flowing in the unity of the Holy Spirit.

(2) A supply of paper tissues and a disposal container should always be on hand. Tears often flow, and mucous is frequently produced when demonic powers are driven out and the emotions released.

(3) Where possible, people should be prayed for in private. They should be spared the embarrassment of others knowing what bondages have been broken, what dominant spirits ejected, and the sight of any display of opposition or emotion.

(4) Counselling sessions and the details of deliverance are strictly confidential. A counsellor's reference to case histories should avoid any clues that could identify the counsellee. A 'person' for example, is a sexless description. 'Some time ago', could be anywhere between five minutes and five years. 'Someone close to me', could be yourself, your wife, your child, a relative, or a friend.

Whatever details a counsellee wishes to disclose about the help received is of course, their personal right. However people who have been let down by the cousellor they trusted implicitly often become resentful and bitter. Consultations between pastors and counsellors concerning counsellees' problems should not be interpreted as a breach of the confidential principle, provided the information is not divulged to others.

(5) Fasting is not essential, but it may open up greater understanding in difficult cases, or release more power in ministry. Isaiah chapter 58, verses 6 and 7, outline the bases and results of fasts which God honours.

(6) Every person involved in deliverance needs special sensitivity in recognizing the difference between direct demonic oppression, and psychosomatically induced symptoms. The former may be traced to heredity, or to a point in time when a bondage or domination occurred. The latter may commence with anxiety, or introverted thinking. With both forms of oppression, prayer for release is necessary. With the latter wise counsel, and the resolution of

contributary causes may also be necessary.

(7) Should a counsellee show unwillingness to co-operate, it is not advisable to try to minister deliverance. This should never be forced. Some presons with mental problems may not be able to consent to prayer, but those who bring them may consent on their behalf.

Sometimes it is necessary to ask a person to speak out willingness to obey God in order to break the strong power of a spirit of unforgiveness, resentment, bitterness, hatred, lust, or an addictive habit. It may go like this: "I choose to forgive my mother", "I choose not to be ruled by lust and I choose to have a clean mind", "I choose to give up smoking, drugs, alcohol, etc."

(8) Counsellees should be seated on a straight-backed chair rather than in an easy chair, for ease of access and control. When laying hands on a cousellee for the breaking of bondages and evicting of dominating spirits, all personnel involved should stand to one side of the person receiving deliverance. This avoids being struck by any sudden movement of arms and legs caused by demonic resistance. It is not a frequent happening, but it does occur.

By standing alongside or behind the counsellee, it is much easier to restrain any show of physical force or violence. Demonic powers must never be allowed to take control. Counsellees must be restrained physically so that they do not hurt themselves, others, or do any damage to property. They need to be told firmly that they must co-operate with the Lord, and not give way to the spirits. They still have choice of will. The assistance of others may be necessary.

4. A few warnings from personal experience.

(1) In casting out demonic powers, be sure you operate within the boundaries of your capabilities. When the Holy Spirit wants to bring you into new levels of revelation and authority, he will give you the faith and confidence to proceed. On the other hand, Satan is always ready to tempt the over-zealous worker to be presumptuous and to operate out of self-confidence. Demons may show their anger towards anyone operating beyond his level of faith, or further afflict the person being helped.

(2) Avoid a demonic 'talk-back show'. Demons lie and cannot be trusted. Challenging them to name themselves or declare their nature is Biblical (Luke 8:30). Some will sidestep the question by challenging your authority, by threatening you, or by remaining silent. Others will mumble their names if challenged, or speak quietly or indistinctly. Persistent challenging will normally get answers, even to confessing the point of entry, which can be used as a basis for their eviction.

(3) Be confident in God's authority, and use it as if you were Jesus Christ himself. The writer has had demons say - "You'll never get me out", "You have no authority over me", and "She has been given to the devil, and you can't have her". My wife, Phyl, heard a demon say through the lips of one young lady, "She's only a woman, take no notice of her". That remark sparked some righteous anger, and one arrogant but bound demon found itself evicted by an anointed woman of God.

(4) Do not be surprised if you hear your contact speak in a tone, or voice quite out of character, such as:-

    (a) A woman speaking with a man's voice.

    (b) Adults speaking or crying like a small child.

    (c) Harsh demonic tongues being spoken against you. Because counsellees are asked to refrain from all speaking during ministry, the compulsiveness of the tongue and the harshness of its sound will quickly identify it as being demonic.

(5) Demonic powers will often cause people to act out of character.
- A small and very thin young lady who was being delivered from spirits of anorexia nervosa, had to be restrained by five men. Afterwards she was so exhausted that she had to be carried to bed. But the Lord had released and healed her.
- An epileptic young lady in her twenties became violent, and used obscenities, but had no seizure.
- A young man with a troublesome thought life, fears, and other problems, suddenly said, "I warn you to put all ornaments away; the spirits in me tonight are furious." His eyes showed he meant what he said. The strong word of the Lord quickly broke the power of those spirits, and he fell on his face, coughing to release them.
- Mild-mannered children will suddenly throw a tantrum, kicking, biting, scratching, and yelling. They need to be restrained until they cease struggling and are quiet and the demonic power in them has been broken.
- Cultural spirits will sometimes put on a show of strength and opposition as they are released, and quiet people will suddenly show a frenzy of activity.

(6) Those who minister in deliverance should pray for their wives and families to be protected by the name and blood of Jesus Christ at all times, but particularly during times of spiritual warfare with needy people. The enemy is subtle enough to try to score through a backlash upon family members.

(7) Beware of any underhand tactics the evil one may try by using defeated people to undermine your faith and authority. Praying for freedom is based on faith, operated in faith, and is victorious by faith. The discernment of the Spirit is more important than the promptings of the senses.

(8) The full benefits of a freedom session may not be seen at once. Some receive total release and healing immediately. Some receive release without feelings, and assurance of their full release comes as they adhere to the follow-up programme. A few find that the benefits from the time of release come as they adhere to the follow-up programme. A few find that the initial benefits from the time of release continue afterwards, but the full results taking months, or even up to one year. God is always faithful to his word. Our responsibility is to trust him.

(9) The degree of manifestation and release varies from person to person. This is because the degree of oppression varies. It has been found that there are often strong spirits present which control the activities of other demonic powers in the mind, emotions, and body. They need to be released first. If there is a controlling spirit over the whole personality, it must be discerned and removed before the lesser powers can be dealt with. Prayer priorities should therefore be determined by the Holy Spirit, and he may use the discernment of others to assist you. Always be open to this.

(10) At the conclusion, one question should never be asked. It is, "How do you feel?" It focuses on feelings, not on faith. God's effectiveness will be manifested in his time. At the end of the deliverance session, the degree of release is normally evident in the counsellee's face. There is often spontaneous praise expressing inner assurance, peace, and joy. When I am confident that God has done a deep work, I will often say, "I am sure that God has done a deep work in you today." This is positive and faith-building, avoiding emphasis on feelings. Should the counsellee reply, "I didn't feel a thing", I usually reply, "Who said you should? Successful Christian living is based on making right choices, not on feelings."

Regrettably, some Christians have lost the ability to gather their own spiritual food because they have been spoon fed. What they require is the spiritual equivalent of physiotherapy. They need a follow-up programme which will restore full function and mobility. The use of such materials, plus the submission of progress reports to the counsellor, will normally release the full effects of their deliverance into daily life.

CHAPTER SUMMARY.

1. This work requires preparation of heart, divine wisdom, genuine love, unwavering faith, special protection, and strict discipline.
2. The Holy Spirit is the Divine Professor of Truth. He is able to cope with any situation you may encounter. Hear him, heed him, obey him, then honour him for all he has done.
3. Never allow Satan to discourage you, limit your authority, make a counsellee violent, or rob you of total victory which is your blood-bought right.

"In my anguish I cried to the LORD and he answered by setting me free"

(Psalm 118:5).

CHAPTER 21.

How to set people free
using divine authority and power

1. Some preliminary suggestions.

Deliverance sessions should commence with giving glory to God, exalting Jesus Christ, and submitting to the sovereignty of the Holy Spirit. If the counsellee is a born-again believer, he or she should be asked to repeat the following prayer:-

"I confess Jesus Christ to be my personal Saviour. I confess and renounce every iniquity, transgression and sin that I, my parents, or ancestors may have committed and which has brought bondages and dominations to my life, and ask for forgiveness and cleansing. I repent from any action, attitude or habit which does not glorify Jesus Christ. I renounce the devil, and all of his works, influences, bondages, dominations, afflictions and infirmities in my life. I claim the release and freedom promised by Jesus Christ, that he may be Lord of my whole life. Amen."

A few simple explanations and instructions need to be given to the counsellee before commencing prayer so that he or she will understand the procedure, and know how to co-operate.

(1) The ban on audible prayer.

Ask the counsellee to refrain from praying audibly during ministry, and particularly from speaking out the name of Jesus Christ. This is for two reasons. Firstly, it becomes confusing when two people are speaking at one time, and it can be noisy. Secondly, the spoken name of Jesus is always a barrier to demonic powers who are ordered to leave.

A simple illustration explains this principle. When a bird gets trapped inside a room, the best way to release it is to open a door or window then stand aside so that the way of escape is clear. To stand in the doorway or in front of the window will only frighten the bird and make it fly around. In the same way, demonic dominations (spirit forces inside the body) are fearful of the name of the conquering Saviour, and its use by the counsellee will only delay or hinder their leaving.

(2) Control of the counsellee's thoughts.

It is important for people receiving deliverance to concentrate their thinking on the Lord Jesus. If they wish, they may pray silently. Again, there are two reasons. Firstly, an inert mind can become Satan's playground. Sin is conceived in the mind, and a 'No Vacancy' sign will discourage unwanted callers. Secondly, dominant spirits sometimes try to manipulate minds with thoughts of unbelief and scepticism, fantasy, distraction, or even to resist what is happening.

(3) The need to speak out.

Counsellees should be encouraged to speak out anything significant that comes into their minds during the session.

(a) A sudden recall of a forgotten event may provide a clue as to the type of domination which may be causing problems.

(b) When seeking to identify strongholds which resist the lordship of Christ, the counsellee should be asked to tell you whatever comes to mind.

(c) When demonic powers try to dominate a mind during deliverance, it is important for the counsellee to declare this so that authority can be taken over them.

(4) Explain the Biblical significance of the laying on of hands.

This procedure may disturb certain types of people:

(a) Believers with reservations.

There are usually two objections. One is that by laying hands on the demon-possessed, "you might become possessed yourself". Well, Jesus Christ wasn't affected, and the Spirit-filled believer is just as safe (Luke 4:40, 41). The other objection is that the laying on of hands is unnecessary. "All you have to do to demons is to renounce them, bind them, and tell them to go away." A few may indeed respond, but by far the majority are more defiant than a bunch of naughty boys, and will remain entrenched until they are evicted by the name of Jesus and the power of his anointing. Both of us have seen experienced counsellors encircle a needy person, naming and binding spirits, without the slightest evidence of release being received. With the laying on of hands, results begin immediately. Demons cannot stand the power of the Holy Spirit being released into the life they have been dominating, and are usually glad to leave. We long for the day of God's power, when the mere presence of a holy life, or a simple command in the name of Jesus will cause demons to flee.

(b) Those who have not previously experienced the laying on of hands.

Before praying for either unbelievers or believers, it should be explained that this was the practice of Jesus Christ, his disciples, and the early church. Only two days before writing this chapter, I had the joy of leading a man to Christ and praying for his release from spirits of Freemasonry and rejection. He had no problems about the laying on of hands, although it was completely new to him.

Many times before deliverance actually begins, demonic powers have become so restless because of the counsellee's renunciation and prayer, that they have begun to leave before hands can be laid on the one oppressed. They certainly know what their future state will be (Matthew 25:41; Revelation 20:10).

(5) The manner of demonic releases.

Demons leave the body in a variety of ways. When demonic bondages are broken, there is usually no evident sign unless they are particularly strong, but spirits of domination normally leave in an obvious manner. This includes coughings, sighing, yawnings, and belching. It is wise to forewarn a counsellee about this so as to save him from later embarrassment. The following explanation has helped people understand the reason for this. The engines in our cars need air to aid the fuel combustion, and draw this in through the air filter and carburettor. The waste products are then blown out through the exhaust pipe. This process illustrates the need to get rid of the demonic powers (spiritual impurities) by coughing, or other means, before the Holy Spirit (as the breath of God) is able to cleanse and heal.

2. THE RELEASE PROCESS, STEP BY STEP.

(1) Aim to remove root causes rather than just pick bad fruit.

There are many spiritual 'fruit inspectors' around who can tell us what bad fruit they can see on the trees of our lives. However, few of them are 'tree-doctors' capable of diagnosing and removing causes in order that we may bear good fruit.

Counsellees are often not able to diagnose the causes of their own problems, although they are acutely aware of their presence. They usually do not want to disappoint those who pray for them, and may even pretend to have been helped, even if they do not feel so. If their problems have not been actually discerned and dealt with they may give way to hopelessness and despair and remain defeated Christians.

The 'Tree of Rejection' in chapter eleven, is here harmonised with the diagnostic questions set out in the questionnaire in chapter nineteen. This will highlight some of the most commonly encountered root-fruit systems to be dealt with in deliverance.

THE TREE AND ITS ROOTS	THE QUESTIONNAIRE INFORMATION
The basic causes of rejection: At conception In utero The manner of birth A baby not being bonded at birth Being an adopted child Hereditary rejection Causes in the family home School teachers or students One's own attitudes Other causes later in life	Questions one and two will reveal not only the causes of rejection, but also the branches that need attention, item by item.

THE INPUT
IDENTIFIES

THE ROOT SYSTEMS OF REJECTION
WHICH REQUIRE REMOVAL

The list is not exhaustive. It may be amended as the Spirit of God directs.

1 REJECTION (Aggressive reactions)	2 SELF REJECTION (Negative reactions)	3 FEAR OF REJECTION (Counter-actions)
Rebellion Anger, temper, etc. Stubbornness Aggressive attitudes, by words, or use of force Refusal, or inability to communicate Inability or refusal to receive comfort	Low self-image Inferiorities Apathy, disinterest Self-accusation FEARS OF ALL KINDS Doubt, unbelief Self-pity Negativity Emotional immaturity caused by a childish or adolescent spirit	A spirit of striving for friendship or achievement. Perhaps performance or competition. Withdrawal, a desire to be alone. Independence, isolationism Criticism, judgement Envy, jealousy. The self syndrome: self-righteousness self-defensiveness, protectiveness perfectionism

The following root-fruit systems have been developed from the other problems highlighted by the questionnaire. They will be of assistance in diagnosis, and as a guide to the release of root causes which may be hidden, or are inter-related with other problems.

The central boxes contain the names of problems. The surrounding boxes contain contributory root causes.

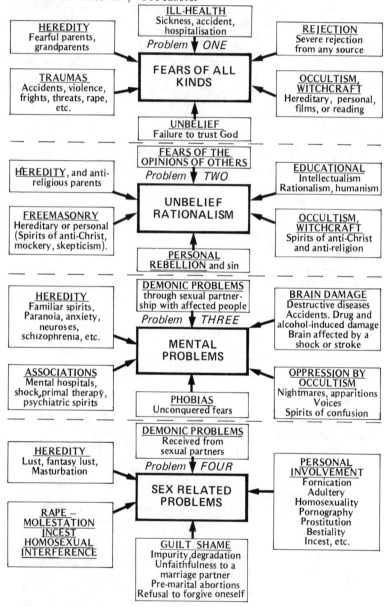

ILL-HEALTH
Sickness, accident, hospitalisation
Problem ONE

HEREDITY
Fearful parents, grandparents

REJECTION
Severe rejection from any source

FEARS OF ALL KINDS

TRAUMAS
Accidents, violence, frights, threats, rape, etc.

OCCULTISM, WITCHCRAFT
Hereditary, personal, films, or reading

UNBELIEF
Failure to trust God

FEARS OF THE OPINIONS OF OTHERS
Problem TWO

HEREDITY, and anti-religious parents

EDUCATIONAL
Intellectualism
Rationalism, humanism

UNBELIEF RATIONALISM

FREEMASONRY
Hereditary or personal
(Spirits of anti-Christ, mockery, skepticism).

OCCULTISM, WITCHCRAFT
Spirits of anti-Christ and anti-religion

PERSONAL REBELLION and sin

DEMONIC PROBLEMS
through sexual partnership with affected people
Problem THREE

HEREDITY
Familiar spirits, Paranoia, anxiety, neuroses, schizophrenia, etc.

BRAIN DAMAGE
Destructive diseases
Accidents. Drug and alcohol-induced damage
Brain affected by a shock or stroke

MENTAL PROBLEMS

ASSOCIATIONS
Mental hospitals, shock, primal therapy, psychiatric spirits

OPPRESSION BY OCCULTISM
Nightmares, apparitions
Voices
Spirits of confusion

PHOBIAS
Unconquered fears

DEMONIC PROBLEMS
Received from sexual partners
Problem FOUR

HEREDITY
Lust, fantasy lust, Masturbation

PERSONAL INVOLVEMENT
Fornication
Adultery
Homosexuality
Pornography
Prostitution
Bestiality
Incest, etc.

SEX RELATED PROBLEMS

RAPE – MOLESTATION INCEST HOMOSEXUAL INTERFERENCE

GUILT SHAME
Impurity, degradation
Unfaithfulness to a marriage partner
Pre-marital abortions
Refusal to forgive oneself

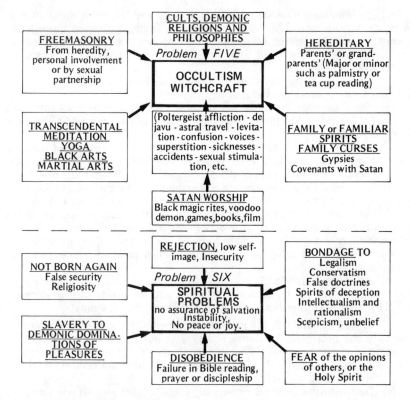

CULTS, DEMONIC RELIGIONS AND PHILOSOPHIES

Problem **FIVE**

OCCULTISM WITCHCRAFT

FREEMASONRY
From heredity, personal involvement or by sexual partnership

HEREDITARY
Parents' or grand-parents' (Major or minor such as palmistry or tea cup reading)

TRANSCENDENTAL MEDITATION YOGA BLACK ARTS MARTIAL ARTS

(Poltergeist affliction - de javu - astral travel - levitation - confusion - voices - superstition - sicknesses - accidents - sexual stimulation, etc.

FAMILY or FAMILIAR SPIRITS FAMILY CURSES
Gypsies
Covenants with Satan

SATAN WORSHIP
Black magic rites, voodoo demon. games, books, film

REJECTION, low self-image, Insecurity

Problem **SIX**

SPIRITUAL PROBLEMS
no assurance of salvation Instability, No peace or joy.

NOT BORN AGAIN
False security
Religiosity

BONDAGE TO
Legalism
Conservatism
False doctrines
Spirits of deception
Intellectualism and rationalism
Scepicism, unbelief

SLAVERY TO DEMONIC DOMINATIONS OF PLEASURES

DISOBEDIENCE
Failure in Bible reading, prayer or discipleship

FEAR of the opinions of others, or the Holy Spirit

(2) Distractions of the evil one.

Every person involved in releasing spiritual prisoners develops his own style with which he feels comfortable. Final results are of course the only objective evaluation. With this in mind, and with gratitude to the Lord, we share what he has taught us. We are conscious of our mistakes and failures, and realize that the Holy Spirit has so much yet to teach us. We trust it may encourage others to step out in faith, trusting the Spirit of the Lord for increasing insight into causes of spiritual problems, and new ways of meeting personal needs.

The enemy has tried to prevent effective deliverance by a number of activities:

(a) by trying to bring about the cancellation of an appointment. His favourite tricks are sickness, an accident, severe oppression, appointment confusion, and unreasonable fears of what may happen.

(b) by bringing an onset of distracting pain during prayer. One woman suddenly doubled up in agony when the pain of an operation performed ten years previously returned. The demon of pain was cast out, and immediately she felt normal.

On other occasions, headaches, dizziness, and a sense of imminent fainting have threatened to hold up ministry. Each feeling has been a demonic delaying tactic, and ceased when authority was taken over it.

(c) by bringing unreasonable feelings of panic and fear while the counsellee is being prayed for. The fear is a demonic feeling expressed through the counsellee. During deliverance, women have become terrified of me as a male, and have clung to Phyl until they were set free. Remember the Boy Scout motto and 'be prepared'.

The stages of the deliverance process are as follows:-

(1) **The binding, breaking, and loosing.**

(a) The counsellee should be seated on an upright chair without arms, well clear of surrounding furniture. The paper tissues and waste container need to be close at hand.

Your prayer partner should be asked to hold the completed questionnaire so that you can easily read the negative problems for which bondages must be broken, and the names of the dominating spirits which must be evicted.

Examples of a bondage are an inability to forgive, or express love. Examples of a dominating spirit would be bitterness, anger, hatred and lust.

As stated previously, we have found that by naming specific spirits which produce root causes of problems they can be evicted, and cleansing and wholeness received. This is probably the key to understanding the difference between verbal counselling, and counselling which leads to freedom through deliverance.

(b) After the prayer and renunciation, one hand should be placed on the forehead, and one at the back of the head, and the power of each demonic force by name should be bound, broken, and loosed one at a time.

Unless the Holy Spirit indicates otherwise the rejection syndrome is normally the best place to commence prayer, not just because it heads the questionnaire, but because it is the key to releasing other parts of the personality. Where strong spirits of witchcraft and anti-Christ are resisting ministry, they should be tackled first.

(c) Deal with the demonic powers of several related areas at one time, and be sure there has been a release before proceeding to the next group. This procedure is followed until the entire list compiled from the questionnaire has been dealt with.

(2) **How to know that demonic forces have been driven out and bondages broken.**

Once the power of the demons have been bound and broken, and their hold over the life loosed, they no longer have any legal right to remain. Although demons are always illegal squatters, they are seldom keen to vacate the premises under orders of the rightful owner. Some however can't leave fast enough, and the person receiving prayer may burst into spontaneous coughing, as soon as the authority is taken.

When there is no immediate manifestation, the writers have found it most beneficial to ask the counsellee to bend forward slightly, from the waist up. We then place our hands on each side of the waist above the hips, the two thumbs pointing towards the spine, and as close to it as possible. It is important that the hands avoid the stomach area. The activity of demon powers may actually be felt in the hands. They may move and jump around, sometimes quite strongly, or gather in a knot. The counsellee may or may not be aware of this. Sometimes the whole area under the hands becomes rigid, and the counsellee finds it most difficult or even impossible to cough even if he desires to do so.

The power of 'holy hands' added to what Jesus Christ has given us is certainly most effective. Normally, one of the following reactions will take place:

(a) The counsellee will spontaneously cough deeply, and continue coughing until each demonic power named in the root-fruit systems has gone. Other manifestations may include yawning, belching, sighing, gagging, or retching.

(b) Nothing happens. In this case, suggest that the counsellee try a good strong cough. This normally triggers the process of release, which should continue until the spirits named have gone. When the coughing commences, the named spirits can again be commanded to leave.

(c) A counsellee refuses to cough, saying "Why should I cough?" This may be because he does not understand why he needs to do so. When the reason is repeated, there is usually co-operation. But if the response is more of a challenge to authority, or an expression of no confidence in the method, it should be explained that coughing is an act of faith and co-operation. The counsellee needs to understand that confidence in the person who is ministering is important, and although the act of coughing may seem irrelevant, it is a method which God has blessed. Spirits of unbelief, doubt, and scepticism should then be bound, broken, and loosed, and the request to cough repeated. In almost all cases, the process of freedom commences, and the person is able to be fully released. The spontaneity of coughing, after it has been commenced by an act of the will, builds faith and expectation.

Should a counsellee still refuse to co-operate after an explanation and further prayer, it is obvious that it is not God's time for release. Further counselling may be necessary.

(d) A counsellee genuinely tries to cough, and is unable to do so. Some make noises which are more like clearing the throat, but cannot cough at a deeper level. Normally this is caused by strong spirits of resistance. Often they come from occultism, witchcraft, or Freemasonry. Authority should be taken strongly over every spirit of anti-Christ, rebellion, resistance, stubbornness, and spiritual darkness. Where there is mocking laughter, a spirit is causing it. It is important that the counsellee co-operate by attempting to cough, and with persistence by both counsellor and counsellee, the coughing will begin and increase until the pent-up demonic powers literally rush out. The counsellee will then usually express relief from the inner tension and pressures. The best advice, in difficult cases, is simply, "Hang in there".

It is seldom that people who have received deep releases do not spontaneously confess their sense of freedom when the session is completed.

(3) Points to remember:

(a) **Persistence is important.** Demonic powers will bluff, pretend not to be there, or to have gone when in fact they still remain. They use every trick possible to resist eviction. Their resistance can only be temporary; remember your legal rights over them, purchased at Calvary.

(b) **Reassure counsellees** that when you voice strong opposition to demonic powers, you are not speaking to them personally, but to what is in them. Some sensitive people may feel crushed unless they understand this.

(c) **Demonic noise can be and should be controlled.** Some people scream unexpectedly while they are being freed. If this continues, the spirits need to be commanded to be silent. Their talkback can be similarly controlled.

(d) **The final check.** When you have worked through your problem list and believe all the demonic forces have been driven out and all bondages have been broken, a final check is necessary. Paul tells us that we have weapons which destroy strongholds and make Jesus Christ Lord of the life (2 Corinthians 10:5). Use that power to challenge any authority which may still remain to hinder Lordship. By commanding all such demonic powers to name themselves, or reveal their work, they will either speak out through the mouth of the counsellee, or will name themselves in the counsellee's mind. By asking that anything of this nature be spoken out, even if it has already been dealt with, what surfaces is sometimes surprising. Deal with each item, so that there is a clear release before renewing the challenge. Even if a word or name shocks the individual, deal with the demonic power behind it in faith.

(e) There is one important rule in ministering freedom in Christ. When the Holy Spirit gives any inner conviction that a certain demonic spirit is operating within a person's life, **always act upon his advice.** It may not make sense to you, but act upon it, and you will always see results. The more teachable you are, the more you will be shown and the greater will be the glory brought to the name of Jesus Christ.

So, when completing the release portion of the session, be open to what the Lord may reveal as well as what comes into the mind of the counsellee. Time taken is an investment. Do not proceed to the cleansing process until you and the counsellee have the inner witness that the enemy has gone. Then proceed to clean up the battle field.

3. Cleansing, receiving forgiveness, forgiving others, and inner healing.
(1) Cleansing.
Jesus said a life becomes clean when an evil spirit leaves it (Luke 11:25). John sets out the process in his epistle. First there is confession, then forgiveness followed by cleansing from all unrighteousness caused by that sin (1 John 1:9).

It appears that few believers really believe this promise and claim the blessings of inner cleansing. Most of us re-confess our sins time and again to make sure we have been thorough. The evidence is that many Christians continue to live in the bondage of guilt for sins that have been forgiven. We can delude ourselves into thinking that our low self-image is a sign of repentance and humility - some form of penance imposed on ourselves to make us feel better! All this is contrary to what our merciful and gracious God has provided in Jesus Christ.

Inner cleansing through the blood of Jesus Christ may also become very real during the laying on of hands. Ask the counsellee to receive this by faith in every area which has been defiled. This involves mind, heart, conscience, will, and each physical system affected by demonic powers.

(2) Receiving forgiveness.
When God forgives, he wipes out all record of the wrong doing. That means that there are only two persons who still have that information, and who can use it wrongfully. One is the devil who constantly enjoys accusing us and making us feel guilty. It is one of his really bad habits and counsellees should be warned not to listen to the world's most incorrigible liar. The other knowledgeable person is the forgiven sinner who often battles with past memories, and doubts forgiveness. That memory needs to be dealt with in two

positive ways. Firstly, forgiveness needs to be established by being declared openly. Here is a simple prayer:

"I thank you Father for your forgiveness for .... (name), and for your total release from the grip and accusation of the evil one, and the completeness of your inner cleansing. Because I am clean in your sight, I now forgive myself for all I have done in sinning against yourself, myself, and others. I release myself completely from bondages to people and past events. Amen."

Secondly, the counsellee needs to believe that there is no longer any basis for anyone to cause condemnation (Romans 8:1). All lying accusations from the memory or from Satan need to be resisted by praise to God for his total cleansing.

(3) Forgiving others.

When spirits of unforgiveness, resentment, bitterness, and hatred have been driven out, a counsellee has no trouble in expressing forgiveness to parents, children, a marriage partner, and friends. A prayer of faith should be framed so that the counsellee can specifically name the people who are being forgiven and released from troublesome memories. Forgiveness of others is basic to all spiritual blessing (Matthew 6:14, 15; Mark 11:25; Colossians 3:13b).

(4) Inner healing.

Much has been written about the healing of memories. It has been the experience of the writers that complete healing cannot be received or retained until the causative factors have been removed. It is like trying to heal a finger without removing the wood splinter which has caused an infection. Once every form of demonic oppression has been removed, cleansing taken, and forgiveness received and extended to others, there is no hindrance to a person receiving full healing in all affected areas. This should harmonise the thoughts and emotions, produce a healthy self-image, and allow the Spirit of God to direct bodily appetites and habits. Physical healings will also be manifested when spirits of infirmities and afflictions have been cast out. Many people testify to physical healings received in this way after public ministry.

It has been found that the average time taken to diagnose and release problems using the questionnaire is about ninety minutes. Those who come with a clear understanding of their problems and causes may take a little less, and the more complicated may take thirty minutes longer. A few may take several hours. Before concluding, follow-up literature is explained, and given to the counsellee. This contains an address if future contact is needed. The details are given in chapter twenty-three.

(5) Dealing with a small or large group of people at one time.

Sessions of this nature are normally preceded by a teaching session giving some understanding about the demonic causes of personal problems. There should be prayer which exalts Jesus Christ, and authority should be taken over every spirit of the enemy, including spirits of false deliverance. People desiring release should then be led in a prayer of confession and renunciation of the devil and his work.

Demonic spirits should then be systematically named, bound, broken, and loosed from the lives of those present in much the same way as in personal exorcism. When they are called out, a variety of manifestations will occur. There could be crying, coughing, retching, and every other manifestation seen in private sessions. The following guidelines should also be observed:

(a) Demonic noise such as wailing and screaming should be stopped.

(b) People involved in, or understanding deliverance, should move around amongst the individuals needing help, assisting those who are having difficulty in being released, and supplying paper tissues to those in need.

(c) Physical violence must be restrained, and demons made to leave, as commanded.

(d) The time taken to deal with each problem spirit will be determined by how long the group dominated by that problem needs to receive freedom. Stragglers should be dealt with individually, or at the conclusion so as not to delay the others.

(e) When you have dealt with all the bondages and dominations, and obeyed every prompting of the Holy Spirit, cleansing and healing should be sought in prayer.

(f) All prayer in public should be done with open eyes, so that the devil will not be able to spring any surprises.

An advantage of this type of group activity is that more people are able to receive freedom in a shorter time. Somewhat surprisingly, few people show self-consciousness. Most willingly open themselves to receive every blessing the Spirit of God wishes to impart. But it may be necessary to minister further to them in private.

Although deliverance is time-consuming and very demanding because of the numbers constantly requesting appointments, it is the most thrilling confirmation of God's presence amongst his people.

Here are three of many written testimonies which have been received:

● "I have been a born again Christian for 33 years, Spirit-filled for 11 years, married for 29 years, 26 years of it just hell, and a defeated Christian for 30 years, knowing what I should do, but unable to do it.

Because of rejection through heredity, and receiving rejection throughout my life, I couldn't give or receive love from anyone, particularly my wife. I would retreat into a hiding place within myself at any hint of criticism, and not communicate to my wife or children often for weeks at a time, even although I was a deacon of a local church. I was a workaholic and put work before my family. I had so many walls up no-one could ever get near me to hurt me.

Three years ago through Noel and Phyl the Lord delivered me from rejection, self-rejection, fear of rejection, and workaholism. They described to me the filling in of the black hole into which I would go and hide whenever I was threatened with rejection.

The first few weeks after ministry I felt like a crab caught in the sunshine, and any time a threatening situation arose, I would scuttle around looking for my hole in which to hide, there was none; it was filled in! I found there was really no danger at all. For the first time in my life I was able to give and receive love.

I have grown more, spiritually, in the last three years than the previous thirty years. My married life gets better every day. Praise God. He has set me free."

● "I received Jesus Christ as Lord of my life five years ago. Through Freedom in Christ Ministries I have been gloriously freed from alcoholism, drug addiction, Freemasonry, nicotine, suicide, death, many addictions, obscenity, adultery, pornography, rejection, and fear.

They are now so far behind me that I have trouble remembering the person I used to be. Now I know the reality of the fruit of the Holy Spirit in my beautiful life with friends and family relationships, all unimaginable in the past! I not only received prayer and deliverance through the Gibsons' ministry, but patient and constant loving follow-up. Their teaching and guidance have been so vital to my relationship with my Lord. I truly know the contrast the black life of the world and the sweet life with the Prince of Peace. Hallelujah!''

● "I wish to share some wonderful news. Your ministry has been priceless, not only to myself, but also to my husband. When he saw the change in me, he wanted the same for himself.

A week after my visit to you, with the guidance of our pastor's wife, he committed his life to Jesus and was filled with the Spirit.

To describe the many blessings that our Lord has bestowed upon us, not only as a married couple, but individually, would take up too many pages. Suffice to say, that our wonderful God has blessed us beyond our dreams! My husband received much prayer over the years, but the turning point came when he saw evidence of God's greatness.''

CHAPTER SUMMARY.

1. The Spirit of God has given the spiritual therapist great advantages over traditional psychological and psychiatric processes. They are the word of God, the power and authority of Jesus Christ, and the understanding and guidance of the Holy Spirit.

2. The aim of deliverance is not to pour oil on troubled waters, but to detect and remove sources of trouble. The goal is to free people, then see them healed and renewed.

3. The process of freeing people to the glory of God is no twentieth century invention. Its theological basis is orthodox, but unorthodox methods of release do not invalidate the ministry. Fear of what others may say will not only prevent the application of Biblical truth, but may condemn some of God's people to needless continued slavery.

4. God wants his people out of the wilderness and into his land of blessing!

"By wisdom a house is built, and through understanding it is established; through knowledge its rooms are filled with rare and beautiful treasures"

(Proverbs 24:3, 4).

CHAPTER 22.

Demolishing brick walls

(Part 2 of Ministry to children by Phyl Gibson)

I would like to commence by writing to parents, and particularly to mothers. No one is as close to a child as the mother. From the moment of conception, the mother is committed, whether she desires to be or not.

Thousands of books seem to have been written on what to do and how to think before childbirth, and on how to handle the rearing of children. Some have been helpful, and some confusing. Modern thinking agrees that "Mum and Dad know best most times - especially Mum". Jesus spoke many times about the importance of children, and if we could learn to understand their value from God's point of view, we would enjoy our children more while they are young. The film of childhood can never be remade to correct the mistakes the parents make.

Children are influenced by both good and bad examples, just as blotting paper absorbs whatever is spilt upon it. Professor Wilson, a New York criminologist, says the two dominant things that continue from childhood into the teenage years are affection and consistency. They both reflect the character of God. He is all loving, and always consistent in his dealings with his children.

1. The need for physical love. Genuine love is a vital key. We will never fool a child about the true quality of our love. Giving gifts is no substitute for caring love. Until children reach the age of understanding and accountability, we as parents are responsible for their spiritual, moral, and physical well-being. The best way for them to learn to love Jesus is by seeing the example of our love to him and our enjoyment of him.

Physical love given from a caring heart is an essential ingredient in the growth of the whole child. It has been proved that babies who are not physically loved and handled, do not grow or develop emotionally like those who are.

Mothers, please hug your sons right through their teenage years. Many think that a ten year old boy is too big for physical love, but this is not so. Sons who are hugged by their mothers become used to a female body, and are not 'turned on' by a girl's femininity on their first date.

Emotional starvation causes a child to feel unloved, unwanted, and unvalued. This has caused many teenagers to take the exit ramp to drugs and suicide. When talking to a group of teenagers, I asked them how they felt about parental discipline. Nine out of ten said that their parents never set guidelines. Their parents didn't enquire where they were going at night, with whom they were going, or set any time limit for their return. They generally felt that their parents didn't love them enough to care. They said: "We like set boundaries; they make us feel secure."

This type of love always programmes a child for problems when he grows older. He then finds it difficult to believe that God's love is unconditional. Fathers who have not shown physical signs of love for their children (particularly sons) and have not spent time with them will inhibit them in relating to God.

A mother is the first representative of God that a child meets. All of us mothers can look back to times when we have been poor examples of God's love to our children. I have a magnetic card on my refrigerator door which sums it up: "Thank you, Lord, for granting me this new day, especially since I loused up yesterday so badly!" So take heart.

Many of us do not realise that even the things we say may harm our children. We do not mean them seriously, but the child who hears us believes that we mean them.

In counselling adults, we are often amazed by the amount of negative expressions which are remembered from childhood. It has not only been a stumbling block to self-acceptance, but also to accepting God for who he is. Some of the common examples are:

"You are no good." "You are a failure."
"You are ugly." "You are a bird-brain."
"You are a nuisance." "You're dumb."
"You will never make anything of your life."

Dogmatic statements do not go in to one ear and out of the other. In many cases they leave an indelible mark and programme the life for failure. We need to keep in mind Reuben's advice to his brothers when they were about to reject Joseph: "Do not sin against the child" (Genesis 42:22).

● A man of thirty who came for ministry had a history of constant failure each time success was in sight. When he shared his childhood background, it was obvious that his father had favoured a younger brother. As a child of seven, he was continually told that he would never be a success, and that he was of no value. This became so deeply rooted in his sub-conscious mind that he was permanently programmed for failure in everything he did. Self-rejection was the ruling factor of his life.

● Rene walked in to a room where her mother was talking to a friend, just in time to hear her say, "Rene is ugly." The mother never knew her little girl had heard the remark, but it created a low self-image which remained until late womanhood.

How often we parents express our negative thoughts, instead of those which are positive and encouraging. Children are also very discerning, and if they do not see their parents practising the principles they demand of their children, they will discard what they say as of no value. To lie to a child is to plant seeds of deceit. "Fathers, do not exasperate your children; instead, bring them up in the training and instruction of the Lord" (Ephesians 6:4).

2. Dealing with the problem of bad sleeping.

If a child does not sleep well, at least one of the parents is not liable to sleep well either. Most adults become quite unreasonable if denied sleep, and desperate parents often bring their children to us. Some of them, after being disturbed for up to nine or ten times per night, finally take the child into their own bed. This often creates more problems than it solves.

The causes of bad sleeping in a child may be quite complex, and the following possibilities need to be investigated:

(1) Ill-health.

The child's health needs to be checked carefully before considering other causes, particularly with babies or very young children who cannot explain what is wrong with them.

(2) Loneliness and anxiety.

Surprisingly, even babies are affected by being left alone. Remember, for nine months they have had the companionship of their mother's heartbeat and voice.

Little Ruth kept getting up at night, going into her parents' bedroom, and asking for a cuddle. Some nights she would do this a number of times. She was a much-wanted and much-loved child who was constantly given warm and caring love by both parents. As we waited upon God for his answer to the problem the Holy Spirit revealed that a spirit of loneliness in her bedroom was attacking her at night. The mother explained that a 'latch-key' son of the previous owner had used the room her daughter was occupying. The boy's mother had worked on a full-time basis and he let himself into the empty house each day, after school, with a key he kept on a cord around his neck. He had no friends to play with and spent much time alone in his room. When the room was cleansed by the blood of Jesus Christ from all influence of the spirit of loneliness which had oppressed the boy, Ruth slept soundly, needing no extra comfort.

(3) The effects of a disturbed pregnancy
may surface in bad sleeping patterns in a baby, and continue into childhood until the habit is broken and healing ministered.

(4) A constant change of homes, schools, and friends
may unsettle a child and result in interrupted sleep. Some children have felt so rejected through these experiences that they have in turn rejected their parents whom they blamed for the changes and consequent insecurity.

(5) Unreasonable fears.

Some children become frightened of wind, rain, the noises of creaking house timbers, and shadows on the wall. Some have 'bogey-man' fantasies, and even a small spider on the wall can disturb sleep. The grip of spirits of fear needs to be broken, and the children prayed over for cleansing and healing to their minds.

(6) Bad dreams.

Children often tell us of being chased in their dreams by monsters. Dreams involving violence and death are not unusual with children. The power of the dominating spirits causing these problems must be broken, and the children prayed for.

(7) Reactions to insecurity in marriage.

Marriage harmony gives a child security. When constant arguments take place within earshot of the family, a child may look for security in attachment to one parent, and end up being manipulative.

(8) Sexual molestation and incest.

This demonic spirit of perverted lust has been operating under cover for centuries, but in these days of unrestrained sensuality, restraint and secrecy seem to have been abandoned. In Australia it is estimated that there are between thirty thousand and one hundred thousand cases of incest per year. It is also believed that for every child molested, there are four cases of incest. Estimates are rarely accurate, but these offences are on the increase. Jesus spoke some very strong words of condemnation against anyone who sins against a child (Matthew 18:6, 7).

If as a parent you become aware of a change of behaviour in a child without a known cause, you should investigate the possibility of molestation or incest. The symptoms may be an anti-social attitude, a noticeable drop in school grades, a bad sleeping problem, or anxiety. Fear usually keeps a child from speaking about the cause.

If you are suspicious, speak very gently and lovingly to the child and ask if someone has been 'doing naughty things' to the child. Listen to every detail given. You may not be inclined to believe all you hear, but it is as the child sees it, and this is the important factor. Never convey a feeling of guilt by attributing to the child blame for what happened. Do not ignore what you have been told, investigate it.

Many adults have told us how their mothers refused to believe them when they told them what a father, brother, or favourite relative had done to them sexually. Some have been actually punished by their mothers for 'making it up'. The results are always deep rejection and guilt, which very often cause considerable problems in later life and marriage. Spiritual release is the best possible help.

A nine-year-old boy went to a boys' camp for a week. Afterwards he became withdrawn, slept poorly, and was generally fearful. After two weeks of this, the mother gently asked what had happened at the camp. He then told her that one of the camp leaders had got into his bed at night and 'did things' to him.

Thankfully, God does release and heal not only children who have suffered from such traumas, but adults also, who suffered them in childhood. We parents certainly need to be in our 'watch towers', praying for spiritual preservation for our God-given treasures. The word of God tells us, and we certainly know from personal experience, that our human nature is sinful. In addition, we also become victims of what is passed on from parents and grandparents. But, praise God, good and positive influences are also hereditary.

3. Positive hereditary influences.
(1) Timothy is a perfect example of how the faith of a godly grandmother was passed to him through his mother, Lois (2 Timothy 1:5).
(2) We are told that John the Baptist was filled and controlled by the Holy Spirit in, and from, his mother's womb (Luke 1:15).
(3) The scriptures assure us many times that our children will be blessed if we honour God. " .. the seed of the righteous shall be delivered" (Proverbs 11:21).
(4) The man who worshipfully and reverently fears the Lord will be blessed by his children following in his footsteps. This should encourage and motivate fathers to honour God in all their ways, for their children's sake (Psalm 128:3, 4). Other Old Testament passages which confirm this parental blessing, are Deuteronomy 12:25, 28 and Isaiah 59:21).

4. How can we best help our children?
After meeting the first priority of being a good example, we should:
(1) Instruct them in the Word of God.
When our own children were young, we tried to ensure that our family devotional times were not boring. We had interesting Bible readings, stories, question-and-answer sessions, and family prayer, which each of the girls led in turn.

(2) Pray for them.

Prayer is a most powerful weapon in the hands of parents. In praying with a child, ask what he or she would like to ask or tell Jesus.

Interecede on their behalf during your private devotions. Only eternity will reveal how many wonderful things have happened because of the faithful prayers of a Mum or Dad, and how many times Satan was prevented from taking control, especially in the rebellious teenage years.

A young man who had been on drugs for five years, later told his parents that he had been prevented from doing many evil things because of their prayers. He said, "I know, Mum and Dad, that you have put Jesus in my mind since I was a little boy, and I had to come back to him as Saviour."

(3) Speak into the sub-conscious mind.

When children are anxious about school work or relationships at school, talk the problem over without criticism, and make positive suggestions as to how they can be overcome. Then at night, after they have been asleep for about ten to fifteen minutes, go and speak quietly into their sub-conscious minds, which never sleep. Speak direct assurances, such as: "You CAN do your (spelling) (maths) . . etc." Reassure them of your love, and how precious they are to you. Their spirits and souls are at rest, and are very receptive to all the love and positive assurance you can give them. Replace the 'can'ts' with 'cans', disobedience with a desire to obey, and negative thoughts with assurances of confidence.

The Lord taught me this principle when our eldest daughter was only five years of age. She was apprehensive about her school work. She often came up the stairs in the morning after prayer, and repeated the assurances I had given the night before, as if they were her own ideas. In a few months they were being carried out, and she was confident and able to cope. She never knew that I had spoken to her in her sleep, until I told her about it when her own little one needed help; now she does it with her own children. The Lord leads his children in right paths.

(4) Guard against hereditary influences.

Godly parents, take your stand against harmful hereditary influences. "The Father has delivered and drawn us to Himself, out of the control of the dominion of darkness and has transferred us into the kingdom of the Son of His love" (Colossians 1:13 Amp.). The name of Jesus is our weapon, the blood of Jesus is our means of cleansing, and the Spirit of God is the source of our healing.

5. The matter of infirmities and allergies.

Most doctors agree that at least 75% of sicknesses are psychosomatic, with physical symptoms which are not pathogenic. The Lord has proved to us, even in our lack of deep medical knowledge, that if children are freed from basic causes, healing can be received and beautiful things happen.

'Andrew', a six year old, was a very very serious case of hypoglycemia. He could not take the slightest amount of lactose. As a baby he was at death's door for weeks and as a child he was on a restricted diet. He was also hyperactive. When the Lord freed 'Andrew' from rejection and the hereditary influence of the spirits of Freemasonry, healing followed. He became completely normal in his lifestyle. His recovery timetable went something like this. At 11 a.m. he was prayed for. At 2 p.m. his mother gave him a chocolate candy bar, as she was confident that he had been healed. At 5 p.m. an excited mother knocked on our door. Her face told the story. 'Andrew' had shown no sign of the usual diarrhoea and vomiting. He was immediately put on a normal diet, and over the past two years has shown no sign of his problem. And his special delight now? Chocolates of course.

"The weapons of our warfare are not physical (weapons of flesh and blood), but they are mighty before God for the overthrow and destruction of strongholds" (2 Corinthians 10:4 The Amplified Bible).

Children are often more spiritually aware of what is going on than we think. Ask a child what he thinks is the cause of his problem, and you may be surprised by the answers. One little four year old replied to a question by saying, "It's my wildness inside that makes me naughty." Another five year old said that he had asked Jesus why he was like he was, and Jesus had said to him, "It is Satan's helpers that makes you do bad things." Most children love to be prayed for, especially when they realize that someone is trying to help them with their problems.

May I say a word to grandmothers. You have a high calling in God to pray for your grandchildren. It is a rich, rewarding privilege. May we all be able to pray, "Lord grant me the willingness, patience and love to let the children come to me."

Finally, I would like to share a prayer which has been a blessing to many parents who have not known how to pray for their children:

A special prayer of protection over children.

"I take authority over you Satan in the Name of Jesus Christ, and render you powerless in the life of . . . . (child's name).

"I bind your power, break your influence, and loose . . . . (child's name) from your grip. All harmful hereditary, and other spirits . . . . . . (name them, such as rejection, etc.) I break in the name of Jesus, and by faith I now take the blood of Jesus and cleanse the conscious mind, the sub-conscious mind, the emotions, the imaginations, the heart and will of . . . . (name child).

"I thank you for the power and authority of your name and blood, Lord Jesus, and ask you to keep the heart of . . . . . (child's name), open and tender to the leading of the Holy Spirit. Please fill . . . . . . (child's name) with your everlasting love, your peace, and your joy, for your glory. I ask this in the name of Jesus. Amen."

This prayer was given to a group of ladies attending a seminar. One of them had a nine year old boy who woke up screaming the following night. The mother didn't know what to do, then suddenly remembered the prayer she had written down during the day. She quickly found it, and simply read the prayer over the boy who had stopped screaming, but was too frightened to go back to bed. When the prayer was finished, the boy said, "I feel good now!" It may be an old motto, but its truth hasn't changed: "Prayer changes things".

CHAPTER SUMMARY.

1. Children need warm and spontaneous expressions of love to preserve them from emotional starvation, which may produce tragic results.
2. Parents should think before speaking negative, unkind, or soul-destroying remarks. They may emotionally cripple a child for life.
3. Changes in behavioural patterns, particularly in sleep, should be carefully investigated.
4. Parents can bless their children by their godly examples, their openness, availability and their prayers.

"We know that anyone born of God does not continue to sin; the one who was born of God keeps him safe, and the evil one does not touch him. We know that we are children of God, and that the whole world is under the control of the evil one" (1 John 5:18, 19).

CHAPTER 23.

Follow-up and the importance of after care

The normal hospital routine for patients requiring surgery is thorough preparation, the surgery itself, then appropriate nursing care during recovery. Before the patient is discharged, a number of specialists may have been involved in helping the patient regain and retain health, strength and mobility.

The whole deliverance process has similarities. There needs to be careful preparation for the release procedure which many have later described as 'spiritual surgery'. Nurses who also experienced deliverance describe the follow-up materials as filling the role of 'post-operative recovery procedures.'

Written guidelines have been found to be of immense practical value in stabilizing and encouraging those who have been set free. The Lord revealed them, and has confirmed their value over a number of years through the testimonies of those who have applied them. The blessings gained through deliverance need to be consolidated by adhering strictly to spiritual principles. Disobedience and lack of co-operation with the Spirit of God could cause a person who has been freed to be brought back into bondage or domination. Every blessing of God is conditional. Our co-operation is essential.

Regrettably, there are some weak-willed people who expect everything to be done for them. But unless they are willing to accept responsibility for their own actions, and make their own right choices, they will never make spiritual progress. This type of 'self-help' follow-up is unlike normal counselling which involves regular sessions of sharing and giving advice. After deliverance, personal counselling should be limited to necessary encouragement, or providing answers to unusual questions. In fact, overmuch after-counselling can cause introspection and insecurity. Both my wife and I have avoided providing an on-call counselling service for adults who need to learn to walk in maturity, rather than remain dependant upon others. Of course, every assistance is offered those who have genuine difficulties and need encouragement. Most people whom the Lord has freed find the follow-up materials sufficient.

The evil one is an expert at crushing counsellors with an overload of work and we need to avoid that kind of bondage. The criterion of success in counselling is not the number of 'regulars' who continually return for help, but the number who do not require further assistance, and walk in victory.

After each deliverance session the counsellee is given the following programme with the strong recommendation that it be placed in the front of their Bible and used daily until spiritual strength and stability have been achieved. There is nothing special about the counselling details, but they have been included because of the spiritual pressures which are known to follow a session of deliverance.

The following fifteen points may be photo-copied and given to people who have been freed. This section of the book is exempted from copyright.

1. Declare aloud in prayer, positively and gratefully, the major areas in which you have received freedom.

For example: "Thank you Lord for taking away my rejection / my low self-image / my anger / my lust / my bondage to Satan / the memory of my past" etc.

Never offer to Satan the keys of doubt or of negative thinking. Without hesitation he will use them to oppress you. Remember:

God's forgiveness and cleansing give you self-acceptance.

God's restoration and renewal give you self-respect.

God's boundless love, joy, and peace, give you self-worth.

2. Commence each new day, and continue through each day by making right and positive choices.

Never let your feelings dictate your behaviour as they can be deceptive. Spirit-filled living is based on right choices.

(1) Jesus Christ has called you to discipleship which means denying yourself, taking up your cross, and following him (Matthew 16:24). Discipleship brings the knowledge of truth, and truth sets us free (John 8:31, 32).

(2) Paul emphasizes that right choices are the basics of victorious living. "Put OFF your old self . . . put ON the new self created to be like God in true righteousness and holiness (Ephesians 4:22, 23 emphasis added). "Count yourselves TO BE DEAD to sin . . . count yourselves ALIVE to God" (Romans 6:11-13 emphasis added).

(3) Peter defines the 'how' of making right choices:

"MAKE EVERY EFFORT to add to your faith goodness . . " He then defines other virtues which are gained by choice. These are knowledge, self-control, perseverance, godliness, brotherly kindness, and love, which keep us from being ineffective and unproductive (2 Peter 1:5-10 emphasis added).

. .Right choices release faith and control feelings.

. .Right choices will deny Satan a foothold (Ephesians 4:27).

. .Right choices will discipline the flesh and bring it under control. The flesh can never be cast out, but it can be subject to the Lordship of Christ (Romans 8:12-17).

. .Right choices give glory to God; obedience reveals our love for him.

3. Expect continuous and increasing freedom in areas where Satan has previously exploited you.

When the Hebrews came out of Egypt, a minority kept complaining about God's diet of manna. They had nostalgic memories about the delicacies they had left behind. God became exasperated with their grumbling, so fed them quail flesh for breakfast, lunch, and dinner, served with plague (Numbers 11). What caused their problems? **Living in the past, instead of looking forward to all God had promised for the new life.** Lot's wife became a salt memorial for the same reason, **longing for the past which God was destroying,** instead of accepting a new lifestyle.

From the time of experiencing freedom, there must be no more post mortems, but a reaching forward to all that God yet has in store. Never exhume the past from which God has delivered and cleansed you. Don't satisfy those over-zealous people who want to check you out to see if a real work of God has been done! Freedom and renewal should not be rationalized but enjoyed and shared.

The writer once said to a woman, when explaining this point, "Throw away your rear vision (view) mirrors." She laughed, and said, "You mean the ones on my shoulders!" I certainly did. She had taken the point.

Allow yourself time to grow into the new image in Christ. It takes time to change habit patterns, and to re-programme thinking and responses. Even if it takes weeks or months, press on in faith and obedience. Remember that perfection is neither promised nor possible in this life.

4. Never forget that the devil is an incorrigible liar.

He is a liar by profession, and he is highly skilled at it (John 8:44). Everything he whispers in your ear will turn out to be sugar-coated poison aimed at your defeat. Should he counter-attack after deliverance, trying to convince you that you were not really freed at all ("It was only a psychological or emotional trick"), reject both the suggestion and him. Your shield of faith will preserve you from those fiery darts. When John Wesley was supposedly confronted by the devil with pages of his past wrong-doings, he told him to write all over them in red ink: "The blood of Jesus Christ, God's Son, cleanses me from all sin". The devil then made a hasty exit.

Resist the devil but avoid conversing with demons, particularly those who have been hearing voices. Resist them by the shield of faith, then concentrate on praising God for the completeness and permanency of the freedom he purchased for you at Calvary. Let the Spirit of God renew your mind, and keep it renewed.

5. Remember, Jesus Christ has freed you from all condemnation.

One of Satan's most destructive weapons is condemnation. He will try to make you stumble over some misunderstanding or imaginary hurt, then when you have lost your balance he will push you down the slide of discouragement. At the bottom, the spiritual bullies of guilt and condemnation are waiting to pummel you. Then someone has to drag you up that hill again, little by little. It could all have been avoided by refusing to allow anything to come between Jesus Christ and yourself. No one was more misunderstood and had more hurts than Jesus, and he refused all self-pity. Live in his freedom.

There is an old saying: "You can't stop the birds from flying over your head, but you can stop them from nesting in your hair." The moral is: refuse to accept doubt and discouragement and you won't be filled with condemnation.

"There is therefore now NO CONDEMNATION for those who are in Christ Jesus, because through Christ Jesus the law of the Spirit of life set me free from the law of sin and death" (Romans 8:1 emphasis added).

'No condemnation'! What a slogan for victory! Learn to hold it high, wave it around, and rejoice in it. No more unworthiness, guilt, hopelessness and despair. No more bondage to the past, no more false interpretation of Scripture. No more isolationism. "So if the Son sets you free, you will be free indeed" (John 8:36). Claim your blood-sealed rights, and reject even the fear of condemnation.

6. Don't play with deliberate sin; it is a poisonous snake.

Believers are forbidden to sin deliberately. But, should you unintentionally sin, then repent, confess it immediately, and receive forgiveness and cleansing.

Remember:

(1) God expects us to live holy (set apart) lives. "Be holy, for I am holy" (Leviticus 11:44, 45; 1 Peter 1:16).

(2) Guilt is the shadow cast by sin. When the cause is removed, there is no longer any basis for guilt. Don't fool yourself, or let the evil one stand between you and the Light.

(3) **Never save sin up for later confession,** like dirty washing in a clothes basket. Have spiritual contamination removed immediately.

(4) Don't generalize your confession of sin such as "Lord forgive my sins". Itemize them, name each horrible thought or act separately. God requires genuine repentance.

Never leave the presence of God without consciously receiving his cleansing. Go away free of defilement, burdens, guilt, stain, and know you are beyond condemnation.

7. Invite the Holy Spirit to enable you to make Jesus Lord of your entire personality every day.

The act of consecration in Romans chapter twelve, is threefold:

What you give to God is yourself, 'lock, stock, and barrel' as we say. In other words, Lordship means the willing subjection of spirit, soul, and body to the Spirit of God (v. 2).

What you receive from God is a renewed mind able to understand and carry out the will of God (v. 2).

What you do for God is to fulfil what he has appointed you to do within the Body of Christ (vv. 3-8), and bless his world (vv. 9-21).

Remember, God is not asking you to fit the Kingdom of God into your objectives. Your life should be a means God uses for fulfilling his objectives.

Being filled and controlled by the Holy Spirit never stops with what is so loosely termed a 'charismatic' experience. Many people who are filled and controlled by the Holy Spirit have never experienced the charismata, and many who have received them are not filled and controlled by the Holy Spirit! Being ever filled and stimulated with the Holy Spirit (Ephesians 5:18, Amplified Bible), not only brings a new relationship with God, but with friends, a marriage partner, family, and the work force of which we are part. Paul lists the total effects of being filled and controlled by the Holy Spirit right through to Ephesians Ch. 6, verse 9. It is shallow living to claim to exercise the charismata, without the moral evidence of victorious living to back them up.

When Paul wrote to the church at Colosse, he said the same things as he did to the Ephesians, except that he substituted the words "the Word of Christ" for the words "Holy Spirit". This shows the divine partnership between the two (also in 2 Timothy 3:16; 2 Peter 1:21). It is not a question of one versus the other, or one preferred to the other, but of one in unity with the other.

The word 'charismatic' has lost its basic meaning, and a service might be done to Christians if it were to be removed from circulation. Firstly, it is impossible to reach an acceptable definition which would satisfy all shades of opinion. Secondly, it polarizes attitudes, and separates believers. Thirdly, the ministry of the Spirit of God is to glorify Jesus Christ and the charismata are but a part of that ministry. When Jesus Christ is given Lordship, God can do everything he desires in and through that person. Any other attitude is a denial of the abundance of life Jesus came to give (John 10:10). So be renewed by God (Romans 12:2; Titus 3:5), and let him refurbish that inner life, now that the squatters have gone!

8. Make time to read, learn, and meditate on God's word, and communicate with him constantly.

Probably the first casualty of an over-busy lifestyle is our two-way communication with God. Bible-time, prayer, meditation, and worship, are spiritual food and breath.

Satan tolerates Christians as long as they skimp on spiritual necessities. He fears them having God's wisdom and strength, or finding out his subtleties. The old saying is still very relevant, "Either God's Word will keep you from sin, or sin will keep you from God's Word".

(1) God said to Joshua: "Do not let this Book of the Law depart from your mouth; meditate on it day and night, so that you may be careful to do everything written in it. Then you will be prosperous and successful" (Joshua 1:8).

(2) The Psalmist said, "How can a young man keep his way pure? By living according to your word. I seek you with all my heart; do not let me stray from your commands. I have hidden your word in my heart that I might not sin against you" (Psalm 119:9-11).

(3) Paul said, "Study and be eager and do your utmost to present yourself to God approved (tested by trial), a workman who has no cause to be ashamed, correctly analyzing and accurately dividing - rightly handling and skilfully teaching the Word of Truth" (2 Timothy 2:15, Amplified Bible).

C. H. Spurgeon, a prince amongst preachers, said: "The word of God is like a lion. You don't have to defend it, just open the cage door". God's Word alone is strong enough to defeat 'you-know-who', prowling around like a lion looking for food. Don't allow yourself to become lion-fodder; use the word of God to repel the evil one. Jesus Christ defeated him by quoting Scripture three times (Luke 4:4, 8, 12).

Meditation will produce spiritual growth as a growth stimulant affects a plant. You will certainly be blessed by reading "Alone With God" (Bethany House), a manual of Biblical meditation, written by our beloved friend, Campbell McAlpine. The book explains his own beautiful and powerful relationship with God.

One thing more. God-talk does not have to be heard. Speaking from your spirit to God through his Holy Spirit keeps the mind positively occupied, glorifies God, and strengthens you. It also gives Satan the 'busy-line' signal he needs to hear. You don't want any more of his free loading lodgers!

9. Put on, or affirm the protection of the armour of God daily.

God's spiritual armour is both offensive and defensive against Satan's attacks. Jesus himself prayed for the protection of those who believed in him (John 17:5). He also taught the disciples to pray for their own protection (Matthew 6:13). The Apostle Paul, who appeared to have had more demonic opposition than his fellow apostles, described each item needed to cope with the constant assaults of demonic beings (Ephesians 6:10-18). Each article was first tested and proved by Jesus Christ in defeating every demonic power (Hebrews 2:17, 18).

The power to withstand Satan and to remain standing when the attack is over, comes from prayer directed and energized by the Holy Spirit (v. 18).

When youthful David opposed the giant Goliath, he wore that armour. Goliath never knew what had hit him. If he had been able to give a post-mortem interview, doubtless he would have said something like this: "It never entered my head that the little squirt would stone me out of my mind!" Put simply, the advice means, 'Be enamoured with that armour and no one will harm you!'

10. Train yourself to be constantly thankful and full of praise.

"Praise the LORD, O my soul, and forget not all his benefits" (Psalm 103:2).

"Always giving thanks to God the Father for everything in the name of our Lord Jesus Christ" (Ephesians 5:20).

Praise disturbs the enemy. When King Jehoshaphat found that the Moabites and Ammonites had declared war on him, he called his people together and asked God for help. The prophet Jahaziel then said - "This is what the LORD says to you: Do not be afraid or discouraged because of this vast army. For the battle is not yours, but God's . . You will not need to fight in this battle. Take up your positions; stand firm and see the deliverance the LORD will give you" (2 Chronicles 20:15, 17). The Levites then praised God with a very loud voice, and the king put singers who praised and worshipped God in front of the troops. "As they began to sing and praise, the LORD sent ambushes against the men of Ammon and Moab and Mount Seir who were invading Judah, and they were defeated" (vv. 21, 22).

Never, never be ungrateful for what God has done for you. Of the ten Samaritan lepers who were healed, only one returned to give glory to God (Luke 17:12-19). Your song of gratitude will be a warning to Satan to back off from any take-over bid he might have in mind. He fears a praising saint.

11. Keep your eyes and ears open for the devil's camouflaged traps.

Often the devil cleverly dresses up his temptations so that you don't realize that they have come out of his workshop. Avoid anything which looks or sounds as if it might lead you back into prison. That includes old friends, places you once visited, things you used to do, books and magazines you used to read, films and videos you used to look at. It would be foolish to walk into a bar, order a drink, take the first sip and then call upon the Lord for help. Victory is won by refusing temptation in the first place.

(1) "Resist the devil, and he will flee from you. Come near to God, and he will come near to you" (James 4:1-8).

(2) "No temptation has seized you except what is common to man. And God is faithful; he will not let you be tempted beyond what you can bear. But when you are tempted, he will also provide a way out so that you can stand up under it" (1 Corinthians 10:13).

(3) "The Lord knows how to rescue godly men from trials (A. V. temptations)" (2 Peter 2:9).

Λ

12. Don't forget that you are NEVER alone.

God is to be trusted without qualification. Faith, not the mind or senses, brings him close to us. He has never broken a promise yet, and his character will never allow him to do so. He has said:

(1) "Never will I leave you; never will I forsake you. So we may say with confidence, The Lord is my helper: I will not be afraid. What can man do to me?" (Hebrews 13:5, 6, a repetition of Deuteronomy 31:6, and Psalm 118:6, 7).

(2) " . . and surely I will be with you always, to the very end of the age" (Matthew 28:20).

The writer once had a card on a breakfast tray which read: "Good morning. Jesus is looking forward to spending the rest of the day with you". I liked it then, and still do, because I continuously enjoy his companionship.

No wonder Paul very confidently wrote that we are more than conquerors, despite trouble, hardship, persecution, famine, nakedness (being stripped of everything we rely upon), danger and sword. Being more than a conqueror means knowing that we are on the winning side before the conflict begins. It means that we have been given the victory over every evil power which may try to keep us captive to the past, or in fear of the future. God's love will hold us to him in any and every circumstance (Romans 8:38, 39).

13. If necessary, break wrong friendships, and choose clean-living, positive, and Christ-honouring friends.

(1) "You adulterous people, don't you know that friendship with the world is hatred towards God? Anyone who chooses to be a friend of the world becomes an enemy of God" (James 4:4).

(2) Friendships can be hazardous. A good friendship is one is which each party blesses the other. Parasitic associations in which one party leans on and drains the other, are not of God. True friendship means mutual sharing.

14. Constantly draw upon your available spiritual resources.

Jesus Christ said he could do nothing without his Father (John 5:19, 30). He also said we could do nothing without him (John 15:5). In 'tree language' this means without a root system, fruit will never be produced. The fruit God wants to 'pick' from our lives can only grow as we are deeply 'rooted' in Christ (Colossians 2:7). The grace of God is the sap which produces the fruit. The fruit has the same nature as the tree, which in our case is the fruit of God's Spirit (Galatians 5:22,23). Not only does God's grace produce fruit which reflects the moral excellence of Jesus Christ, but it also deeply satisfies each need of the human soul which original sin interrupted. So, drink deeply.

Daily supply is needed for daily growth. Yesterday's grace has already been used. All that branches do is to remain in position; the sap will stimulate growth. And so it is with the food of the Word, and the water of the Spirit.

15. Finally, set yourself free if the need arises.

After a time of major deliverance, it is possible for a demonic manifestation to occur. This will usually be from one of two sources.

The first is that some bondage or domination overlooked at the time of ministry has come to light as a result of the new work of grace in you. It is similar to what happens after a garden has been carefully weeded. The sun and rain cause roots which were not removed to begin to sprout. They usually come out easily.

The second cause is a new spirit of oppression which has entered because of deliberate unbelief or disobedience. To remove a bondage, or domination:

(1) Repent from any deliberate sin, name it and confess it, and by faith claim and receive spiritual cleansing.

(2) Renounce aloud the devil and all his work in your life, naming the problem or problems which have recently gripped you.

(3) Successively bind, break, and loose each demonic power which has asserted or re-asserted itself over your life in the name of Jesus Christ. Command each power to leave you, and expel it by an act of your will accompanied by a deliberate cough. Keep this up until you know you are free.

(5) Receive your cleansing and renewal by faith.

(6) Rededicate that re-cleansed portion of your life to Jesus Christ, for his use and glory.

(7) Give praise to God for what he has done in you.

(8) Continue this follow-up schedule until it becomes part of your daily spiritual preparation. These are rules for daily living, not just for times of freedom. AND enjoy the milk and honey of the Land of Promise.

"In my anguish I cried to the LORD, and he answered by setting me free" (Psalm 118:5).

CHAPTER SUMMARY.

1. The freedom Christ gives is for believing, receiving, maintaining, and preserving.

2. Continuing personal follow-up by a counsellor is not necessary if counsellees will faithfully adhere to the written programme. Counsellees should not become counsellor-dependent.

3. The kiwi used to fly. Now it forages in the dirt and undergrowth (mainly in the dark) to satisfy its voracious appetite for worms. Don't be a spiritual kiwi!

"No one knows the thoughts of God except the Spirit of God. We have not received the spirit of the world but the Spirit which is from God, that we may understand what God has freely given us" (1 Corinthians 2:12).

CHAPTER 24.

Answers to some frequently asked questions

Few subjects call forth more questions than deliverance. The writer makes no claim to having all the experience necessary to answer every question, or to having all the right answers, but the following answers to common questions may prove helpful:

1. "Can demons be consigned to hell?"

There does not appear to be any Biblical authority for this. No instance is reported in Scripture. Legion repeatedly begged Jesus not to be sent to the Abyss (Gr. Abussos - bottomless pit, Luke 8:31). The king of this demon-filled place is Abbadon (Gr. for destroyer, a synonym for Satan, Revelation 9:11). Jesus Christ did not order the demons into that place of torment, as it was not yet the time to do so. He was on earth as Saviour, not as Judge.

2. "What happens to demons when they are cast out, or driven off?"

When demons are bound in the name of Jesus, they no longer have the power to bind or dominate people. Jesus Christ drove out demons because he had all authority (Mark 7:29). The apostles cast out demons in the authority Jesus had given them (Mark 6:7). The seventy were taught by God the Father to exercise authority using the name of Jesus, and demons were subject to them (Luke 10:17-20). Christ has given us express permission to use his name in casting out demons (Mark 16:17). We also have a clear illustration of how to use that name. " . . . how can anyone enter a strong man's house and carry off his possessions unless he first ties up the strong man? Then he can rob his house" (Matthew 12:29). This verse is given in the context of Biblical deliverance. In some cases, spirits who have been bound and ordered to leave have not moved because the persons they were indwelling were only half-hearted in their desire for deliverance. When those individuals had returned for further prayer determined to be released, they were quickly set free as the demonic powers had remained bound during the time of indecision. Demons of unbelief often strongly resist deliverance.

Jesus taught that evicted spirits seek rest, and if they find none, they will return to their previous human home. If they find it clean and empty, they gather seven more evil spirits and re-occupy the unfurnished house (Luke 11:24-26). So it is important that people are not only cleansed but filled with the Spirit to prevent other demonic family members from entering. People who are obedient after being freed, have no fear of further possession.

3. "Why do you lay hands on demon oppressed people? Isn't it dangerous?"

Firstly, by doing so we follow the Biblical example. Jesus did it (Luke 4:41; 13:12, 16). He promised his disciples that nothing would harm them in dealing with evil spirits (Luke 10:19). Secondly, the power of delegated authority and the divine anointing makes demons fearful and subject to control.

4. "Can a sickness like cancer be cursed?"

There does not appear to be any Biblical authority for this. People, not sicknesses were cursed in the Old Testament. Before the curse of sin, there was no sickness, and demons inflict people with sicknesses. Jesus Christ is victorious over causes, results, and afflicting spirits. He also has power over life and death. There is an appointed time for each person to die, and if a particular illness, or cancer, is permitted by God for this purpose a curse would not be in accordance with the will of God (Psalm 139:16). Demons, and evil workers are already under God's curse (Matthew 25:41).

The writer confidently prays against any spirit of infirmity which may be interfering with God's will for a particular person, at the same time asking God to glorify his name in the person concerned. All human ministry is by delegated authority, and that delegation does not extend to making demands on God. God is sufficiently loving to want to give, and give generously. As God reveals his will, then faith and delegated authority can make demands of Satan.

5. "How much truth is in the statement, 'The devil made me do it'?"

It may well be true. A dominant spirit can cause uncontrollable actions. But very often the statement is an excuse or an attempt to avoid responsibility. Except in very strong cases of domination, oppressed people are able to exercise their will-power if they so desire.

6. "How do you determine who needs deliverance and who doesn't?"

Basically, people fit into one of five categories:

(1) Those who do need deliverance (freedom).

(a) Unbelievers bound by sin and Satan. Some need to be freed before they can trust and be saved.

(b) Believers who have never gained victory over their pre-Christian thought life, habits, and desires, and who were not freed when they were born again.

(c) Believers who have never been able to live the victorious life in the power of the Holy Spirit. They have tried, but have always failed miserably.

(d) Believers who have hereditary and cultural problems which they cannot overcome.

(2) Those who may need deliverance.

(a) People who have not responded to prolonged counselling.

(b) Believers who respond to every altar call, talk to every visiting speaker, and consistently avoid taking personal responsibility for their actions.

(c) Believers who seem unable to make and stand by their own deceisions.

(3) Those who do not need deliverance.

(a) Believers who have genuinely made Jesus Lord of their whole life.

(b) Believers who, having received deliverance, are changing habit patterns, but have the occasional doubt, or failure. What they require is a 'faith-lift'.

(4) Those with whom a deliverance should NOT be attempted.

(a) Any person who is unwilling to repent from known sin and renounce every demonic grip upon their life.

(b) Those who are receiving medical or psychiatric care for mental health problems, (unless they come by referral).

(c) Those who refuse to believe that their problems are from demonic causes.

(d) Those who have no faith to believe that Jesus Christ can release them.

(e) Any person who refuses to co-operate.

(f) Christians who are against deliverance.

(5) **Those for whom special wisdom is needed in determining whether deliverance is the appropriate answer to their problem, such as:**

(a) Counsellees who have suffered a mental breakdown, have been in psychiatric institutions, or have had shock treatment.

(b) Christians who have had prayer for deliverance but have shown no improvement. Believers who have had 'bad' experiences in past deliverance sessions. This includes the embarrassment of long or highly emotional and noisy sessions, or the trauma of suffering sexual interference by unscrupulous manipulators.

A special comment needs to be made concerning those people whose mother tongue is not English, and who may question the effectiveness of prayer because they cannot understand all that is being said. Fortunately, demons are multi-lingual. (Unfortunately, they not only know good English very well, but are also fluent in English blasphemies and obscenities). Even when the basic information has to be obtained by interpretation, and the counsellee does not know a word of English, demons obey all commands given in the English language, to the glory of God.

7. "What do you do when people don't know what is wrong with them, and ask you to diagnose their problems?"

Ask one or two diagnostic questions which can lead to causes. "Do you have a problem with low self-image? Anger? Fears? Lust?" With a knowledge of the root-fruit systems, positive answers will give you some basic information. The more you are controlled by the Holy Spirit, the more understanding you will have of a counsellee's spiritual condition. The ultimate ideal for every counsellor must surely be to have the Spirit communicate everything he needs to know just as Peter knew about Ananias and Sapphira. But presumption will always remain a possibility. Some have sought help after being deeply hurt by a counsellor who has wrongly accused them, saying "The Lord has told me .. "

8. "How do you distinguish between problems which can be 'worked through' and those for which release is needed?"

When a recurring problem does not respond to normal counselling, there is usually a demonic cause. Compulsiveness, a total inability to overcome a specific problem and a desperate desire to be able to live in victory, all show that the enemy needs to be dealt with. Matters which require only discipline and determination should be overcome by the Word and the Spirit of God.

9. "If a person has difficulty in exercising faith, does this indicate a need for deliverance?"

Faith is really a 'package deal'. It requires a choice of the will to believe, and to expect results before God answers. Unbelief may be caused by fear, lack of understanding, disobedience, and sometimes the influence of other people. If so, counselling should help. If not, there may well be a stubborn spirit of unbelief or of anti-Christ from heredity, occultism, or witchcraft. This spirit must be driven out.

10. "Some say that acupuncture has occultic overtones; others say it is a medical science. Which is it?"

Acupuncture is an electrical stimulus to nerve centres throughout the body by means of needles. Infra-red photography has shown that traditional acupuncture points on the surface of the skin show up as glowing red dots, which brings a scientific confirmation of discernible nerve centres. This dispels the air of mysticism that has surrrounded this treatment for centuries.

Because the Chinese were the first to practise acupuncture centuries ago, the method has been associated with Buddhism and religious spirit practices. It is not the treatment which is a problem, but the practitioners. Deeply religious Buddhists, Taoists, and worshippers of Chinese ancestral spirits, often do mix rites with acupuncture and this is what causes problems. We have prayed for Christians who have been adversely affected by these and other western holistic practitioners.

Christian doctors and practitioners certainly have no such spirit, or holistic pollution. Believers receiving acupuncture, sonic acupuncture, or acupressure treatments, should have no spiritual problems. A few, regrettably, have come to us because they have been sexually interfered with during treatment.

12. "Can unbelievers be freed from demonic problems?"

Yes, provided they understand what is at stake and are willing for God to exercise his authority in their lives. Once released they should be challenged to put their faith in Jesus Christ for salvation. I have personally led a number to the Lord AFTER deliverance. Only one, a woman, refused to respond.

With those who are held by a spirit of unbelief, and who want to respond to Christ but can't, the bondage needs to be broken so that they can willingly trust him.

There are two different spirits of unbelief. One binds a person, and the bondage must be broken before faith can operate. The other is a spirit of control or domination within the individual. It must be cast out because it is a spirit of anti-Christ which does its own thing, and the person concerned cannot control it. The former bondage is mostly encountered in unbelievers, and manifests itself as spiritual blindness. Dominant spirits love to trouble Christians.

13. "How do you reconcile the all-sufficiency of the salvation Jesus offers with the need for deliverance after salvation?"

What we have by inheritance in Christ needs to be appropriated by faith. We must volitionally give his Spirit control over every function of our lives. Jesus Christ should be given the key to every room in our spiritual home, and not confined to the 'guest room'. If some squatters need ejection first, then that must be done. Salvation is not simply a certificate of membership in God's kingdom, but a life which must be experienced. Deliverance is just the means of releasing that life.

14. "How may we avoid becoming demon-oppressed, or re-oppressed?"

Always believe what God says. Never rationalize God's word. Don't add to it, or take away from it; just obey it, and its truths will protect you.

An Indian national whose daughter lay dying went to a local chemist to seek help. After listening to the girl's symptoms, the chemist told the father that there was no known cure for his daughter's illness. As the despondent man turned to leave, the chemist said: "Someone once told me of a god who is said to have allowed his son to die for the sins of people. It is also said that the son came alive again. If you could contact this god, maybe he could save your daughter."

The man hurried home, only to find that his daughter had died in his absence. He went into the room where her body was lying, and said something like this: "If the god who allowed his son to die for the sins of people can hear me, please heal my daughter". The girl then opened her eyes, sat up, and appeared completely well.

In due course, the girl's uncle heard of the miracle and came to visit them. He told his brother that he had been a witch doctor for a number of years and wanted to be free from the power of the evil spirits who constantly troubled him. He asked if his brother would pray to the same god who had healed his daughter and ask that he would be set free. The father prayed with the same simplicity to the god whose name or whose son's name he did not know, and his brother was immediately set free.

17. "Is there anything which should be avoided in this work?"

Avoid anything that will not harmonise with Biblical principles, or would dishonour Jesus Christ. Three examples come to mind:
(1) Some 'practitioners' believe that demons must come out of the oppressed through the body of the counsellor. They personally do all the manifesting and coughing for the oppressed person. This has no association with the principle of substitution, and is a dangerous practice.
(2) Sadly, some 'practitioners' have even prostrated their bodies on top of women as a means of 'deliverance'. One woman who came to us was so repulsed by the sexual overtones of this that she shrank from being prayed for again. God graciously freed her from the effects of that experience, her fear of further prayers, and the problem for which she had originally sought help. Moral and ethical purity is basic to all effective ministry.
(3) Male counsellors should exercise care not to touch a woman in a way which dishonours Jesus Christ. Personal holiness means avoiding anything which may be wrongly interpreted.

18. "How many people should be present during ministry?"

There is no reason why a spiritually mature and experienced person should not pray alone with a member of the same sex. Phyl and I do this when time is limited and many people are requiring help. When praying separately, we prefer to be within sight of each other so that we can join one another for extra discernment, authority, or restraint, if needed. From experience, the ideal team is a husband and wife who flow together in love and in the Holy Spirit. Men and women are set at ease, and marriage problems can be dealt with from both points of view.

Generally speaking, two people of the same sex and spiritual outlook should be able to work together. There needs to be some mutual agreement as to taking the lead, and apportioning responsibility. The devil likes to create confusion or jealousy, so misunderstandings need to be avoided.

Groups of people can indeed be effective, providing there is no confusion. Silent prayer is strengthening for whoever is taking the lead.

Very often, it is godly women who discern the need for people to be freed from demonic problems. If they can't get a man to do this for them, they sometimes pray together, and in this way groups of women have found themselves involved in praying for deliverance. For their protection, there should be some competent pastoral oversight. This ministry is spiritual warfare and care needs to be taken to avoid potential deception or wrong practices. Another important principle is that whatever is done by members of a local church, whether individually, or by groups of men or women or mixed groups in private homes or in the church building itself, needs to be with the knowledge and blessing of the pastor, or spiritual leaders.

The major objective of this book is to provide the Body of Christ with what the Holy Spirit has taught and confirmed so that pastors, counsellors, and church leaders will be able to effectively meet all the needs of their congregations.

19. "How do people know for certain that they are absolutely free?"
By being able to:-
(1) Love God and other people spontaneously and without conditions.
(2) Read, pray, and worship without limitations.
(3) Be a disciple of Jesus Christ without questions.
(4) Live a moral and ethical life without accusations.
(5) Make right choices to the glory of God without constant battles.

CHAPTER SUMMARY.

1. Questions will always be asked about this ministry. Some are from those who are opposed and inexorable, so answers are irrelevant. Some are from those who are in deep need, but are unsure of the method. Your answer to them may be very relevant. Seek wisdom, and be honest.
2. Avoid being adamant and authoritative on subjects about which the word of God is silent.
3. Be open at all times to the divine professor of all truth, the Holy Spirit, and never hesitate to do exactly (and only) what he tells you.
4. Discouragement, frustration, and the fear of failure, are evidences of the evil one's desire to move you out of his way. Take your instruction from the God of eternity, not the god of this world.

"Fear of man will prove to be a snare, but whoever trusts in the LORD is kept safe" (Proverbs 29:25).
"The LORD is my light and my salvation - whom shall I fear? The LORD is the stronghold of my life - of whom shall I be afraid?" (Psalm 27:1).

CHAPTER 25.

Be warned

The contemporaries of John the Baptist looked at his severe lifestyle, felt the cutting edge of his fearless denunciation of their sin, and said in self-defence, "He has a demon" (Matthew 11:18).

The contemporaries of Jesus Christ were offended at the learning he showed without having graduated from the Jewish schools. In claiming to have been taught by God, Jesus challenged the Jews to fulfil God's will and prove the truth of his claims for themselves. Then he asked this simple question: "Why are you trying to kill me?" (John 7:19b). Their self-defence was immediate. "You are demon-possessed. Who is trying to kill you?" (v. 20).

Later, Jesus exposed their true spiritual lineage as being from the devil himself because they were intent on carrying out their spiritual father's will (John 8:44). Without the strength of logic, the Jews could only make wild, baseless allegations against him. "The Jews answered him, 'Aren't we right in saying that you are a Samaritan and demon-possessed?'" "I am not possessed by a demon" said Jesus, "but I honour my Father and you dishonour me. I am not seeking glory for myself: but there is one who seeks it, and he is the judge. I tell you the truth, if a man keeps my word, he will never see death."

At this the Jews exclaimed, "Now we know you are demon-possessed!" (John 8:48-52). When the last piece of truth expressed by Christ had fallen on deaf ears, the Jews picked up stones to assault him, but he hid from them, slipping away from the temple grounds (v. 59).

Then, after the discourse about the good shepherd laying down his life for the sheep "the Jews were again divided. Many of them said, 'He is demon-possessed and raving mad. Why listen to him?' But others said, 'These are not the sayings of a man possessed by a demon. Can A DEMON open the eyes of the blind?' " (John 10:19-21 emphasis added).

Even the power Jesus used to cast out demons was attributed to Satan. The Pharisees were stung to the quick when the people thought Jesus was really the son of David because of the deliverance and healing of a blind and dumb demon-possessed man. They said, "It is only by Beelzebub the prince of demons, that this fellow drives out demons" (Matthew 12:24).

The disciples were clearly warned that what had been said and done to their master would happen to them.

"A student is not above his teacher, nor a servant above his master. It is enough for the student to be like his teacher, and the servant like his master. If the head of the house has been called Beelzebub, how much more the members of his household!" (Matthew 10:25). Summarising:

HE was called a Samaritan, and 'demon-possessed'.
HE was referred to as 'a demon'.
HE was accused of working for Beelzebub, (a synonym for Satan).

The personal cost to be considered.

A friend of the writers once spoke lovingly to a prominent pastor about the moral implications of some of his relationships with the opposite sex. He was promptly rejected and accused of being demon-possessed, resulting in much hurt over a number of years. But the pastor lost his church and reputation because of the very moral indiscretions he so strongly denied.

The truth of divine revelation may be resented, denied, rationalized, or postponed, but eventually we will all be judged for our response to it.

Because Phyl and I have determined to serve God without fear of man, we have certainly lost friends. Situations for teaching and preaching previously wide open have been slammed shut when it became known that we were involved in deliverance. People who have been pleasant to us have criticized and talked about us behind our backs. But none of this really concerns us. Jesus said, "Follow ME." He warned that the same treatment would be given to students and servants as was given to teachers and masters (Matthew 10:24, 25). After all, we are now serving a spiritual apprenticeship which will determine the future levels of eternal servanthood.

Is it worth it?

Yes, a thousand times over. God loves his people more than we will ever understand. He needs channels through whom he can bless not only his own children, but a needy world. King David grasped that fact. "David knew that the LORD had established him as king over Israel and had exalted his kingdom FOR THE SAKE OF HIS PEOPLE ISRAEL" (2 Samuel 5:12 emphasis added).

It is worth it when we read what people have written to God's glory such as:

* "Our own time with you, when we truly met with the Lord was two years ago now. The great release from bondage and the blessing we received both as a family and as individuals has not diminished; it has remained a truly 'turn-around experience' for both of us . . "

* "I am well and continue in the deliverance and release which came about last time you were here. Several people have commented that I have changed and am more cheerful and positive. As I have declared and spoken about my release it has become a clear-cut reality."

* "You and [. . .] ministered deliverance to areas in my life that had held me bound since I was very young. It's been almost nine months now and I wanted to write to tell you (and thank you) that I have walked freely in those areas of which I had despaired. The freedom has been so great that if I've since been tempted in those areas I didn't even notice it. Those 2½ hours of ministry have had a profound effect on my life and my relationship with the Lord."

* "I wish to express the feelings of deep joy experienced over the past 5 months since I received ministry from you.
  While my mother was carrying me, the many traumatic experiences of her life must have been weighing heavily upon her.
  For this reason, I believe that I was born with a 'Tree of Fear' in my life. In subsequent years that was reinforced, as my mother had not come to terms with her fears. It wasn't that she tried to make me fearful, but that in reacting to her problems I reinforced my own fears more deeply.

Since receiving ministry from you, I have been released from this 'Tree of Fear' which Satan had used many times in deceiving me and which has stopped me from receiving the full blessing of my Heavenly Father's love, provision and guidance."

* "During my teenage years I allowed the hurt given to my parents by my sister's behaviour to damage me too. I decided never to do anything which would cause my parents anxiety, and so I allowed my emotions to be bound by a juvenile spirit. Outwardly I was complacent, but inwardly constantly hurt by injustices.

Since you released me from all this, and from an emotional schizophrenic spirit, I have been living out my freedom in these areas, and the release has been wonderful. The follow-up sheet of directions that you gave me, has proved a great blessing. The steps of spiritual warfare linked with the daily breathing in of the fruit of the Spirit have proven to be wonderfully effective, and liberating. I thank God for your ministry, I thank you both for your obedience."

TO GOD BE THE GLORY, GREAT THINGS HE HAS DONE - IS DOING - AND WILL CONTINUE TO DO!

"But each one should be careful how he builds . . the fire will test the quality of each man's work. If what he has built survives, he will receive his reward. If it is burned up, he will suffer loss; he himself will be saved, but only as one escaping through the flames." (1 Corinthians 3:10b, 13-15).

CHAPTER 26

RESOURCES

APPENDIX "A"   THE DEVIL, his names, activities, and destiny.

1. HIS NAMES.

The names used to describe this fallen angelic being provide much information concerning his degraded nature and activities both in heavenly realms and on earth.

(1)   **The devil.** Gr. 'diabolos', means false accuser, slanderer (Matthew 4:11; Revelation 12:10).

(2)   **Satan.** Heb. 'satan', the adversary. Gr. 'satanas', the hater or accuser (Luke 4:8).

(3)   **Beelzebub** - Beelzebul. (Lord of the fly, a heathen deity thought by the Jews to have supremacy amongst evil spirits, and whom they described as 'the prince of demons' (Mark 3:22). When Jesus replied to the Jews who accused him of being possessed by Beelzebub, he made it abundantly clear that Satan himself was Beelzebub (v. 23).

(4)   **The king** of the kingdom of darkness (Luke 11:18; Colossians 1:13).

(5)   **The prince** of this world (John 13:31).

(6)   **The god** of this world (2 Corinthians 4:4).

(7)   **The prince of the power of the air** (Ephesians 2:2).

(8)   **The spirit of disobedience** (Ephesians 2:2).

(9)   **The dragon** (Revelation 12:7, 13). The enormous red dragon (Revelation 12:3). The great dragon (Revelation 12:9).

(10)   **The serpent** (Genesis 3:1; Revelation 12:3).   That old serpent (Revelation 12:9; 20:2).

(11)   **The deceiver of the world** (Revelation 12:9).

(12)   **The tempter** (Matthew 4:3; 1 Thessalonians 3:5).

(13)   **The evil one** (KJV 'wicked one' Matthew 13:19; John 17:15).

(14)   **Abaddon** (Hebrew), Apollyon (Greek) meaning the destroyer (Revelation 9:11).

(15)   **The enemy** (Matthew 13:39). Your enemy (1 Peter 5:8).

(16)   **The beast of the Abyss** (Revelation 11:7; 17:8).

(17)   **The angel of the bottomless pit** - king of demonic beings which look like locusts (Revelation 9:11).

(18)   **Belial.** The worthless, reckless, or lawless one (2 Corinthians 6:15).

(19)   **The ruler of spiritual darkness** (Ephesians 6:12).

(20)   **The father of desire** (John 8:44).

(21)   **The thief, killer, destroyer** of the sheep (John 10:10)

(22)   **A murderer** from the beginning (John 8:44).

(23)   **The spirit** who works in those who are disobedient (Ephesians 2:2).

(24)   **A liar** and the father of lies (John 8:44).

(25)   **A masquerader** as an angel of light (2 Corinthians 11:14).

(26)   **The accuser of the brethren** (Revelation 12:10).

(27)   **The lawless one** (2 Thessalonians 2:8).

(28)   **The strong man** (Mark 3:27).

(29)   **Leviathan.** The title of the gliding and coiling serpent in Isaiah 27:1, an allegorical picture of Satan (Revelation 20:2).

(30)   **The devil is also a trinity of evil,** manifesting himself as dragon, beast, and false prophet (Revelation 16:13).

2. HIS ACTIVITIES.

In these the devil is always subject to the will of God. (1 Samuel 24:1 with 1 Chronicles 21:1; Job 1:12; 2:6; Revelation 20:3, 7, 10).

(1) He challenges and opposes God's will. (Genesis 3:1; 1 Timothy 6:4, 5).
(2) Is the first cause of sin, and inspires its practice on earth (1 John 3:8).
(3) Tempts people to sin (1 Chronicles 21:1; John 13:2; Acts 5:3; Matthew 4:1, 3, 5, 6, 8, 9).
(4) Blinds the minds of unbelievers to spiritual truths (2 Corinthians 4:4).
(5) Prevents people from responding to the Gospel (Matthew 13:4, 19).
(6) Traps the souls of the ungodly (2 Timothy 2:26).
(7) Devises schemes to snare God's people (Ephesians 6:11; 2 Corinthians 2:11).
(8) Holds the world in his power (1 John 5:19; Acts 26:18).
(9) Produces signs and lying wonders (2 Thessalonians 2:9, 10).
(10) Prowls around seeking to devour Christians spiritually (1 Peter 5:8).
(11) Restlessly walks around the earth (Job 1:7; 2:2).
(12) He disguises himself, and is full of deception (Genesis 3:1).
(13) Sets an example of pride (conceit), to lead people into judgment (1 Timothy 3:6).
(14) Oppresses people (Acts 10:38).
(15) Binds people with infirmities (Luke 13:16).
(16) Uses the power of death and the fear of death (Hebrews 2:14,15).
(17) Has the power of entry into lives (John 13:27).
(18) Produces spiritual 'tares' or counterfeit Christians who will be cast into the fiery furnace in the final harvest of souls (Matthew 13:37-40).
(19) Resists the Lord's anointed in carrying out their duties for the kingdom of God (Zechariah 3:1; Luke 22:31; 1 Thessalonians 2:18).
(20) Deceives the nations by spurious miracles, signs, and wonders (2 Thessalonians 2:9).
(21) Directs the activities of the hordes of evil spirits referred to as 'his angels' (Matthew 25:41; Revelation 9:11).
(22) Like a wolf, he attacks and tries to scatter God's people (John 10:12).
(23) Acts as a spirit of betrayal (John 6:70; 13:27-30).
(24) Exercises rage and destructive anger (Revelation 12:12).
(25) By sovereign permission, may act as God's agent in punishing extreme cases of disobedience in Christians (1 Timothy 1:20; 1 Corinthians 11:30)
(26) Fires flaming arrows of temptations and afflictions at Christians in attempting to defeat them (Ephesians 6:16).

3. HIS TOTAL DEFEAT.

At Calvary, Jesus Christ triumphed over every rebellious and fallen demonic deity, disarming them (Colossians 2:15). The time is coming when they will be destroyed, or done away with entirely (1 Corinthians 15:24).

(1) Satan has already been judged and condemned (John 12:31; 16:11).
(2) Satan is to be cast into eternal fire (Matthew 25:41; Revelation 20:10).
(3) Satan may be successfully resisted by the believer (James 4:7).
(4) Satan may be overcome by faith in the blood of the Lamb and the testimony of God's people (Revelation 12:11).
(5) Satan's power over death, hades, and the fear of these, has been totally broken (Revelation 1:18).

4. HIS FINAL OVERTHROW.

In Revelation chapter twenty, verse ten, the devil, or deceiver, will be thrown into the lake of burning sulphur where the beast and the false prophet will have already been sent (Revelation 19:20). With him will be his angels (Matthew 25:41), death and hades (Revelation 20:14), and every person rejecting God and his Christ (Revelation 21:8).

APPENDIX "B"

DEMONS, their origin, names, activities, future, and the use of the sign gifts in combating their oppression.

1. THEIR ORIGIN.

Demons like their leader, Satan, began their existence as spirit beings created to fulfil the will of God.

"For by him were all things created: things in heaven and on earth, visible and invisible whether thrones or powers or rulers or authorities; all things were created by him and for him" (Colossians 1:16).

Some believe that when God removed the rebellious Lucifer from his position of trust and authority, one third of the angels were cast out of heaven with him. This is suggested from the verse which says, "Then another sign appeared in heaven: an enormous red dragon with seven heads and seven crowns on his heads. His tail swept a third of the stars out of the sky and flung them to the earth" (Revelation 12:3).

Numbers are not important, but it is very evident from the New Testament that demons must have originally been in the presence of God, and were fully aware of spiritual realities:

(1)   Demons are stated to be angels who sinned and did not retain their original state (1 Peter 3:19; 2 Peter 2:4; Jude 6).

(2)   Demons, like Satan, are evil, wicked, and unclean - a reversal of their former glory (Ephesians 6:12; Mark 7:25; 9:25).

(3)   Demons show an intimate knowledge of the deity, authority, and power of Jesus Christ (Mark 1:24; 3:11; 5:7; Luke 4:41; Acts 19:15).

(4)   Demons fear their future judgment and confinement in the Abyss (Luke 8:28, 31).

(5)   Demons showed that Jesus Christ had total authority over them on earth, by obeying every command he gave (Matthew 8:31, 32; Mark 1:25).

(6)   Demons still fear and obey the name of Jesus when it is used in faith (Mark 16:17; Acts 8:5-7; 16:18). In this way they submit to the authority of the one who conquered them. This confirms the timelessness of spiritual beings and the 'power of Attorney' believers have on behalf of Jesus Christ.

2. THEIR NAMES.

The King James Version used the word 'devils' for demons. It comes from the Hebrew 'shed[im]', or the Greek 'daimon', meaning a supernatural spirit of a malignant nature (Deuteronomy 32:17; Psalm 106:37; Matthew 8:31; Revelation 16:14). The modern use of 'demon' distinguishes them from the devil, their leader. Other names are:-

(1) **The sons of God** (Genesis 6:2; Job 1:6). Peter said they were spirits (1 Peter 3:19)

(2) **Every idol** in the Old Testament had a name. Each one was a front for a demon (1 Corinthians 10:20). Examples are Molech (Jeremiah 32:35); Ashtoreth (1 Kings 11:5); Dagon (Judges 16:23), etc. Baal (1 Kings 16:31) was a chief deity and represented Satan himself.

(3) **Satyrs** (NIV - 'goat idols, or demons'; Amp. - 'goat-like gods or demons or field spirits' Leviticus 17:7; 2 Chronicles 11:15; | Isaiah 13:21; 34:14).

(4) **Satan's angels** (Revelation 12:9).

(5) **Rulers** (KJV 'principalities'), powers of this dark world, spiritual forces of evil in the heavenly realms (Ephesians 6:12).

(6) **Princes** in authority in countries opposing God's work (Daniel 10:13, 20).

(7) **Evil or unclean spirits that look like frogs** (Revelation 16:13, 14).

3. THEIR ACTIVITIES.

(1)   As spirits, they seek host bodies through whom they can fulfil their desires, as:

    (a) **Spirits of jealousy.** The Amplified Version adds "and suspicion" (Numbers 5:14, 30).

    (b) **Familiar spirits** (1 Samuel 28:3, 8, 9; Deuteronomy 18:11; 2 Kings 23:24; Isaiah 8:19). Because demonic spirits are familiar with the unregenerate during their life-times, and indeed dictate many of their activities, it is no problem after death to deceive relatives with identical voices and personal details, spurious messages.

    (c) **Spirits of impurity in a land** (Zechariah 13:2).   •

    (d) **Spirits of religious control,** which are anti-God in the countries of the world, e.g. the prince of the Persian kingdom (Daniel 10:13), the prince of the Grecian kingdom (Daniel 10:20).

    (e) **A sorrowful spirit** (KJV) - Bitterness of soul (1 Samuel 1:10).

    (f) **Proud spirits** (Proverbs 16:18). A proud spirit can manifest itself as impatience, self-centredness, rebellion, and stubbornness. Saul, in 1 Samuel 13:8-14, 15:14-23).

    (g) **Deceiving spirits** 'seducing', (1 Timothy 4:1).

    (h) **Spirits of heaviness** (KJV) - 'spirit of despair' (Isaiah 61:3 N.I.V.).

    (i) **Unclean (impure) spirits** 'evil', Mark 7:25, etc. The Gr. 'akathartos' is used 28 times, being translated in the KJV twice as 'foul' and 26 times as unclean. A derivative of this word, 'akathartes' is used only in Rev. 17:4.

    (j) **Sexually seductive spirits** (Genesis 6:4). They are known as Incubus (male spirits), and Succubus, (female spirits).   ·

    (k) **Spirits of anti-Christ** (1 John 4:1-3).

    (l) **Evil spirits** (Gr. 'poneros') used six times (Luke 7:21; 8:2; Acts 19:12).

    (m) **A spirit of falsehood** (1 John 4:6).

    (n) **Spirits of divination** (Gr. 'python'), 'predicting the future' (Acts 16:16).

    (o) **An enslaving spirit of fear** (Romans 8:15).

    (p) **Spirits of error** (1 John 4:6; 1 Timothy 4:1).

    (q) **Spirits of infirmities** (KJV) Gr. 'asthenia' (Matthew 8:16, 17). Also translated:

    (i)   **Sicknesses** (Luke 5:15).

    (ii) **Diseases** (Luke 8:2).

    (iii) **A crippling spirit** (Luke 13:11).

    (iv) **A spirit of invalidity** (John 5:5 - for 38 years).

Other spirits causing bodily ailments:
- (v) **Dumb spirits** (Matthew 9:32, 33).
- (vi) **Deaf and dumb (mute) spirits** (Mark 9:25). These spirits also caused a convulsion like epilepsy, endeavouring to injure the child.
- (vii) **Spirits of insanity, loss of decency, violence** (Luke 8:26-39).
- (viii) **Spirits of injury and death** (Mark 9:22).
  Dake's Bible, page 435, states: "There are demon spirits for every sickness, unholy trait and doctrinal error known amongst men. They must be cast out or restricted in order to experience relief from them"

(2) All demonic spirits are subject to the will of God.
Some may be directed to fulfil his sovereign will:
- (a) **A spirit of treachery** (Judges 9:23).
- (b) **An injurious spirit** (1 Samuel 16:14).
- (c) **A lying spirit** sent to mislead (1 Kings 22:21-23).
- (d) **A spirit of slumber, or deep sleep** (Isaiah 29:10). This causes a dullness, or spiritual blindness in those who deliberately reject the truth. A new Testament example is in Romans 11:8.
- (e) **A spirit of perverseness.** The Amplified version adds 'confusion' (Isaiah 19:14).

3. THEIR FUTURE.

Everlasting fire is their appropriate and final destination, for eternity (Matthew 25:41).

(1) So great was the sin of some, that they have already been chained in darkness (Tartarus). (Genesis 6:2-4; 1 Peter 3:19, 20; 2 Peter 2:4; Jude 6).

(2) Some are already in the Abyss (Gr. Abussos, KJV - 'deep' Luke 8:31); or the bottomless pit (Revelation 9:1; 20:1). When they are released (Revelation 9), they will be likened to locusts, with great power to afflict physically and torture those without the seal of God on their foreheads. In verse 11, Satan is described as their king. He is the angel of the Abyss - Abbadon (Hebrew), or Appolyon (Greek). He is also termed the 'beast of the Abyss' (Revelation 11:7; 17:8).

(3) Some are already bound by the word of the Lord through his servants, and remain ineffective (Matthew 16:19; Mark 3:26).

(4) Their final destiny is the lake of fire, prepared for them and their spiritual leader and overlord (Matthew 25:41). The beast and the false prophet join them (Revelation 3:20). Finally Satan himself is cast in with them (Revelation 20:10).

THE USE OF THE CHARISMATA (SIGN GIFTS) IN COMBATING SATANIC AND DEMONIC OPPRESSION IN CHRISTIANS
(1 Corinthians 12:8-10).

(1)   verse 8, **the message (AV 'word') of wisdom,** or the spiritual insight needed for knowing how to diagnose and combat demonic oppression.

(2)   verse 8, **the message (AV 'word') of knowledge,** or the divine revelation of truth about a counsellee who has not known or has not disclosed needed information.

(3)   verse 9, **faith,** or the 'spiritual fuse' between the person ministering and God, enabling the freeing power of God to flow to the counsellee.

(4)   verse 9, **gifts of healing,** for rehabilitation and renewal after Satanic power has been broken.

(5)   verse 10, **miraculous powers,** which give the servant of the Lord the authority and power to cast out demonic spirits. Jesus called this a miracle (Mark 9:38, 39).

(6)   verse 10, **prophecy,** or the ability to provide words of warning or encouragement that the Spirit of God intends for the counsellee before or after deliverance.

(7)   verse 10, **the ability to distinguish between spirits,** so necessary in discerning what is a genuine work of God, and what results from the deceptive work of the evil one.

(8)   verse 10, **the ability to speak in different kinds of tongues,** or use of the organs of speech by the Holy Spirit in praise and intercession, or in asserting divine authority over demonic powers present in a counsellee's life. Demons often express displeasure at the use of this charisma.

*   verse 10, **the interpretation of tongues,** particularly useful in discerning the difference between the utterances of the Holy Spirit and those of demonic spirits.

BIBLIOGRAPHY.

'War on the Saints'
Jessie Penn-Lewis with Evan Roberts, 'Overcomer' Bookroom

'Demon Possession'
John Warwick Montgomery, Bethany Fellowship

'Christian Counselling And Occultism'
'Between Christ and Satan'
'Occult Bondage And Deliverance'
'The Devil's Alphabet'
'Day X'
Dr. Kurt Koch. Published by Kregel, and Evangelization Publisher, Germany.
"
"
"

'His infernal Majesty'
Dave Breese, Moody Press
'Satan - his personality-power-overthrow'
E. M. Bounds, Baker Bookhouse
'Spiritual Warfare'
Michael Harper, Hodder & Stoughton
'The Authority of the Believer'
J. A. McMillan, Christian Publishers
'The Authority of the intercessor'
'Whom Resist'
F. J. Perryman, 20 Chessel Avenue,
'He must reign till - '
Boscomby, Bournemouth, England.
'A Manual on Exorcism'
H. A. Maxwell-Whyte, Whittaker House
'Pigs in the Parlour'
Frank & Mae Hammond, Impact Books
'Satan' (Papers)
C. H. Spurgeon, Pilgrim Press
'From Witchcraft to Christ'
Doreen Irvine
'The Fourth Dimension'
Pastor Cho
'The Programme of Satan'
C. T. Schwartze, Good News Publishing
'Angels of Light'
Robert E. Freeman, Charisma Books
'The Ouija Board - Doorway to the Occult'
Edmond C. Gruss, J. G. Hotkiss Moody Press
'Beyond the Crystal Ball'
Merril F. Unger, Moody Press
'The Adversary'
Mark I. Bubeck, Moody Press
'The Cult Explosion'
Dave Hunt, Harvest House
'Peace, Prosperity, and the Coming Holocaust'
"
'Christian Set Yourself Free'
Graham and Shirley Powell - available from Center Mountain Ministries, Box 120. Westbridge, BC VOH 2BO, Canada.

'Demons in the World Today'
Merrill F. Unger, Tyndale
'Setting the Captives Free'
Bob Buess, Box 959, Van, Texas 75790 USA
'The Brotherhood' (The explosive expose of the Secret World of Freemasons).
Stephen Knight, Granada
'The Hidden Dangers of the Rainbow'
(The New Age Movement and our coming Age of Barbarism)
Constance Cumbey, Huntington House
'Demons Defeated'
Bill Subritzky, Dove Industries Ltd.
'Battling the Hosts of Hell - Diary of an Exorcist'
Win Worley, H. B. C., Box 626, Lansing, Ill. 60438, USA
'Conquering the Hosts of Hell - an open triumph'
"
'Demolishing the Hosts of Hell - Every Christian's Job'
"
'Annihilating the Hosts of Hell - The Battle Royal'
"
'Should a Christian Be a Mason?'
E. M. Storms, New Puritan Library
'Principalities and Powers'
Gordon Powlison, Power Fellowship Ministries Inc. P.O. Box 32752 San Jose Calif. 95122 U.S.A.
'In God's Name'
David Yallop, Corgi
'The Acquarian Conspiracy'
(Personal and Social transformations in the 1980's)
Marilyn Ferguson, Paladin
'Devil Take The Youngest'
Winkie Pratney, Huntington House Inc.
'Turmoil in the Toybox'
Phil Phillips, Starbust Publishers